THE ONLY BIOGRAPHY OF AMERICA'S GREATEST STORY-TELLER SINCE MARK TWAIN!

"Meticulous...A fine book about the elusive Keillor."
—Philadelphia *Daily News*

"A great deal of new information concerning Lake Wobegon's famous son...Fedo suggests interpretations that help us understand Keillor's work and help clear his personality of much that is enigmatic."
—*Library Journal*

"Far higher toned than the gossip purveyed by most celebrity bios."
—*Booklist*

"Gives great insight into...the mild-mannered, gentle storyteller."
—Charleston (SC) *Post*

"I _____ have wanted to _____ hat produced A _____ own—story-te _____ raphy for us curious fans."
—*Nashville Banner*

THE MAN FROM

LAKE WOBEGON

MICHAEL FEDO

ST. MARTIN'S PRESS/NEW YORK

Grateful acknowledgment is given to the following authors and publishers for permission to quote from their previously published material.

"America's Hottest New Storyteller," by Dan Cryer, from *Newsday Magazine*, October 13, 1985. © Dan Cryer.

"The Distance Between Gopher Prairie Paririe and Lake Wobegon: Sinclair Lewis and Garrison Keillor on the Small Town Experience," by John E. Miller, paper presented at Dakota History Conference, 1986. © John E. Miller.

"Door Interviews Garrison Keillor," from *The Wittenberg Door*, December-January 1985–86. © *The Wittenberg Door*.

"Interview with Garrison Keillor," from "Fresh Air" hosted by Terry Gross, and produced by WHYY Radio in Philadelphia. © WHYY Radio.

"Interview: The Met Grill," by Michael Walker, from *Metropolitan Home*, November 1985. © *Metropolitan Home*.

"Plowboy Interview," by Peter Hemingson, from *The Mother Earth News*, May-June 1985. © *The Mother Earth News*.

"Sharing the Laughter with Garrison Keillor," by Michael Schumacher, from *Writer's Digest*, January 1986. © Michael Schumacher.

THE MAN FROM LAKE WOBEGON

Library of Congress Catalog Card Number: 87-13136

ISBN: 0-312-91295-1   Can. ISBN: 0-312-91297-8

Printed in the United States of America

St. Martin's Press hardcover edition published 1987
First St. Martin's Press mass market edition/November 1988

10 9 8 7 6 5 4 3 2 1

To my father,
Michael A. Fedo,
who was always there
when needed

PREFACE

SHORTLY after I moved to the Twin Cities area in 1970, a local columnist touted an off-the-wall early morning disc jockey, a freewheeler whose eclectic musical tastes ranged from the Beach Boys to Bach, and who told amusing, whimsical stories between records. No hype, no self-promotion—the guy never even mentioned his name on the air—no jingles, no commercials. The subject of the column was Garrison Keillor, at that time toiling in relative obscurity as host of a program on KSJN, a listener-starved Twin Cities public radio station.

I located the station on my clock radio and for years after would wake up to music, live as well as recorded, and "commercials" from Jack's Auto Repair and other related Jack's enterprises in a mythical Minnesota community called Lake Wobegon. The program quickly became a habit, and each morning while kibitzing with colleagues at work, I discussed and enjoyed again the sketches or observations Garrison Keillor had made on his broadcast. Those of us who listened to that program felt special, because we could listen to a guy who was making radio programming both intelligent and literate. He was sensitive, and on his best days, as penetratingly humorous as Twain or Thurber. He would never have had a chance on a commercial outlet, we told ourselves, but how great it was to be able to have him at all. His appeal was to the educated, but we felt that if the quasi-literates could dominate the commercial bands with ungrammatical commercial messages and music, we were entitled to at least one personality who spoke well and assumed his audience also was both literate and intelligent. As his career ascended over the years, we were delighted and gratified that a wider audience would be reached by one we felt was a certified genius.

Many years later, I was approached to write a book about Garrison Keillor, the man who made it okay for people with graduate degrees to indulge in hero worship. Keillor's shyness was by now well known and well documented, and it was one of the few personal characteristics he possessed that he was willing to talk about on the air and in interviews. But he was not ready to have his life documented—at least not in a book. I would not be able to meet him, nor did he wish me to meet with employees of his popular weekly public radio program, "A Prairie Home Companion," and accordingly, he had his attorneys send letters to many performers and musicians requesting they not grant interviews for this book.

Other performers were not sent letters, however, and Maury Bernstein was one of them. Bernstein is both a folk music performer and a broadcaster, whose folk and ethnic music programs have reached national audiences. His weekly hour-long "Folk Music and Bernstein" at one time played on more than a hundred National Public Radio stations. Bernstein's program was produced at Minnesota Public Radio studios, and he had been a guest on "A Prairie Home Companion." Also, he'd hosted Keillor's daily morning program during Keillor's 1974 trip to Nashville, which resulted in the *New Yorker* story on the Grand Ole Opry, as well as providing the impetus for Keillor to begin what would become the most popular program on public radio. Bernstein sent me a letter which read in part:

You must be wondering why Keillor's attorneys have sent out letters amounting to gag orders to former members of [his] cast. After all, his radio persona is a nice guy around the corner, and what could be his concern? That the former cast members might tell you what a warm, wonderful person he is, just like it says in his PR? . . . No, that is not what this silly letter from Keillor's attorneys is all about. It is intended to be a gag order—with no case law to back it up. . . .

Bernstein is no fan of Keillor's, nor of MPR, but he was not far off the mark. Several persons contacted about participating in this project voiced fear about their futures as performers if they agreed to be interviewed. Others said they were told this book would be an invasion of Keillor's privacy, and they didn't want to be hassled about lawsuits.

But when a citizen of the United States achieves celebrity status, be it through athletics, show business or politics, he or she is understood to relinquish a certain degree of privacy accorded ordinary persons. Not so with the celebrity, who has chosen to make a mark in the public arena, seeking widespread public approval and, in the case of Garrison Keillor, public funds. His employer, Minnesota Public Radio, has been at least supported by public money—government grants—and as a result of his nationwide exposure, he has become one of the most admired and adored men in this country. Certainly his fans are among the most slavishly loyal anywhere. He is loved because of his genuinely unique talent, a sort of talent that had seemed dormant in our culture for several generations. Keillor became our most celebrated storyteller, striking a universal chord among the millions of Americans hungry for stories that chronicled their own experiences and rooted them to a specific place, where their names and faces were known, where others cared if they lived or died and wished them Godspeed when they became ill or took long journeys.

Shortly after Keillor turned down my request for an interview, I received notice from the law office of Tanick and Heins (see page x).

Further, when I placed a brief announcement in the staff bulletin of School District 11, where Keillor had been a pupil, requesting that teachers who may have known him contact me, attorneys sent a letter to the district superintendent, Lewis W. Finch, advising him that the biography was unauthorized, and Finch responded by immediately sending each of the district's more than one thousand employees a memo (see page x).

Each year there are scores of celebrity biographies published

PREFACE

TANICK & HEINS

PROFESSIONAL ASSOCIATION
ATTORNEYS AT LAW
701 FOURTH AVENUE SOUTH, SUITE 1800
MINNEAPOLIS, MINNESOTA 55415

MARSHALL H. TANICK
SAMUEL D. HEINS
BARBARA ZIEGLER ASHLEY
SHERRI L. KNUTH
TERESA J. AYLING
MARTIN D. MUNIC

(612) 339-3395

October 10, 1986

Mr. Michael Fedo
15740 Hedgehog Street
Anoka, MN 55303

Dear Mr. Fedo:

The undersigned represent Garrison Keillor.

On behalf of Mr. Keillor, this is to advise you that St. Martin's Press and Michael Fedo do not have Mr. Keillor's authority to publish, print, or quote any written work of Mr. Keillor or any other intellectual property of Mr. Keillor. Mr. Keillor specifically denies to St. Martin's Press and to Mr. Fedo the right to make any use whatever of correspondence, memoranda, stories, poems or any other written material of Mr. Keillor whether it has heretofore been published or not.

Please be advised also that Mr. Keillor's right to privacy, and the right to privacy of his family, will be protected by all appropriate means.

Very truly yours,

TANICK & HEINS

Samuel D. Heins

SDH:msc

MEMO

DATE: October 10, 1986

TO: All Staff

FROM: Superintendent Lewis W. Finch

The October Staff FOCUS contained an item indicating that a local author is working on a biography of Garrison Keillor and would like to talk with teachers who knew Garrison when he was a student in our schools.

Keillor's attorney has since informed the school district that he has not sanctioned this biography and is, in fact, discouraging it. Keillor considers such a biography would be an invasion of his privacy.

Lewis W. Finch

Lewis W. Finch, Superintendent

LWF/az/Ds6

x

in the United States. Few subjects have gone to such lengths to discourage publication, however. And Garrison Keillor had previously been quite generous in granting interviews to major magazines and newspapers. His life and work habits could hardly be termed a closed book, leaving the curious to wonder why this much loved figure would so adamantly oppose a biography.

Unfortunately, some of those who may have provided useful insights did not respond to requests for interviews, including Mary Keillor, Garrison's first wife, and Bill Kling, President of MPR.

It is rare for a person to achieve prominence in more than one area of artistic expression, and rarer still is the individual who, upon achieving that prominence, knows when to step aside gracefully. Too many continue past their primes, embracing Dylan Thomas's dictum to "rage against the dying of the light." In leaving his successful radio show, Garrison Keillor may rest awhile and rekindle that light. But this is mere speculation. What is fact is that he is no longer the shy, relatively friendless, awkward boy floundering through the halls and classrooms of Anoka High School but has—like the literary godfather of his wife Ulla's native Denmark, Hans Christian Andersen—emerged from ugly duckling to swan. This book is about that journey.

Throughout my sojourn writing this biography, many people have contributed material and inspiration. Without them this book would not have been completed. Among those to whom I am particularly indebted are my wife, Judy, for her unswerving emotional buttressing and editorial wisdom; my agent, Jeanne K. Hanson; Reverend Charles Kolk; Richard Sheehan; and Dennis and Patricia Tkach for their suggestions, encouragement and counsel. To them and to those who did agree to help with this book go my deepest thanks.

ON the sports page of a newspaper beginning to yellow and crinkle with age is a headline reading TORNADOES SWAMP RAMSEY 40–0. The newspaper is the Anoka *Herald,* and the story appears in the September 25, 1958 edition. It is an unremarkable, workmanlike piece, running several hundred words, highlighting the previous Friday evening's football triumph of Anoka High School over its suburban conference rival. This story marks the first professional appearance in print of a shy, gangly sixteen-year-old high school junior named Gary Keillor.

Shy—almost a byword regarding author and broadcaster Garrison Keillor—was more than applicable to him in 1958. Nearly thirty years later, the editor and publisher of the *Herald,* Warren Feist, didn't remember Keillor had worked there and had to be reminded that the young, almost anonymous sports reporter had eventually become this nation's most famous shy person. "To be frank, I didn't know who he was," said Feist, who thinks that a printer hired Keillor to cover high school sports for three dollars a game.

Though high school sports was and is a staple of small-town life, many weekly newspapers entrust the reporting of athletic events to teenage stringers. Such stringers were hired not because they wrote particularly well, but because they were willing to do the job. Thus Keillor, for whom writing had already become a consuming passion, may not have received compli-

1

ments for work he sought so eagerly in those days, no matter how well done.

At this point in Gary's life, acceptance was precious. He was a young man without friends; he was unmotivated in many of his classes at the high school and would seriously consider dropping out of school within a few months. But because the *Herald* would publish him and, better yet, pay him for his writing, there was a tacit acceptance of the fledgling writer.

Young Gary was not encouraged in his creative endeavors at home, where he was the second son and third child born to John Keillor and Grace Denham Keillor on August 7, 1942. Descendants of Scottish immigrants who first landed in Nova Scotia and came eventually to Anoka County, Minnesota, the Keillors were members of a tiny fundamentalist sect called the Plymouth Brethren. Brethren eschewed use of tobacco and alcohol, and forbade dancing, gambling, unnecessary work on Sunday, motion pictures, and for a time, when the medium was young, television. If a Brethren were to be outstanding, to be noticed, it was most acceptable for that attention to stem from his doing the Lord's work: active witnessing to the faith among sinners, bringing the gospel to drifters and derelicts in the slums of Minneapolis. To write—even to write well—was not worthy of the Brethren's attention.

Gary's mother felt there was nothing especially wrong with writing about sports per se, but if one were to make a profession of it, others on a newspaper might exert unsavory influence on a young Christian and lead him away from the Truth. This despite the fact that the newspaper happened to be a weekly hometown journal published in the solidly conservative middle-class city of Anoka, Minnesota, where men were strong, of sturdy Scandinavian and German stock, and women were strong too, if not universally good-looking.

Anoka, usually credited with being Gary Keillor's hometown, is a burg whose history was forged by logging companies and flour mills at the junction of the Rum and Mississippi rivers. Both industries have long since disappeared, and the city survives now as a suburb of Minneapolis, fourteen miles to the southeast. Anoka's present population of nearly 16,000 is up from 10,562 in 1960, when Keillor graduated from high school.

The first white men to set foot in Anoka were missionaries, as were the initial settlers of Lake Wobegon, the mythical Minnesota community of 942 souls where Keillor's monologues for "A Prairie Home Companion," his hugely popular public radio program, are set. But instead of the Unitarians who hoped to convert the Indians around Lake Wobegon to the New England style of Christianity through interpretive dance, it was Father Louis Hennepin, a Franciscan monk who, with two colleagues named Accault and Augelle, landed in what is now Anoka, after being detained by Dakota Indians at Mille Lacs, about fifty-five miles upstream on the Rum River. In early July, 1680, Father Hennepin's band was released by the Dakotas and traveled by canoe down the St. Francis River, since renamed the Rum. Their discovery led to the establishment of a trading post by French trappers, Anoka being ideally situated near the dividing line between territories claimed by the Dakotas and the Chippewas. As undeclared neutral ground, it was a safe location for the trading station.

During its pioneer days, Lake Wobegon—then called New Albion—boasted a college, and so did Anoka during the 1880s, when the Anoka Business College thrived. It was located on the corner of Main Street and First Avenue, a site which is presently occupied by a florist.

There are no lakes in Anoka. However, Anoka, which translates in the Dakota language as "on both sides," straddles the Rum River, before it empties into the Mississippi.

Unlike many of the suburbs ringing the urban Twin Cities, Anoka has the ambiance of the archtypical small midwestern town. Until recently its downtown buildings reflected the prairie-school architecture of the early twentieth century. Old-timers take morning coffee and fried apricot twists at Han's Bakery, near the old high school, which is now Fred Moore Junior High. This is where Gary received his secondary education, a building he once described as a dismal piece of 1950s architecture. The beige tile and fluorescent lights reminded him of a hospital, and it remains largely unchanged. Pink seats in the school's auditorium face a pink and turquoise stage curtain. Adjacent Goodrich Field, the football stadium and track, is scooped out of a mound, somewhat resembling an open pit mine. There are curious murals depicting Halloween on the concrete retaining walls beyond the western end zone, homage to the city's image as self-proclaimed Halloween Capital of the World. The annual Pumpkin Bowl game climaxes the Tornadoes' football season.

The city's professional middle class—bankers, lawyers and doctors—occupy sprawling homes along Rum River Drive or Benton Street, which runs east to west along the Mississippi River. They park pontoon boats at the docks and on lazy summer evenings journey upstream to grill steaks on board, knock back a couple cool ones, and float back downstream, children in tow on large inner tubes tied to the boats.

The new high school is on Seventh Avenue, away from residential neighborhoods, and with student enrollment of nearly three thousand, is the largest high school in Minnesota. It is located near the Anoka State Hospital, a treatment facility for persons with substance abuse and other emotional or psychological disorders. Though it is a resident lockup center, the hospital more closely resembles a small New England college campus, with turn-of-the-century two- and three-story buildings interspersed among graceful pines and gnarled oak trees. Both school and hospital are on the east bank of the Rum River.

During Keillor's years at the old school, enrollment peaked at about twelve hundred students, despite drawing from a much wider geographic area. The district then was considerably more rural than today, and many students lived on farms throughout Anoka County and northern Hennepin County. Those same farms today have been carved into developments with tract homes, where both husbands and wives work at nearby factories, and where snowmobiles are conspicuously present in garages and driveways. During the winter months the evening atmosphere is pungent with the odor of overrich snowmobile fuel, as children as young as eight rip across lawns and into ditches, grinding, whining through the neighborhoods.

Downtown Anoka is home to only two legitimate taverns now, where clientele wearing thick down vests and baseball caps with factory or seed company logos sip beer and munch hamburgers. They squint over the tips of lighted Marlboros, as younger men play video games and pool. When a young woman saunters in, the beer drinkers extend deep, appreciative glances. But like true Wobegonians, they only nod or quickly look away, returning to concentrate on beer foam, toying with how it might be if they were not married with nearly grown children; perhaps ten or fifteen or thirty years younger.

The Anoka *Herald* is gone now, it's old downtown offices on Second Avenue home to a music store. The paper was absorbed in 1959 by the larger *Anoka County Union,* which occupies a new high-tech plant on the edge of town. No smells of ink and newsprint. Instead there's the soft clicking of video display terminals, every bit as fine and fancy as the downtown daily papers.

Yet to most fans and observers of the Garrison Keillor phenomenon, Anoka is the model for Lake Wobegon—minus, of course, the lake.

Though there are elements and characters of Lake Wobegon in and around Anoka, this is not Garrison Keillor's home. He was raised in a trim, two-story house that his father built in 1947 on an acre carved out of one of Fred Peterson's cornfields in Brooklyn Park, eight miles away.

Gary attended high school in Anoka because School District 11 encompasses more than a dozen suburban and exurban communities. Brooklyn Park did not have its own high school until much later.

Because Gary lived some distance from most of the schools he attended, he had to ride a bus, a factor contributing to the isolation he felt as a child. Riding a bus to school meant you lived in the sticks, the boondocks. You had to be a hick to live so far away. You couldn't hang around after school for sports and other activities because the buses left immediately. Those who rode buses could only envy peers from town, who enjoyed all the benefits of extracurricular activities, visits to friends' homes after school, or a stop at Tiernan's Confectionary at 205 East Main Street for ice cream sundaes, malts or cherry Cokes.

As cliques developed in schools, those who rode buses were most often excluded. Carolyn Thompson was raised in Brooklyn Park, too, and was a year behind Gary in school. Now editor of the Blaine–Spring Lake Park *Life* weekly paper, she recalls that "the worst thing of all was to be a bus kid. Since you didn't live in town, you were looked at differently by the kids who did. Because you rode a bus, your opportunities to participate at school were limited. And if you were shy, as Gary was, riding the bus isolated you even more from other kids."

From the start, Gary was almost never like anyone else. He was truly shy and introverted. Then there was his religion, a strong and potent force in his life that draws him still, though he no longer attends services at an assembly, as Brethren gatherings are called.

He grew up at 200 Brookdale Drive about a block west of the Mississippi River, where he occupied a basement bedroom. However, most of the first five years of his life were spent with his mother, older brother and sister, in Bettendorf, Iowa, while his father served in the army.

At the time John Keillor purchased the Brooklyn Park lot, that city was semirural, dotted with large potato farms. At age ten Gary, his siblings, and other neighborhood kids would find jobs pulling weeds for area farmers at fifty cents an hour. Gary remembers dawdling somewhat as he worked, so others would move far ahead down the rows, leaving him behind to sing or let his imagination run free.

His father was a skilled carpenter who moonlighted at that trade while working as a railway mail service clerk on the Minneapolis to Jamestown, North Dakota, run. He made certain the home was sturdily constructed, with the foundation laid on eighty-pound blocks of concrete. John told the home's present owner, Morgan Kjer, that he was surprised at purchasing cement blocks so cheaply, until he discovered they were oversized.

John Keillor fell off the roof three times during the building of the home, and though not seriously injured, recounted landing one time in a stairwell and splattering himself with a can of red paint that had been stored there. His family looked on horrified as he slowly emerged from the stairwell covered with fresh red liquid.

The Keillors, adhering to Saint Paul's New Testament dictum to lead quiet, peaceable lives, were always respectful in their dealings with others, sustaining a persistent witness to their religious faith throughout the neighborhood. One area resident said that when a neighbor fell gravely ill, John was moved to speak to the man about matters of sin and grace, hoping for a deathbed conversion.

"John used to talk about one of the neighbors," said Kjer. "The man used to mow his lawn on Sundays, and John said, 'I know he did that just to irritate me.'"

Gary attended elementary school through the fifth grade at Benson School in Brooklyn Park. That school has since been converted into an apartment building. At the end of that fifth-grade year, it was announced that Benson would be closing and that its students would attend the Riverview School. But when school started the next fall, renovation hadn't been completed at Riverview, so the former Benson pupils were bused to the Sunnyvale School in Dayton, a nearby community. There these youngsters felt removed, apart from the kids who lived in the community. To ease the isolation and to finagle his way out of certain class assignments, one ex-Benson student David Olsen started a student choir, in which Keillor participated. "He was probably the only sixth-grader who could sing baritone," recalled Olsen, now a business instructor at North Hennepin

Community College in Brooklyn Park. "Gary wasn't a soloist, but he sang well."

Olsen, who lived in the same neighborhood as Keillor, used to play with Gary during their preadolescent years. "On West River Road in those days there weren't a lot of kids to play with," Olsen said. "Gary and I weren't close, but we were friends. I was never once inside his house, though we went through school together from fifth grade through high school. He used to sneak over to my house sometimes, to play records—the new stuff by Elvis Presley and so on, because he couldn't listen to that at home. My mother called him the Professor because of his studious appearance. He wore horn-rimmed glasses, and looked like a professor, I guess."

Olsen remembers Gary was not much for participation in many of the kids' activities, but was at all times an observer. "Once, during lunch at school, all of us were fooling around with the food, pretending to be gagging and throwing up over this terrible meal. There must have been about twenty of us involved, but Gary didn't participate. He just watched. All through school, Gary was distant and acted independently. He did things on his own."

Early on, the notion that Gary was different was apparent to neighborhood kids. During the fifties and sixties, Brookdale Drive was an unpaved gravel road. Homes in the vicinity tended to be distant, constructed on one- and two-acre lots. The youngsters got around on their bicycles. "We didn't have ten-speed bikes back then, but everybody had the old standard bikes with balloon tires," recalled Gerald Sundberg, a former neighbor of the Keillors and now a professor of vocal music at Bethel College in St. Paul. "Bikes didn't have gears, but now and then you'd see one with skinny tires, which we called English bikes. They were very impractical for the kinds of surfaces we had to ride on then, but Gary had one of those English bicycles. Already, I guess, he was in a category of wanting to be different."

Sundberg remembered, too, that Gary was something of a

burden to his mother, who was concerned that he spent so much time by himself, writing. "She used to want him to get out and do something," Sundberg said. "But he was probably in his room writing."

Gary developed a musical interest early on, singing the Brethren hymns with family and the rest of the assembly, and Olsen, a prominent musician during his school years both as a vocalist and instrumentalist, recalls that musical interest too. "Gary often told me he'd like to be able to play an instrument," Olsen said. Since Brethren did not use instrumental accompaniment for their hymn singing, playing instruments or having music lessons was not a priority among Brethren families.

"Now when he picks up that Autoharp and pushes a button that plays chords, he's not just looking for something to do with his hands," Olsen said. "I think he's exhibiting that real longing to play an instrument."

Linae Haase, a former area resident, recalls that John and Grace Keillor weren't particularly close to neighborhood children, "but they were always good to us and welcomed us in their home. I always thought of Gary's mother as old, though, because she wore those black grandma shoes and kept her hair in a bun. She doesn't seem any older to me now than she did when I was a little kid. John had a twinkling sense of humor, which Gary probably picked up on.

"The family's deep religious faith was obvious. They used to invite neighbor children to vacation Bible school in the summer. Their children all had chores to do, like work in their large garden." Haase's younger brother, Gerald Sundberg, who played with the younger Keillor siblings—twins Stan and Steve and sister, Linda—remembered that the Keillor family garden was a big thing with them. "The kids had to weed so many rows before they could play. So if you wanted them to play ball or whatever, you went over and helped out to free them up."

The time Gary scored a direct hit on his older sister's bottom with a rotten tomato is described in his book, *Lake Wobegon Days*. That garden occupied nearly half the Keillor lot, which was also dotted with four apple trees, maple trees and grape vines.

Haase, who was several years younger than Gary, said she and her friends didn't see a lot of him during those early growing-up years. "Sometimes though, we used to play in this large ravine near the river. It was a place where kids could get away. We couldn't even see the houses from there. We played imaginative games that Gary would dream up. We'd be pioneers off on an adventure, maybe." The youngsters would also build camps and forts with large boulders and branches in the dry creek bed. "We used to put on plays from the Jack and Jill books in garages for our parents," Haase said. "Gary once directed us in a play about Lincoln. Some of the kids remember that incident about his being a king and the rest of them his subjects, like he wrote about in his book.

"Later, he baby-sat for us a few times and told us very interesting stories. I remember he used our pandas as detectives and used to turn a chair around and put them on it and use it as a stage. He told us about a witch that stole all the silverware in Minneapolis and stuffed her house with it."

Sundberg, who was about five years old at the time Gary occasionally took care of him and his sister, remembered that the teenage Gary made up "incredible stories for us, utilizing neighborhood characters and wedding them with fictitious characters. We were sworn to secrecy though. He used to say, 'The only way I'll tell you this story is if you promise not to tell anybody.' Then he'd put people we knew in the stories, and they were just wild schemes. We were completely mesmerized."

Gary's was an imagination fueled by stories told by his great-uncle, Lew Powell. One, about the fire that destroyed his grandfather's wealth, found its way into a monologue, and into *Lake Wobegon Days*. Powell told great disaster stories, Keillor remembers. "In one of his house-fire stories, there were strong intimations of a family fortune that went up in flames, which hurt, and appealed to my imagination," Keillor told Dan Cryer, in *Newsday Magazine*'s October 13, 1985 cover story. In the piece, entitled "America's Hottest New Storyteller," Keillor also said that Powell's stories were also rambling monologues, often about himself and his family, but that the young relatives "hung on every word."

The imagination would be furthered through the medium of radio, which was a constant in the Keillor household. Gary's earliest memory of radio was of sitting on Uncle Lew's lap as a New York announcer proclaimed the end of World War II. The boy practiced radio announcing himself, using the curved handle of a Hoover vacuum cleaner as a microphone.

"My parents loved radio," he recalled. "But it was limited. You could only listen to a little bit at a time. You had to select your shows. I'm not clear on this, but perhaps my family included such wonderful talkers and storytellers because we didn't have television, we didn't have movies. Newspapers didn't play a big part in our house. We didn't have many magazines come in. We really cut ourselves off from a lot of entertainment. Our entertainment was talk."

The family owned a Zenith console radio with shortwave and police bands. Keillor later reminisced about that old radio:

> In the evening, you could pull in clear-channel stations with amazing, strange stuff on them. As a kid in Minnesota, I'd get rhythm and blues out of Little Rock, and I had to play it at low volume in fear that my parents would come. . . . The raunch on the air! I'll say that as a young man I couldn't stand to listen to it for a very long time.

For Gary, that big Zenith floor model seemed to contain the whole world.

The world "out there," away from Brooklyn Park and Anoka, away from the world he knew, was an escape for a lonely boy who often would tell his favorite high school teacher, Deloyd Hochstetter, that he had no friends. He compared himself to his older brother, Philip, a straight-A student, and found himself wanting. He sought parental and peer approval but was drawn toward activities which didn't merit that approval. In this and other regards, he compares strikingly with another chronicler of life in a small Minnesota town, Sinclair Lewis. Both Keillor and Lewis were second sons whose older brothers were achievers. Claude Lewis was strong, handsome, athletic, an excellent student. Sinclair, or Harry, as he was called, was none of those. The older brothers made their families proud. Philip Keillor would become a soil engineer, and Claude Lewis followed his father into medicine. Writing prizewinning, best-selling books never impressed the Lewis family, and neither are the Keillors unduly impressed with Garrison's successes, as he has often admitted.

Where Lewis excoriated small-mindedness, Keillor would satirize, but gently. And because of his shy nature, Keillor would become what Lewis never did—a cult hero to millions of shy, retiring people, for whom life is solidly Sisyph n. The mundane, the banal would provide Keillor grist for human comedy, tragedy and endurance.

Though Keillor professes to loathe the word *nostalgic* in connection with "A Prairie Home Companion," it is nonetheless appropriate. His own recollections of the radio programming he grew up with were recounted in a sustaining column he wrote called "Broadsides," for *The Ivory Tower*, a student magazine at the University of Minnesota. He wrote of hearing Fanny Brice as Baby Snooks, and Lionel Barrymore reading *A Christmas Carol*; of listening to "Let's Pretend," and Smilin' Ed McConnell and Froggy, or Fibber McGee and Molly at 79 Wistful Vista, "Corliss Archer," "Life With Luigi," and Arthur Godfrey. And Cedric Adams. Always there was Cedric Adams, the most popular, best-known media personality in the Upper Midwest. At the height of his popularity in the 1950s, Adams did a daily five-minute chatter program on the CBS network and occasionally substituted for Arthur Godfrey when Godfrey vacationed. He performed fifty-four radio shows, eight television broadcasts, and wrote seven newspaper columns weekly. He also wrote books, and took variety shows on the road to rural

Minnesota. He was an emcee, talent scout, and top-rated newscaster. Adams, who died at fifty-eight in 1962, was revered by several generations who regularly listened to WCCO-AM, a fifty-thousand-watt clear-channel station. Adams also figured prominently in Keillor's *New Yorker* story, "Drowning 1954." In the story, Adams is followed down the street by the narrator, an awestruck boy of twelve years. He was Keillor's idol.

WCCO's staff was and is a smooth, polished blend of professional broadcast personalities, who are at once urbane and witty but who recognize that their urban audiences migrated to the Twin Cities from small towns in Minnesota, the Dakotas, or Wisconsin—or wish they had. The station still serves a wide and rural constituency throughout the state. Thus cornball humor remains a part of the station's appeal. This audience was carefully nurtured over the years by sending personalities such as Adams or Bob DeHaven out to the farm country for personal appearances and live broadcasts.

Though definitely not cornball, Keillor's laid-back, just-folks approach to his own program is patterned after the successful shows he listened to on WCCO as he grew up.

"Garrison mentioned that he used to come to 'CCO to see this Friday night lineup of shows, and there were four of them back to back," said Bob DeHaven, now retired from the station. The amiable, avuncular DeHaven was also one of Keillor's early broadcasting heroes and is mentioned in the drowning story. "These shows were really a bonanza for radio fans," he said. "If you came early enough you could see them rehearse and he [Keillor] indicated that he would do this. Cedric did one called 'Stairway to Stardom,' which was an amateur talent show. That was followed by a quiz program called 'The Quiz of the Twin Cities,' and then there were two country-western shows: 'The Red River Valley Gang,' and 'The Murphy Barn Dance,' sponsored by Taystee Bread, Cargill Feeds, and Phillips Oil. I eventually emceed both of those shows."

An element of "The Red River Valley Gang" program, fermenting over the years in the deep recesses of Keillor's mind, may account for the concept of his Lake Wobegon monologue with a format opening and closing. "We had a banjo player named Irv Wickner," DeHaven said, "who doubled as a sort of comic foil. I'd use him because of his Scandinavian accent. We had a standard opening. I'd say, 'Well, Irv, where've you been?' He'd say, 'To see my uncle in North Dakota.' And then he would tell what was going on out there. Wasn't nearly as effective as the letter from Lake Wobegon. These pieces were always about bad luck, bad news and disaster, piled one on top of the other. The standard close was always, 'It ain't a very pretty picture.'"

WCCO may have also generated the concept of spoofing commercials, because as a CBS network affiliate it carried the daily Arthur Godfrey program. And Godfrey frequently trifled with sponsors. He might say, as he sometimes did when confronted with a spot for Monarch peanut butter, "Peanut butter—yech. Who wants to talk about peanut butter at this time of the morning?"

Keillor had said that in his Brethren household, radio ranked next to the Minnesota State Fair as the gaudiest, most extravagant entertainment around. "Nowadays, I guess, people think back to radio as something sort of benevolent, and they have warm, nostalgic feelings. But to me it was a great source of violence and horror—and comedy, of course.

"I remember 'Fibber McGee and Molly' as being funny to me at that age. 'My Friend Irma.' 'Amos 'n' Andy.' We all tried to do the 'Amos 'n' Andy' accents." Comics such as Jack Benny or Fred Allen were a mite over Keillor's head back then, though the Benny program was on Sunday evenings, and on Sunday nights the Keillors were at assembly services. As with most mainline fundamentalist bodies, Brethren attended services twice on Sundays and usually went to prayer meetings during midweek as well.

In a Los Angeles *Times* story, Keillor said that when he was fourteen he heard the Brethren talk of the Lord's coming as if it were imminent. "I hoped he didn't come until I'd had sex once because I wasn't sure sex would be part of heaven."

He also said that the men in the assembly were lawgivers, who tended to be hard on transgressors. Brethren women, he remembered, were mostly forgiving. "If you broke a rule, a male elder would come around and lecture you, and then an aunt would come around secretly and put her arms around you.

"These people were wonderful storytellers, and the purpose of their stories was to imbue us with compassion."

Some of the stories told by the Brethren were to be recalled years later as tales of life in Lake Wobegon. And Keillor tried his hand at telling stories too, early on; his first efforts reached fruition in elementary school, where he began a paper called *The Riverviewer* at the Riverview School on West River Road. He was in the sixth grade.

Those efforts were not encouraged by his family, especially the poetry, as they believed it was not appropriate for a Christian to persue. Keillor told the Los Angeles *Times* that his family thought that writing "led to a life that was fraught with temptation. And of course, they were right."

"ALL Gary really knew of Anoka was the school and taking a bus from home and back." Deloyd Hochstetter grins and shakes his head. Keillor was a student in his English and journalism classes from 1958 to 1960 at Anoka High School. A pleasant, bookish man in his middle fifties, Hochstetter is full of face and wears dark horn-rimmed glasses after the fashion of his protégé. He speaks rapidly; ideas, concepts, reminiscences come tumbling, pouring forth, his brain, his mouth working like a corn shucker. He is a man of enormous enthusiasm, recalled by former pupils as almost hyper in his excitement about teaching students to think. Learning and good writing were precious to him. He was a man to latch on to some student's vague wisp of a notion, and before the student was off the hook that notion would have been hewn to precision. Keillor and other students thought Hochstetter an immensely encouraging teacher, one who always tested and challenged. "Why do this?" Hochstetter would ask. "Defend this—why should it be so?" He was of an old school, a teacher who maintained that the classics of world literature influenced activities and philosophies at least as much as politics or military engagements, so he immersed his wards in the study of great literature. He had all pupils select classic works to read on their own. Despite relatively large classes, Hochstetter was Socratic, and each student up to the challenges set forth by this instructor believed himself or herself special, because Hochstetter cared deeply about each one's thoughts and opinions.

He has been on extended sick leave from the Anoka school, recuperating in a book-and-magazine-cluttered efficiency apartment. A vibrant, energetic man, as he discusses his own career and influence on Keillor he freely perspires; his bathrobe is damp. He reaches for packets of old magazines from his floor-to-ceiling bookcase, remnants of the early days and the emerging talent of Garrison Keillor. "I always thought it funny he picked Anoka as a model," Hochstetter says. "But with all the publicity he's gotten he thought he had to have a hometown. Brooklyn Park is just a bedroom suburb with no real identity, and this is where he went to school. When he was a kid, this was sort of a country town—bigger, of course—but country, like Lake Wobegon."

Hochstetter remembers that Gary was on fire to write. "It was his life, you know. At the first parent-teacher conference, his poor mother came to me and said, 'You know, all Gary does is write and write.' He had his room down in the basement, and he was just a monk down there. Seven days a week. One of the things I tell my students is if you want to be a writer, you have to write and write and write. She wondered if the kid was going to grow up to be normal. I said, 'Just let him do that. One day something special's going to happen.' But he didn't get encouragement at home and he felt insignificant and shy."

The family subscribed to several magazines, including *National Geographic*, and the omnipresent Christian publications, but there was nothing of literary merit to inspire the youngster. In 1956, however, Gary happened upon a copy of *The New Yorker* in the Anoka Public Library, a typical small-town, single-story building situated off an alley two blocks from downtown.

In 1956 he submitted poetry to his junior high school newspaper, using for the first time the byline Garrison. He later recalled that he wanted to use a name that sounded "a little bigger. Flags flying. I think I was trying to hide behind a name that meant strength and 'don't give me a hard time about this.'"

By the time he entered Hochstetter's journalism class as a junior, writing already consumed him. He began handing in essays and features that hadn't been requested by editors. "We didn't let juniors write right away, because we wanted them to learn the ropes first," said Hochstetter. "But he did it anyway, because he couldn't not write. He wrote under the byline Garrison Edwards. It came like an avalanche. He started handing this stuff in, and then he was pushing stuff under the door for me. We found out who it was right away, and I started talking to him. The more interested I was in him and his work, the more he opened up—to me, at least.

"But he wouldn't say a word in class. Sometimes he'd leave written answers to questions I'd asked, at the end of the period. He would never volunteer answers. I think he had trouble in every class but mine. He was always being compared to his older brother, Phil, who was a straight-A student. When I would mention that I thought this kid had tremendous potential, other teachers would just shake their heads and say they didn't see how in the world he'd ever amount to much."

To be shy is to be consumed by self-doubt, and nowhere in contemporary culture is the burden of being shy more painful than among the young. For Gary Keillor, youthful experiences exacerbated this trait. His religion, with its emphasis on rejecting worldly pursuits and pleasures, was one major factor. Keillor speaks and writes of the anguish of having to sing hymns in public, on street corners and at the Minnesota State Fair, while one of the Brethren exhorted uninterested passersby to forsake their sins and turn to Jesus. A sensitive young person must have lived in dread of being recognized by acquaintances while posed before a sound truck, his face buried in a worn *Little Flock Hymnal*.

His position paper, "Shy Rights; Why Not Pretty Soon?" does not allude to the real angst of the socially awkward and does not address the turmoil endured by one who is painfully shy. For many shy people the affliction is a curse that keeps them from joining organizations or even applying for jobs. Some shy individuals believe that their shyness causes others to notice them, to wonder why such persons rarely speak.

Though Keillor has told reporters that he was a poor student, several of his old high school teachers say he was actually quite good academically. His concept of poor scholastic efforts may have been in comparison to Philip's work. Lyle Bradley, a retired biology teacher, recalls having Gary in sophomore biology during the 1957–58 school year. "Gary was quiet, but a good student," Bradley said. "He was thorough. I had a habit of always asking questions and wouldn't wait for kids to volunteer answers. He never would have volunteered, but he always had a response. He was very sharp, and his written work was excellent. I required kids to keep notebooks. I ran across his several years ago. He did a beautiful job; it was very well organized. Class participation, though, was never his strong point. I think he got A's and B's.

"What surprises me is that he turned into a theatrical person. I never thought he could do that. I classified him as an introvert. Good students are usually outgoing, and it was unusual for a good student to be introverted."

Charles Faust, the eleventh-grade American history teacher, remembers Gary as a quiet and very studious boy "interested in reading and writing. He once wrote a fine paper on the New Deal for me. He seemed interested in twentieth-century history. He was an A student, and was always ready to recite, though he wouldn't volunteer. He had the answers. If all else failed, I could call on Gary. He was always prepared, but I pretty much had to pull it out of him. I remember he sat in the back seat in the first row, and I can still see his dark brown eyes looking over the head of the person in front of him.

"At one point he sent Christmas cards to a few of us, which was unusual for a student to do at that time, because there was more of a barrier between students and teachers back then."

Though Gary's shyness has become legendary and has been often reported in recent years, he seemed determined to overcome it while in high school. He took a public-speaking course in high school, a class that was an elective. His teacher was Lavona Person, who presently teaches at Coon Rapids High School, also in District 11. "Gary was shy, but very clever," she said. "He was quite popular in group things because he created skits for the groups, and I felt he enjoyed those. He may have suffered some in my class due to shyness, and his first few speeches must have been difficult, but he was a good student— A-B, as I recall. A speech class, however, is a creative outlet and a challenge to that part of him which enabled him to overcome his shyness to participate in assignments."

Person also clearly recalls the young exchange student from Denmark, Ulla Strange, who spent her senior year at Anoka High. She excelled in extracurricular speech activities, participating in oral interpretation on the forensics team. "In *The Little Match Girl*," Person recalls, "she handled the language beautifully. She was vivacious and popular, an outgoing person."

Ulla quite obviously attracted the attention of Gary Edward Keillor. But it isn't likely the woman who would become his wife and the subject of love-struck monologues twenty-five years later would have noticed him.

Fellow staffer on the *Anokahi*, the school paper, Carolyn Thompson, said Ulla was very lovely, very popular, "the exact opposite of Gary. He probably wouldn't have said hello to her at the time. She had a lively, bubbly personality. She was very outgoing and quite attractive. Some of the class big shots were interested in her."

Karen Vogel, another classmate, also remembers Ulla as extroverted, a girl whose easy command of English made her part of the class, rather than a novelty member. "She fit right in," Vogel said, "and was even elected to the homecoming court only a few months after she joined us. That was very unusual for a foreign exchange student, but she was immediately and completely accepted by our class."

During much of her senior year, she dated another of the River Road boys, as the group of students from that area of Brooklyn Park came to be called. But no one from the class remembers any sort of relationship between Ulla and Gary, who was perceived by classmates as probably bright, but also odd, a boy who never seemed to participate in anything around school.

"Ulla was an activist," David Olsen said. "She bought into the peace movement in its infancy, and was involved in causes, as a lot of us were in the sixties. The difference between her and some of the rest of us is that she remained committed over the years, while the rest of us sort of drifted into other things."

At the twenty-fifth reunion of the Anoka class of 1960, Ulla gave a speech, Olsen said. "She spoke of the causes we all championed back then, of a world community. She asked us where were those ideals now? What were we doing now? She seemed to have lived the life of an international activist, and her speech affected me tremendously."

In a Minneapolis *Tribune* profile published in 1976, Keillor described himself in high school: "I loped around in the hallways, slouched around, tried not to look so tall, and worried about how I looked. I was very certain I looked just awful and I was real conscious about trying to blend in."

Other students, however, recall the opposite, remembering distinctly a tall, gangly kid with hands jammed in his pockets and a sort of backward tilt when he walked, his nose in the air. He passed from class to class, rarely establishing eye contact with anyone.

"I'd guess he was always in a world of his own," said Thompson. "But no one questioned his talent. He was introspective, and had a very different way of looking at the world. A few years ago he came back to the high school to do a benefit for the orchestra and I was there to do a story on him. At one point he took a break and went to the cafeteria, a huge room, much bigger than our gymnasium at the old school. He said, 'Let's see what kind of stuff they're serving now.' He remembered a food strike we had back then. It was bad food—macaroni and cheese, or tuna casserole, and we were kind of fed up with it. We refused to eat the food for a while, and I think I recall a food fight. He was definitely involved.

"I knew who he was all along but never really knew him. There he was, a young guy with this deep, masculine voice that hardly anyone ever heard, his head up in the clouds, totally engrossed in whatever he was thinking, and he seemed not to notice anyone else."

But he did notice; he always noticed, and more than noticed, he observed. "Gary always just watched us," Olsen said, "and now he's playing back all those idiosyncrasies he's observed."

His observations even then were precise, and the shy young man began to exhibit a sense of power through his writing. Karen Vogel, who participated on the school paper with Gary and wrote a feature column, was also in several classes with him, and remembers that Gary used to write lampoons on faculty members, jocks, and princesses. "These would sort of circulate underground, and some people would worry about what Gary might write about them. I mostly remember one where he really ripped an old teacher, lampooned him as being alcoholic and falling asleep in classes. It was a wonderful satire on a doddering old teacher who would probably die in his test tubes. But I remember thinking, Gary's going to get kicked out of school if someone finds out about this, and if I'm caught reading it, I'm going to get kicked out too. That's how good he was at satire."

He had, Vogel recalled, a real disdain for the "in" crowd at the high school. "And some of them were aware of his power, that he could be devastating in what he wrote," she said. "I was glad he liked me, and we even chatted occasionally. But that was probably just me. I talked to everybody, and I talked to Gary. He had this sarcastic sense of humor, and I could have been the type he would not have liked. I was on the Dayton's [a large Minneapolis–St. Paul department store] fashion teen board then, so he'd make funny comments about fashion. I also wrote a column for the *Anokahi*, and he talked about that too. But I don't remember Gary having a personality. He was just too quiet and withdrawn. A very intense person who was stoic, guarded, and didn't want to get too close to people. He had an unapproachability, and you didn't kid around with him. So I was surprised when he'd pass those lampoon papers to me."

Vogel said Gary's standoffishness contributed to the uneasiness people felt in being around him. "I know he uses those he knows [in his work] and I've always wondered how or when I was going to show up," she said.

She also carries with her the vivid impression of Gary as a tall, skinny, walking caricature of a kid, who was whippet thin and extremely self-conscious. "He never got involved, except to edit our literary magazine when he was a senior. Because he could write so well, and use humor so well, he wrote our senior class prophecy, which made some people uncomfortable. Two class jocks who were close friends were quite upset when they appeared in the class prophecy as being 'married and living in San Francisco.'"

The notation after Gary Keillor's name in the 1960 *Anokan*, the high school annual, reads "*Anokahi* 3, 4, *Anokan* 4, Film operator 2, 3, Young Republicans 4." A caption under a photo of him appearing on page 43 of the year book discusses a sports weekly entitled *Varsity* that he initiated. The caption noted that he "researched, wrote, typed, printed, stapled and sold it. Gary confesses to having discovered that journalism has more problems than his trigonometry textbook." *Varsity* contained stories about Anoka High School athletes and graduates who were succeeding in collegiate sports.

Athletics have always been the chief means of attaining notoriety for a high school student, and Keillor has always been interested in sports. But he lacked the bulk for football and the coordination for basketball, though he would develop a keen interest in hockey later on, because the game, sans its inherent violence, seemed to him a poetic dance—all rhythm, precision, ballet and jitterbug. As a rapidly growing young man, however, Gary was perhaps handicapped by what the old Greenwich Village poet and sage Joe Gould used to call "ambisinistrousness," the opposite of ambidextrousness; being left-handed in both hands. Thus writing about sports gave Gary access to athletes, a chance to be close to those who truly mattered in the world of American high schools.

In addition to covering high school sports for the local *Herald*, Gary picked up added assignments by reporting on city council meetings, in which he had little apparent interest. Sam Clasen, a longtime veteran of Anoka County journalism and former writer and editor at the *County Union*, also covered council meetings and occasionally helped Gary straighten things out. Perhaps bored with proceedings, Gary sometimes seemed not to be aware of what was happening. Now and again he'd have to ask Clasen what was said, or what was meant.

Being raised fundamentalist meant that Gary was a bit more naive than most kids his age. Hochstetter said that Gary had to learn so many things that other kids just knew. "He once told me that the kids were talking on the bus about what their fathers' incomes were. Gary had no idea, but he wanted to be a part of things, so he blurted out, 'My dad makes three thousand dollars a year,' which was nothing even back then, you know. And one of these kids says, 'You're poor.' The kids looked at each other funny, and Gary told me he should have kept his mouth shut."

Hochstetter said that riding the school bus was difficult for Keillor, and since the school district was massive, it was no less so for quite a few others who didn't live in town. Most rode at least thirty minutes each way on the bus, and during class discussions on civil rights, busing was a central issue. "But kids would say, 'Don't mention buses to me.' They'd been riding all their lives and were fed up with it. But there was one incident that was just wild concerning Gary. A student had written for one of the other teachers a paper about a young man who killed his parents. He concluded that paper by saying, 'I'm that guy.' He was a pretty weird kid, and it happened that the teacher had heard a news report earlier that day that a boy had attempted to murder his parents. He'd crept into their bedroom and opened up with a shotgun, but missed hitting them because it was too dark. It created quite a stir at school, and Gary came to me and said, 'You know, that's who they let me sit beside all these years on the bus.'"

While Gary admired Hochstetter—the two would become good friends—he maintained the reserve that characterizes nearly all his social and professional relationships. However, he was desperate for Hochstetter's approval of his writing, and once one of Garrison Edwards's stories was passed around among Hochstetter's senior class editors, who were stunned by the quality of the piece. "I told him, 'You're on your way to *The New Yorker.*' But he said to the kids, 'I don't trust him.'"

Yet Hochstetter was the only person Gary came close to trusting, and on numerous occasions he confided to the teacher—a man eleven years his senior, "You're my only friend."

"I think he wanted to start calling me by my first name after we got to know each other. But he felt uncomfortable about it, so he used my last name instead. Even now, I find myself in some of his monologues. Always the last name, a reference to something that happened out past the Hochstetter farm or something like that."

Keillor admired not only Hochstetter's erudition and qualities as a teacher, but also his rebellious nature. "I always said what I thought in class," Hochstetter said. "I never got in trouble for it either. I said something once about the American Legion, and people were sort of worshipping the Legion in those days. In fact I had gone to Boys' State [a convention for leading high school students, sponsored by the Legion] and won a medal from them. But I said all the militaristic stuff was a bunch of crap, and Gary told his boss, who was a Legionnaire.

His boss said a lot of it was true. He [Gary] sort of liked what I said, but he wanted to see what a member of the American Legion would say. And his boss, who edited the paper, sort of agreed."

Hochstetter's students were required to make an oral presentation in front of the class in order to receive credit. "Naturally he was the last one to do his oral report," Hochstetter said. "It was at the end of the year, and the other kids were wondering about him. Some hadn't even heard his voice before."

A couple decades before anyone thought about the Freedom of Information Act, students records were sacrosanct. No student ever had any notion of what went into the individual files, and none ever expected to see the contents. But often the secrecy surrounding material in those files was the subject of speculation and conversation. Students tended to believe that negative comments in those records would haunt them all their lives, as prospective employers asked the school to divulge information about former pupils. At Anoka, those records were maintained in a large vault. The records and the vault were the subjects of Gary's essay.

"It was an exposé on what was really in student records," said Hochstetter, who chortles at the memory nearly thirty years later. "No one saw records then, and the first thing he said was, 'I got a copy of the records.' He didn't say how he got in or anything, he just said he got a copy. His report was full of anecdotes about students. It got funnier and funnier, this material that he'd written on two or three sheets of paper. He never once looked up at us, you know.

"I was crying, and the brighter kids who got the satire were just rolling in the aisles. He finished and walked back to his seat and the kids clapped. I think he felt pretty good about it. Even though it was funny, it had a bite to it.

"Other kids who'd preceded him had gotten up and talked about being Eagle Scouts and things like that, and he had to be wondering how he'd measure up against stuff like that. He wasn't anything except a writer."

Despite his obvious success in Hochstetter's class, and his relative success in other academic subjects, Gary felt out of place in school and almost quit after his junior year. His parents, however, wouldn't hear of it.

He was continually encouraged by Hochstetter, who critiqued the reams of poetry and essays Gary gave him. "He sent me batches of stuff—always has," said the teacher. He scans his room. "But I couldn't keep it all—there just wasn't room."

During Keillor's senior year, Hochstetter started a literary magazine for students and Gary was one of the editors. "That group started something for us at the school, and within a year or two after they graduated we started winning all sorts of awards for our magazine and newspaper. I've always been grateful to him for his work in getting us off the ground."

Hochstetter was in the habit of giving his journalism staff small gifts—in recognition of their service as they were about to graduate. "I gave them a book of poetry one year, and he kept it. Whenever he came to see me, he always carried it and put it right in a place where I could see it. I think he wanted me to say something. That's another thing about him; he'd always want people to say things, but he'd never ask. But when he started coming to jazz concerts, it got to be kind of funny, you know. One time he came to the Minneapolis Institute of Arts where there was a jazz concert. He always came with a portfolio full of stuff. And my wife and I were down front and he came down about a half hour late, and he said, 'I thought I'd find you here.' So he handed me the stuff and asked me to read it during the concert, which I did, during breaks and intermission."

Hochstetter and his wife, Beverly, helped introduce a socially awkward young man into the world of the arts. At first he was coaxed into attending a Doc Evans Dixieland jazz performance. Later came the movies. Hochstetter especially remembers seeing *Elmer Gantry* with Gary, and how it impressed the young man. "He'd never been to shows before, because of his family's religion."

Hochstetter recalled that at first he'd take Gary to a restaurant in north Minneapolis for coffee and conversation, and eventually to ballet, concerts and plays, all without the apparent knowledge of Keillor's parents. "I'd sneak up there in the dark," Hochstetter said.

But Gary was not a loner by choice or design. One of the stories he asked Hochstetter to critique was called "The Old Man." It was about a boy wandering through town all alone. He walks up to a house and looks in the window to see a party in progress. Everyone is having a wonderful time, laughing and dancing. The protagonist sees life and vitality all about him, but he is not part of it. At story's end, the boy goes home, climbs into bed and pulls the covers up over his head.

"After I'd read it, Gary says, 'I'm that old man.' He felt terrible about being shy and alone like that. But you know, it was true. He didn't have any friends."

He did have one friend, in Deloyd Hochstetter, who remembers how upset John and Grace Keillor were when Gary published a poem in the high school literary magazine. Gary felt like an outcast from the family for some time after it appeared because he knew that writing secular poetry was anathema to the Brethren.

Because of Hochstetter's recognition of Gary's immense talent and potential creative genius, the young man gradually opened up, confiding in Hochstetter, who continued to receive manuscripts to critique for years after Keillor left Anoka High School. "It took him a long time to believe in himself, and develop a self-confidence about his writing," Hochstetter said. But even then Keillor exhibited flights of fancy, dreams he had heretofore not articulated, about a future fraught with the trappings of success. "He's so complex that behind him, inside him is a terrible, driving ego," Hochstetter said. "In other words, he was going to make it one way or another. He told me once, 'I've got to have money, security. I've got to have money to live in this world because there are things I want. And I want a big car.' He'd affect words, mispronounce them. He'd say 'Merkaydes' for Mercedes, or say his name would be Garrison Kyler. He'd already had the Garrison there. He was so involved with his dreams."

Often Gary retreated to a tiny cemetery for solitude. The unnamed burial plot is a hidden half-acre section a few miles north of Anoka, tucked out of the way, off the road between two private residences. The Keillor relatives, to whom Hochstetter said Gary felt particularly close, are buried here in a weedy, overgrown shambles. It is largely unmaintained, and the oldest headstones are no longer readable; others are knocked over, and the earliest visible markers date to the 1860s. Scrub oak dot the land and most grave sites are unadorned. This was a remote, secluded spot during Gary's boyhood, and he often visited it, claiming it was his favorite retreat on summer evenings. The years have brought residential development to the area, however, and current visitors attract the attention of a neighborhood dog, who yaps incessantly over the hum of steady traffic along Minnesota Highway 47. The cemetery is no longer the quiet plot of Gary's youth.

3

IN the fall of 1960, Keillor's talents earned him his first significant recognition after he enrolled at the University of Minnesota to pursue an English major with a journalism minor. Though not particularly anxious to earn a degree, he feared he would be a failure if he did not receive further education. Philip went on to graduate from college and assume a fine professional position as a soil engineer, so this may have additionally spurred Gary. "He felt people were comparing him to Phil," Hochstetter said.

Athletic teams at the University of Minnesota are named the Golden Gophers, and the era during which Gary Keillor was on campus was indeed golden. Vietnam was still in the future, fraternities and sororities played important roles in campus social life, and school spirit was alive and thriving. Students cared about the fortunes of the Gophers, especially the football and basketball teams. The football team's last national championship season was in 1960, when many of its starters were black players. The team played in two consecutive Rose Bowl games, led by a black quarterback named Sandy Stephens, who became all-American. In that period, too, there were other all-Americans: tackles Carl Eller and Bobby Bell and middle guard Tom Brown. Basketball was still a white man's game at the university, and the teams under former Minneapolis Laker coach John Kundla flirted with mediocrity. But students cared;

homecoming was an event. Until the advent of the Minnesota Twins and Vikings, Gopher sports were the only games in town, and tickets to football games at Memorial Stadium, or Williams Arena for basketball and hockey, were precious commodities. Big-time college sports lent an aura of excitement to campus life, heightened by appearances by name entertainers, frequently folk musicians such as Pete Seeger, Odetta, or the Limelighters.

Off-campus folk clubs abounded, certain establishments catering to the button-down crowd—the Padded Cell on Lake Street, where Peter, Paul and Mary performed, or Le Zoo on University Avenue—and coffee houses like the Ten O'clock Scholar, where the clientele was more hip, bohemian, bearded, beaded. Young Bob Zimmerman from Hibbing, Minnesota, tried making his mark here, but went largely unrecognized, and had to flee to New York with a new name, Dylan, before he would be touted a genius.

There was a general feeling of promise; John Kennedy had formed the Peace Corps, and thousands of young people applied. On campuses, students drawn to social activism found a president sensitive to their altruism. For a time, possibilities seemed golden; the arts were respected and prejudice would be defeated. After all, a Protestant country had elected a Catholic president.

The University of Minnesota embraces both Twin Cities of Minneapolis and St. Paul, with Minneapolis predominating. St. Paul is home to the school of agriculture and some social science departments, and resembles a typically pastoral small-college campus. However, the great majority of the more than forty thousand students matriculate to Minneapolis, where the campus is broad, sprawling along the banks of the Mississippi River. It is a school with a strong literary tradition. Max Shulman wrote *Barefoot Boy With Cheek* while an undergraduate there, and Tom Heggen wrote *Mr. Roberts* only a few short years after completing his studies at the university. Journalists Harrison Salisbury and Eric Severeid worked on the Minnesota

Daily, the campus newspaper, while literary luminaries such as Alan Tate, Robert Penn Warren, Saul Bellow, Mark Harris, John Berryman and James Wright either taught here or were in graduate school during the late fifties and sixties.

When Gary began classes, there was a strong literary ferment, equal—at least in the minds of some students and faculty—to the excitement generated by Golden Gopher football. Major-league writers, including Berryman, Wright, Howard Nemerov, novelist Jack Ludwig, and critic Dick Foster, taught undergraduate courses. Students possessed with obsessions to write worked for the *Daily* or the weekly campus magazine, *The Ivory Tower.* The *Daily* was published Tuesday through Friday, and its editors and reporters were paid. These same people also produced the magazine, which served as a catchall for material that couldn't be pigeonholed in the *Daily*—pieces that were too long, or an occasional poem or short story not suited to the newspaper.

"Those were wonderful times to be on that campus if you had literary ambitions," recalled James Delmont, former arts editor of *The Ivory Tower* and now a freelance reviewer and teacher. "There seemed to be great excitement about literature. Salinger was publishing; Mailer and James Baldwin were being discussed and written about by a lot of us. We looked up to the published people on our faculty then. Some of them gave us stuff for *The Ivory Tower* too. We all thought we were in some sort of literary renaissance, and to be part of this was enormously exciting."

"Classes were extraordinary. Berryman was a superb teacher, animated, enthusiastic. A snob, too, but a nice one. He'd say offhandedly that he knew Auden in London, then tell us, 'You don't know Auden at all,' leaving us the option of doing some research and finding out who he was. There was this incredible literary agitation on the U campus at that time, but it had its downside too. These people somehow instilled in us the notion that we could make a living in this field. We became aesthetes and rejected journalism, and wound up, many of us, with no

THE MAN FROM LAKE WOBEGON

marketable skills with which to earn a living. In that sense those men were irresponsible, leading us into an unreal state of mind. But we ate it up and thought the sixties were going to be another decade like the twenties."

Other students gravitated toward journalism, and they discovered an excellent campus daily on which to hone their skills. These people took their work very seriously, often viewing themselves as reporters first and students second. Beverly Kees, editor of the Gary, Indiana *Post-Tribune* and former *Daily* editor, said that as far as journalism students who worked on the *Daily* were concerned, classes kept getting in the way. Staffers hung out at campus joints, drinking beer at Stub and Herb's, eating at Vescio's Italian restaurant in Dinkytown, a small shopping area adjacent to the university with a decidedly bohemian cast; kiosks announced readings, musical performances, or demonstrations; there were also bookstores, coffee houses, and Bridgeman's ice cream shop. "All of us in that crowd had intense discussions," recalled Kees. "In the manner of journalists, we talked. We didn't dance much at parties."

Gary Keillor, of course, neither talked nor danced. Nor was he much noticed at first. Kees doesn't remember him from the era when she edited the *Daily* but recalls his occasional byline. She does remember Jim Wright being invited to student parties, drinking beer and recommending books for students to read. "He was always accessible," Kees said.

So was Berryman, holding forth in hallways, on campus walks, or wherever students gathered to hear pearls of wisdom or waspish gossip. "He was just a wonderful teacher," Delmont said. "He infused religion or God-awareness into his lectures, making students read John's Gospel, and dwelling at length on the Resurrection, which he maintained was genuine—a factor surprising some students who were weaning away from their parents' faiths only to have this brilliant scholar and intellectual in effect tell them their parents were right.

"Wright, as I recall, was released from the university for hiring some uncredentialed person to take over his classes while he wrote his poems."

Keillor absorbed this atmosphere but never seemed part of it. In fact, his initial involvement with campus activities was at WMMR, a closed-circuit student radio station, where he began announcing in 1960. He told a local reporter that he was too self-conscious to walk into the city room at the *Daily* and ask for work. It was easier to slip into the radio station and cut an audition tape with no one else around.

Since he had to finance his own education, he may not have had time to assimilate the literary ambiance about him. He worked for two years as a campus parking lot attendant, earning $1.35 an hour, and he also worked as a dishwasher. The grind apparently wore him down, and he left the university for a time in 1962. But not before he had published two poems in *The Ivory Tower*. His first appearance was in the April 30,1962 issue: *My Child Knew Once Who He Was*, followed by *At the Gallery* in the May 28 issue.

The poems are artfully rendered products of a young aesthete, and the imagery is often striking, decrying lost innocence, expressing alienation in mixtures of religious and grisly images. In *My Child Knew Once Who He Was*, Keillor wrote of a child weeping for mangled cats and being lost upon a flood of chalky Jesus dolls. In *At the Gallery*, he described a dead girl and utilized the grisly again in a line, "He wept and chucked beheaded babies' chins."

Returning to school in 1963, Gary auditioned as a student announcer for KUOM, the university station, which was an educational and classical music service. The staff was professional, with an occasional student hired at $1.85 an hour to augment full-time employees.

Burton Paulu, professor emeritus and director of the university broadcasting service in the sixties, remembers Keillor as playing a "good, but limited role here. He wrote essays that were short, witty and quite good. But his overall role was

minor. He was with us a short period as a student employee—
one among several at the time."

Marvin Granger, station manger at KUOM in the early sixties, however, recalls a burgeoning genius at work. "Educational stations did academically oriented stuff back then, and
deviations from straitlaced programming were not looked on
with approval."

However, there was one program called "Radio Free Saturday," a kind of free-form program of humor, musical variety and
interviews. "It was quite innovative for that time on that station," Granger said. "We had alternate hosts; I did it one week
and Garrison the next. When *Sgt. Pepper's Lonely Hearts Club
Band* came out, Garrison got an early copy and put the whole
thing on the air, which terribly upset Burton Paulu. Paulu
called me at home and said, 'I want to see you in my office at
eight Monday morning.' He said, 'I never want to hear rock
and roll on this station again.'

"Garrision had talked of the significance of the album as a
studio project—as a single piece, not a collection of cuts, as all
rock albums were up until then. And the album, he said,
should be listened to in its entirety.

"We were a daytime station then, sharing the frequency with
WABC in New York, a clear-channel station. We signed off as
early as four thirty P.M. in December, or as late as nine P.M. in
the summer.

"Garrison was one of two or three of us who did the late
afternoon newscast, which was the last program before sign-off.
His first piece of humor at the station was a hot-air-balloon
traffic report. It was totally unannounced, a last-minute thing
that hadn't been cleared with me or anyone. He had a tape
loop of sounds of a hot air balloon and then in his very quiet
voice described traffic conditions of the freeways. It was just
hilarious."

"Radio Free Saturday," the program on which Keillor began
to develop his distinctive broadcast personality, was a five-hour

affair. Connie Goldman, a former KUOM announcer who went to work for National Public Radio in Washington, now runs a nonprofit radio production company, and Garrison sits on her board of directors. She recalls breaking in a KUOM by reading the community calendar at the end of each broadcast day, or five P.M., whichever came later. "It was a five-minute spot," she said. "My first time on I was so scared I could hardly talk. I finished and was wringing wet. I got back to my desk, and Garrison had left a darling little note. He had listened, and said not to worry, that I was doing just fine. Next time, he suggested I don't take it as seriously as *Marat Sade*. It was a sweet way of supporting me, and I've saved the note."

Goldman and Keillor shared an office on the second floor of Eddy Hall, an old red sandstone building that resembles a Victorian castle. It had been renovated to accommodate KUOM's staff and studios, the latter being in the basement. Most of the staff offices were on the first floor, but Goldman said she and Keillor were on the second floor because "we didn't fit in with the classical music mold. Our desks butted up against each other, and we shared a common phone that I was always using. He hardly touched it, and when he did, his conversations were short, of few words. We were different. I mean, he was well over six feet tall, and I'm just five feet. We didn't even breathe the same air. I was always talking, he was always quiet.

"Garrison, Marvin [Granger] and I were all young when we met there. Garrison was attracting the campus poets. Marvin attracted the rebels and revolutionaries, and I attracted the freaks.

"We worked together a lot. On the Saturday show, I did little pieces. He'd send me out with a tape recorder to get man-on-the-street interviews and other silly things. The music was whatever we liked. Garrison would do his comfortable sort of talk, which you couldn't tell from his writing. We did what we thought were important and interesting things. It's strange for me to hear 'A Prairie Home Companion' so upbeat and jovial."

Goldman says she didn't often understand Keillor, but the

two were friends. "I didn't understand a person who was quiet and reserved. He wasn't one for small talk and had no glib answers. Yet he was very creative at the station. And I think the work he did on the old Saturday show was the beginning of the development of the Garrison Keillor everybody has grown to love. He could be very funny. He worked terribly hard. But he never discussed his writing at all."

At least, not with his broadcasting colleagues. He became fiction editor at *The Ivory Tower* in 1963, as his own quality short stories were routinely being published in the magazine. John Skow, in the 1985 *Time* cover story on Keillor, wrote, "At the University of Minnesota, Gary edited the literary magazine and wrote a noisy satirical column called 'Broadsides.' . . . But the storytelling gifts did not immediately appear."

But they did, almost immediately, *Time*'s error of omission notwithstanding. The magazine also erred by photographing Keillor with cheerleaders they indicated were from his old school. They were not from Anoka but rather represented a conference opponent. Keillor no doubt knew this and perhaps enjoyed sardonic delight in putting one over on America's leading newsweekly.

What appears to be Keillor's first published story in *The Ivory Tower* was "The Man Who Locked Himself In," published in the October 7, 1963 issue. It was a forerunner in style of the collected pieces in *Happy to Be Here*. The story's protagonist is a man named Howard Birdie, who spends his daughter's wedding reception locked inside the men's room at the church. While his wife and the minister attempt to persuade him to come out, Birdie contemplates the terry-cloth toilet seat cover upon which he's sitting. Keillor twice used the archaic spelling of *cigaret* instead of the more common *cigarette*.

Deloyd Hochstetter still has copies of the old *Ivory Towers*, which Keillor unfailingly sent him, along with copies of other published pieces and manuscripts. Much of it is in boxes, other items have been discarded. "I'd have needed another room to store it all in," he says.

"He used to say he didn't like college too much," said Hochstetter. "He said it was a waste of time. But he used to skip his last class and come out to visit. He'd always show me stuff he was working on. When I'd compliment his work, he'd say to my students that he didn't trust me. In other words, he thought I was saying that to be nice. He really lacked confidence."

Hochstetter remembers Keillor's first social encounters with a young woman at the university. "He met Mary there," Hochstetter said. Mary Guntzel was a young music major with a concentration in organ performance. She also did some writing and contributed a profile of the organist, Heinrich Fleischer, to *The Ivory Tower* while Keillor was editor. "I was just shocked the first time I met them together," Hochstetter said. "He had his arm around her, and I thought, my gosh, what happened to him? He wouldn't even talk to girls before." Garrison and Mary were married in 1965.

For a four-month period in 1963, Keillor also worked for the St. Paul Pioneer Press as a student intern. He expressed a desire to stay on with the paper, but there were no openings. "I loved newspaper writing," he said in a 1985 interview. "I did my share of weather, lots of obits, called hospitals to see if people in traffic accidents had died, and I interviewed authors. That's no way to live. Interviewing celebrities is just a step above calling the morgue."

This is the true Keillor speaking. He holds reporters in generally low esteem, but on the other hand, he was not cut from reportorial cloth himself. He was much too shy, too retiring, to make it as a hard-nosed reporter. He may have been able to ask tough questions but probably would have taken too long to get around to asking them.

Dr. Mitchell Charnley, Journalism Professor Emeritus at the university, was faculty advisor to student publications while Keillor was a student. He always admired Keillor's writing talents. "I knew he would make his mark with his typewriter," Charnley recalled, "but reporting for a daily newspaper was definitely not his cup of tea."

One story Keillor didn't get to write in St. Paul disturbed him. He told Hochstetter that he'd come upon a traffic accident involving a bus. He started helping with the injured and looking for bodies, and he came across one that had been decapitated. "He was quite shaken," Hochstetter said. "He got right on the phone to me and he says, 'You know what happened?' He wanted to write about it, but the *Press* wasn't interested, and it seemed no one was interested in this important happening, and he was hurt. He wanted to go up to professors and say, 'I saw death.' Even though he's a genius, he's extremely sensitive. He could be hurt easily.

"It was important to him and he may have written about it for a class assignment at least. One of his college professors used to say that he wouldn't hand in the assignments. Instead he would write his own things. Which is sort of nice, but you don't fulfill the class requirements that way."

Keillor began to drift away from his family's religious faith, at least in print, about the same time he became editor of *The Ivory Tower*, in September, 1964. A note in his sustaining, unsigned column, 'Broadsides,' upbraided the organization Campus Crusade for Christ for its huckstering come-on for a magician headlining one of its programs. He called the organization's advertising for the event charlatan Christianity, an insult to serious Christians and the campus at large.

Editing a prestigious publication should have fostered confidence and esteem, but the joy of obtaining this position was tainted. Shortly before he was named to the post, he encountered Deloyd Hochstetter near the campus as Hochstetter was on his way to church. "Gary was dressed up with a suit coat, and I saw a row of cigars in his pocket. I never said anything about his being dressed up, because he had turned into a sort of bohemian then—long hair, and a beard and all—I just asked where he was going. 'To interview for *The Ivory Tower*,' he said.

He'd already prepared himself to look the part of the editor—tie, cigars and so forth. But as it turned out, he was the only applicant for the job. Some of the kids who knew him made fun of that. When people said, 'Isn't it great that Gary Keillor is *The Ivory Tower* editor?' they said, 'Yeah, but he's the only one who wanted it.'"

His sartorial appearance, as noted by Hochstetter, was decidedly nonconformist. Keillor had grown his hair long and parted it in the middle. He would sport a full beard off and on for more than a decade. His dress, save for a white suit that Goldman says he wore occasionally before becoming a household name, was casual—blue jeans, sweatshirts.

Charnley, a pleasant, professorial sort, recalled that seniors with a lot of campus publication experience were normally appointed to the chief editorships and were named by the student-dominated Board in Control of Publications. Even in the days when autocracy was the rule on college campuses, administrators rarely intervened with the board's selections. "Except once," Charnley recalled. "A young man named Severeid wanted the job as *Daily* editor when he was a student. But the dean wouldn't hear of it. Severeid was far too liberal, according to the dean. Otherwise there was a tacit hands-off policy." The position paid $1250 a year, plus a minimum of 10 cents per column inch of copy.

"Gary was a young intellectual, but he wasn't the thin kind. He was a good thick one, I think, whose interest was in literary writing," said Charnley. "I remember he and I had a number of conversations about writing, and especially sportswriting—particularly hockey, because he was a hockey nut, and he had a scorn for many of the hockey reporters, which he unloaded on me."

Keillor's work on *The Ivory Tower* reflects skill and maturity, and many of his pieces stand up today as wonderfully polished and fresh. His burgeoning interest in hockey propelled him to take the plunge into creative journalism, hut it happened almost on a dare.

Dave Mona, a Minneapolis public relations executive and former baseball writer for the Minneapolis *Tribune*, was the *Daily* sports editor in 1965. He and Keillor shared an office in Murphy Hall. "His office and mine had a common wall and it had a pass-through, so we would overhear conversations of the *Tower* staff, and they would overhear us planning *Daily* sports coverage, and there were a number of one-liners traveling back and forth, usually on wildly different subjects. If you were designing an office, you probably couldn't do a better job of putting two more different groups of people adjacent to each other than the *Ivory Tower* people and our sports staff.

"It was our perception that the *Ivory Tower* people were elitist. Truly a different group, clearly an intellectual one. They were older, and a lot of stories were written by people who were not typical undergraduate types. They were graduate students, young faculty members. They looked and talked differently from most college students, and one did not see them at a lot of more social events around campus.

"Keillor was not a great mixer. The *Daily* at that time was a social activity as well as a newspaper, and lended itself to a great number of parties and unofficial get-togethers. Garrison was a little out of the mainstream of the banter and badinage of the day-to-day activities. He seemed a loner. He looked forty when he was nineteen, and not appreciably different than he does today. He also had a certain mystique about him. Everybody knew he was very smart; I think he was pretty shy. Just when you thought he didn't know what was going on, or didn't care, he would come up with a one-liner or something that was absolutely appropriate to the situation. You realized there wasn't much going on in that office that escaped his attention. He was more an observer than a participant."

Part of his mystique had to do with what might appear in any particular issue of the magazine. Unlike the *Daily*, where people posted notices about stories and deadlines, the *Tower* operated in relative secrecy, not with sinister intent; it simply reflected

Keillor's management style. Along with his shyness was an intense need for privacy that continues to the present.

"I remember vividly one story where Keillor had saved examples of sportswriting that he had taken from the *Daily*," Mona said. "He had clipped leads and graphs out of context and gave a humorous interpretation to what they might mean in real English. It was pretty funny, as was most of the stuff he did. It was out of context though, and it hurt a little. I guess we had some pride of authorship, but he kept our bylines intact for all to see. I remember commenting to him that it was a little unfair for him to keep a scissors for a year and clip a graph here and there and take them out of context.

"He said he meant no harm by the story, and I must have suggested that it was inappropriate coming from him, because he wasn't a sports fan. He was offended by that. He said, 'That's not true. I am a sports fan.' He was probably among the people I'd have put among the ten least likely sports fans on campus. I remember saying something like, 'You couldn't tell it from your magazine. You ignore sports in your magazine.'

"He said, 'Well, we would cover sports.' I told him I'd have more respect for him as a critic of sports journalism if he'd written at least one sports story. And he said, 'Well, all right. I'll write a sports story.'

"We didn't hear too much about it, but we knew he was working on a sports piece, and we knew it was going to be about hockey. It came out, and it was the best sports story I'd read in my life up to that time. It was so good but it was so atypical, because it concentrated on the poetry of hockey, the sights, sounds and smells, and was much more centered on the feeling of the game than in just a superficial experiencing of it. It was almost poetic; it was beautifully done."

It was almost a prose poem, and appeared on February 1, 1965, entitled, "Two on Hockey: A Conversation with Minnesota Center Doug Woog." The piece opened with a description of kids playing playground hockey at dusk on a rink on Como Avenue in St. Paul. "He captured the flavor of hockey so well that it dispelled any doubts anybody had about his ability to take on almost any subject and do an outstanding job on it," Mona said. "We didn't have any other suggestions about areas in which he wasn't qualified to write."

Doug Woog today is the head hockey coach at the University of Minnesota, a man with wide experience in amateur hockey. He's coached in high schools and junior divisions, as well as with the national and Olympic teams. But in the 1964–65 season, he was a twenty-year-old junior from South St. Paul, who became an all-American player for the Gophers. Though Minnesota has been a collegiate hockey power for many years, back in the sixties the team struggled against North Dakota and Denver—teams that recruited Canadians, who were often older and more experienced and thus able to dominate the younger, slower Minnesotans. A college player from Canada in that era may have already played one or two seasons of Junior A hockey and so would be about twenty years old before enrolling at an American college.

Seated behind his cluttered desk in the spanking new sports complex on the university campus, Woog recalled that season, his best as a player. "I had a banner year then. Everything went right, and that's where that story comes from."

After a pause, Woog said he remembered Keillor because Garrison spent so much time with him preparing the story. "He was different. He called me on the phone and said, 'Garrison Keillor here.' He spoke differently, dressed differently, his background was more academic than athletic. It was atypical, certainly the most unique interview experience I've ever had."

Woog remembers spending hours with Keillor, instead of the few minutes most sportswriters required to get their stories. Keillor visited Woog at his dormitory, at practice sessions. Woog also recalls having misgivings about doing an interview with a literary intellectual, wondering if Keillor's intentions were to do a hatchet job on a jock or on athletes in general. "It was unusual for a campus intellectual to be interested in hockey or any sport. He looked that part—not at all like a sports figure. I remember thinking when I saw him, How the hell is this going to come out?

"He was very soft-spoken, unlike other local sportswriters, who could be brash. Having come from a successful high school sports background I became very familiar with area sportswriters and got to know them quite well. But here was a guy who was entirely different—a bearded, tall, lanky guy. He wrote just a fantastic piece, very fair, one with more depth and understanding than I would have anticipated. He viewed the game from a sense of beauty, not as a combative, physical game. He could see the beauty of motion."

Keillor described hockey as a dancer's game—a cross-step shuffle of defenders as they skated backward; the long strides of wings and centers on breakaways; goaltenders hopping and sliding. He liked the aspect of the game that stressed skill over size and speed. He wrote that talented players from the neighborhood rinks evolve into lightness and syncopation, lamenting the use of sport as a metaphor for life.

"He had me explain the system of the game," said Woog. "I diagrammed breakouts and other plays. For me to have gone into this much depth, he had to have presented a situation in which I would have been comfortable. He assimilated a lot of information, especially when you consider he came from a nonhockey background.

"I didn't normally get that kind of coverage; it was so extensive and intensive. It took me a half hour to read. I don't remember a story since then of that style. It was about an individual who related to the game, and he was so accurate about how I related my feelings of dancing on ice. As I said, it was my most unique interview experience."

The profile was widely praised around campus, and provided the impetus for Keillor to write another major hockey article, this one about the Gophers' final road swing to Grand Forks, North Dakota, to close out the season with two games against the vaunted Sioux. The series ended with the Gophers losing both games to the Western Collegiate Hockey Association champions, but Keillor captured the road trip ambiance in a story titled, "The People, The Game and The Spirit."

"*The Ivory Tower* was never better than when he was editor," said Denis Wadley, a teacher at a private high school in Minneapolis and freelance book reviewer. Wadley was associate editor at the *Daily* at the same time Keillor was magazine editor. "It had been around for years and used to be a weekly," Wadley said. "He changed it to a monthly, and it was much thicker and much better. After he left, it went straight downhill and was discontinued not long after. He set standards that nobody was going to match."

The magazine took on a decidedly *New Yorker* look, and in place of the "Talk of the Town" column in the front of the magazine, the *Ivory Tower* frontispiece was called "Broadsides," which John Skow called noisy and satirical. More often though, it was an intelligent sort of monologue, or series of short monologues: references to old-time radio, academic freedom, or current popular music—which Keillor held in contempt. His standards for the publication were so high, that there were times when he wrote virtually the entire issue himself, under various pseudonyms, because submissions didn't meet the level of excellence he expected.

"I wasn't sophisticated enough then to recognize his enormous talent," said Carolyn Thompson, who followed Keillor to the university in 1961, a year after he enrolled. "His writing was always mature, and even more so for a college kid."

James Delmont remembers Keillor as a "really gifted writer of high literary quality. He had a grace, a style uncommon for undergraduates, though he was shy and proud. He had uncommon intelligence too, but few people, I think, knew him."

"It seemed to me he was often uncomfortable in a conversation," said Dr. Charnley. "He would hesitate. But I would never question his basic intelligence or sensitivity."

Despite his closeness to the writing scene at the University, Charnley never had Keillor in one of his classes. "He took courses in the department that appealed to his special interests—critical writing or literary aspects of journalism. He asked my advice on occasion, and it was always fun to talk to him. I had great confidence he would make his mark. I was not at all surprised to find his name one day in *The New Yorker*. My impression was that he had quite a lot of talent and he had the character to make use of it.

"One of the last times I saw him when he was in school, it was late spring. He came into my office one day, and he had a paperback book. He laid it down on my desk and said, 'You might like this.' Then he turned around and walked out. It was a book of poems by Reed Whitemore. I thought that act of Gary's coming in here and giving me a book and then turning around before I could look at it and say thank you was very characteristic of him."

Dennis Wadley viewed the eventual decline of *The Ivory Tower* as almost inevitable. "He changed it, made it his own. The faculty and grad students liked it very much. But it was of less general interest to undergrads. It had begun as a general-interest magazine because there were occasional pieces submitted that didn't fit the *Daily* format, and some of these were fairly aimless things. But when he came in, he would seek out these essays and poems, not just the deflected rejects from the *Daily*. He accepted any creative value. No petty sniping, no political stuff either. He was interested throughout in the quality of writing, and I don't think the opinion or the topic meant very much if the style was clever. He set standards that nobody was going to match."

The standards he established, according to Dave Mona, were the toughest possible, "because they were the ones he set for himself. It would have been hard to be his editor, because he had a strong sense of what he would and would not do. There was a sense of purpose about him, to the point where a lot of times you felt he was oblivious of other people who'd come in and out of that office."

The typical *Daily* staffer was genial and made friends easily and quickly among other writers. Those offices were writers' homes on campus. "You'd come in at eight o'clock and didn't have a class until third hour," Mona said. "When you went to your class, you left all your books for your next class there. You came back and you had three hours, so you did your interviewing and started your story before your afternoon classes, and you went to them, came back and finished. Then you probably went over to the Big Ten or Stub and Herb's for a beer at five-thirty, and perhaps you worked night staff and stayed until one o'clock in the morning with a printer. So you got to know everybody well. There was Keillor sharing those offices with all these people who spent so much time there, and yet I would say there weren't three people in the office who knew him well. He was never unfriendly, just standoffish. He was clearly different from the rest of us at that office."

The Keillor persona varied between the man who edited *The Ivory Tower* and the broadcaster at KUOM. "He was first and foremost a writer," Marvin Granger said. "He was and is a very serious writer and a very serious poet as well. Back then I saw him as a trusting, humanitarian type. I'm not surprised by his success but am somewhat surprised by how he relates to business and business affairs. He and I were quite antibusiness then."

Most of those who worked at the *Daily* and *The Ivory Tower* confused Gary's diffidence with unfriendliness. "He wasn't the guy I'd invite to watch a fight on TV," said Delmont. "He didn't seem at ease around people, and I think people were uneasy around him." Yet according to Connie Goldman, Keillor could be funny during informal encounters.

Wadley didn't find him a stimulating conversationalist. "He didn't speak unless he had something to say. He didn't feel any obligation to inject something into a conversation just to keep it going. I'm not sure whether that was an intellectual decision, or whether it was just his personality."

Many who knew him from his associations with the *Daily* and *The Ivory Tower* apparently didn't connect him with the person who broadcast on KUOM. Indeed, that station has never been popular with university students anyway; most have always preferred mainstream popular music, and KUOM was tilted toward the edification of its audiences' minds, which ruled out popular music. Keillor, however, viewed his employment at the station as his basic job, the one that paid for his education. He told *The Mother Earth News*, "Radio announcing is easy, indoor work. You sit in the studio and you say 'We have just heard *Appalachian Spring* by Aaron Copland, and we now turn to the music of Beethoven.' Announcing is much easier than parking cars or washing dishes, and yet it has a kind of status attached to it that I've never understood. I got the job, I think, because I was able to imitate the voice they were looking for. I could broaden a few vowels and get a kind of cultivated funereal tone with a very slight British sound to it."

"He was good at it, no question," Hochstetter said. "And he developed an interest in classical music. He became the best announcer they had pronouncing classical names."

One has to wonder about Garrison's view of the announcer's prestige. Far from being something he never understood, he early on obviously attached great significance to it and seemed to idolize the local broadcast personalities, in much the same manner other youngsters chose to worship great athletes. And the status of the broadcaster is one of celebrity—a job that, simply put, sounds like fun. There's a congeniality about it, a potential to reach people, to make them happy for a time and, for one possessed of ego, to be recognized as significant, to be tendered speaking or emceeing engagements. A broadcaster is one who is acquainted with the political and sports headliners; or with popular musicians, and what shy, lonely young person couldn't relate to the announcer's ease with words, with people, his ability to say what needed to be said?

Keillor's voice—a marvelous broadcast tool, rich, dulcet—is natural. Cedric Adams delivered his little homilies and news in a baritone, too, but his carried a whiskey-edged rasp. Keillor's is buttermilk smooth and has been variously described a soft as corn silk or warm and supple as the soft nap of old corduroy. During his tenure at KUOM he was much appreciated by classical music lovers in the listening area. His sound was professional and erudite, lending credibility to the image of an educational station programing music for an elite audience. It was the voice that would within a few years, though, enrage classical music lovers; for when he appeared on the local public station, KSJN, he replaced the morning classics with hillbilly tunes interspersed with mouth music—strange humming or buzzing sounds that may imitate musical instruments—and nonsensical commercials from Jack's Auto Repair, followed by Bach chorales.

While Granger and Goldman knew Keillor wrote and heard his clever sketches on "Radio Free Saturday," he never discussed it with them, just as he seldom talked about radio with those he knew through his writing.

"He was so shy," Wadley remembered," that the last thing I would ever have expected from him was radio or television. I did anticipate his being a professional writer, and I think everyone did. He had a deft, satirical touch back then, without being ham-fisted. He wrote easily, he wrote well. He seemed impatient with interruptions when he was writing, which is why he seemed to do most of his writing away from the office. And even though I got to know him rather well, he wasn't one to sit around and chat. So it might have been difficult to tell how close you were to him."

That a young artist would deign to study journalism did not surprise Wadley. "You learn more about writing in journalism than when you study English," he said. "And the reason you do is that they insist, for practical reasons and deadlines, that you write briefly, concisely, rapidly, with no time for leisurely revisions. This discipline was important for him. He rarely wastes a word in his writing, and his style is traceable to his experience as a journalism student." And no doubt this was a contributing factor in Garrison's ability to complete a story-monologue each week that achieved or approached true literary excellence.

By spring 1965 Keillor's creative writing began to receive prizes. He won honorable mention in competition for his poems, *On Waking to Old Debts*, and *Nicodemus*, both of which appeared in the April 5, 1965 *Ivory Tower*.

Almost nothing has been revealed of Keillor's relationship with the charismatic, brilliant, alcoholic, Pulitzer Prize–winning poet, John Berryman, but they must have had at least a nodding acquaintance. Berryman contributed a remembrance of the critic Morgan Blum to *The Ivory Tower*. Blum had died while teaching at the university.

In an unusual move, Keillor was reappointed editor of the *Tower* for the 1965–66 academic year, though the effort cost him academically. He apparently received some F grades and was put on academic probation before he decided to give his classes a solid effort and graduate.

"I took one class with him, a graduate class in poetry," Hochstetter said. "He usually arrived first and saved a chair for me every morning, and we'd have dinner later on in the day. I think he wanted us to study together, but I always had so much going, that there wasn't time. We both got B's. I guess it was good for that course, even though I had graduated with honors. He didn't, and a B for him was pretty darn good."

Before graduating, Keillor won the Academy of American Poets contest in the spring of 1966, after relinquishing editorship of *The Ivory Tower*. He received the one-hundred-dollar Fanny Fay Wood Poetry Prize for two poems judged best by the university's English department. *At the Premier* and *This is a Poem, Good Afternoon* were the award winners.

He received his B.A. in English with the journalism minor later that spring, six years after beginning the baccalaureate program. He then started a short-lived attempt to earn an M.A. in English. Keillor later remarked to Irv Letofsky of the Minneapolis *Tribune*, "It was a mistake to have gone to the university, to expend the time I did. . . . It had a corrupting influence on me on what I wrote. It removed me from what I had to write about and what I still have to write about—which is people that I came from and the class of people that I have some feeling about."

"He told me that going to the university was the worst thing he'd ever done," Hochstetter said. "He once wrote me that people had to find ethics or science and technology were going to destroy us. I think he still thinks that."

After graduation, Keillor remained on KUOM while in graduate school. But the rigors of academic life interfered with his creative writing. He was spending long hours at his typewriter, working on a novel, which he eventually abandoned, as well as short pieces he hoped to sell to *The New Yorker*. Because of his great reverence for that magazine and its illustrious contributors, he worked hard and with extreme care on the stories he would show the editors. He told John Bordsen in a 1983 article published by *Saturday Review* that he'd gone through a great many drafts, "and I studied every sentence, and it was work that I enjoyed, but it was also very difficult."

LITTLE has been revealed about Keillor's activities between the time he left the university and November 1969 when he took a job with fledgling MPR, except that he was writing regularly, and just as regularly receiving rejections. He joined MPR and his old KUOM colleague, Marvin Granger, at KSJR in Collegeville, Minnesota. Granger would also later move to KSJN in St. Paul. Garrison and Mary lived in nearby Freeport, a town ninety-five miles west of Minneapolis on Interstate 94, in the heart of Stearns County. The birthplace of Sinclair Lewis in Sauk Centre is a mere ten miles north and west of Freeport on U.S. 52. Approaching from the east, a visitor is drawn to the water tower identifying the town. A large smiling face is painted on it. This is farm country, the acreage rolling gently, broken only by the occasional lines of trees, planted during the thirties as windbreaks, and spherical silos, which bloom like giant mushrooms in clusters of threes and fours close to simple bungalows that house farmers and their families.

Cable television has recently come to Freeport, but like the Norwegian bachelor farmers in Lake Wobegon, who eschew modernity, Freeporters seem reluctant to try it. They've grown used to the twenty- and thirty-foot antennas on their roofs, pulling reception from St. Cloud and even the Twin Cities. And besides, what good is cable if you have to put up with Xrated movies and all those sensual and obscure rock videos that come along with it? Freeporters will spend their hard-earned money elsewhere, thank you.

Freeport is probably the main model for Lake Wobegon, according to Deloyd Hochstetter. "It's about the right countryside," he says. And indeed, it has the small-town ambiance that Anoka lacks. It is smaller than Lake Wobegon, with a population of only 530 and it doesn't have its own lake, but Birch Lake is nearby, and the town is dominated by two structures: the Famo Feeds granary near the railroad tracks and the Sacred Heart Catholic Church, the tallest building, in the heart of town. The only church in Freeport, it is constructed of blond brick with a bell tower below the spire. The bell tolls dully, without resonance, on the hour. There's a sizeable Catholic cemetery on the church property, and a Catholic elementary school is adjacent, located north of the church.

Dorothy of the Chatterbox Cafe doesn't hold forth in Freeport, but Charlie's Cafe will do as well. In rural America value remains a constant, and so portions of noon meals are served on rectangular platters—stout roast beef sandwiches smothered in thick gravy, a double scoop of instant whipped potatoes, canned peas and carrots, a roll; a large bowl of chicken and wild rice soup, a bit heavy on the sage. Regulars and irregulars wolf it down; men off the fields that butt against the city limits barely a quarter mile from the town's center; men who eat with their seed-corn caps on, who take long swallows of Charlie's coffee—brewed rather thin, one would surmise, by Wobegonian standards. Norwegians love nothing so well as sturdy coffee, coffee that causes the lips to curl over the front teeth, eliciting a small aspirate grunt of appreciation and a quick shake of the head. A spoon placed in a cup of Charlie's coffee remains visible clear to the bottom.

In Charlie's a hired hand, hung over, drinks coffee from a pot placed before him in his booth. He is alone, and he chain-smokes unfiltered cigarettes, his hands trembling as he raises matches to his lips. Hair pokes out in wings above his ears, from beneath his old navy surplus stocking cap. Waitresses leave him alone; they know him, know this ritual.

Unlike Lake Wobegon, Freeport is predominately Catholic, and at least one in ten homes has a small grotto displayed in the yard. The houses are an eclectic mix of old turn-of-the-century farmhouses, with newer construction. Some of the older homes feature new siding but retain their old gingerbread brackets and rolls above large, open porches.

Children gambol across a frozen swamp, a springer spaniel in tow. A truck driver visits with a worker from the local creamery, the latter, his foot up on the diesel's bumper, nods, squinting over the smoke from a cigarette dangling between his lips.

The Corner Store is an old-time general store, selling groceries, dry goods, hardware and floor coverings. Clerks politely inquire after the needs of out-of-town customers, and as a line forms at the cash register, the checkout girl chats with a young man recently returned home from college in Bemidji. No one minds. They all become part of the conversation, as he recounts how his dog snatched the steak his mother had fixed for him upon his return for the Thanksgiving weekend.

Freeport bears a striking resemblance to the illustration on the cover of *Lake Wobegon Days*.

Garrison and Mary lived here, outside of town in an old farmhouse that Hochstetter remembers as having no screens and thus attracting a plethora of summer insects when windows were opened. The Keillors occupied the house while he toiled on "The Morning Program" over KSJR-FM. The station was originally operated by Saint John's University, a Benedictine men's school, and is still located on the campus, which is itself pastoral, with streams and lakes.

The university's abbey, however, is definitely contemporary—a majestic Marcel Breuer design, and one of his most noted works. Upon approaching the campus, a visitor's attention is immediately drawn to it and it is one of the region's major tourist attractions.

Saint John's has also given work to and eased the financial

burdens of writers. The National Book Award—winning novelist and short-story writer, J. F. Powers, used to teach classes here between royalty checks, as has novelist Jon Hassler. Keillor, of course, did not teach but relied on his broadcasting ability for a livelihood while he, too, struggled with the muse in an attempt to create stories and sketches that *The New Yorker* or some other major magazines would want to publish.

Before settling in Freeport, though, he made his well-known excursion out East, applying for a job at *The Atlantic Monthly*. He was not hired, and as he has often told reporters, he felt the folks at that august publication could tell that he had changed into presentable clothing in a public rest room.

Though Freeport is the most logical setting for Lake Wobegon, Keillor has also included another Minnesota village—Marine on St. Croix—as part of the mythical town. Like Freeport, Marine's population is about 530, and the two villages' combined populations barely exceed Lake Wobegon's 942 souls.

Marine on St. Croix is one of Minnesota's oldest settlements, established in 1839 on the west bank of the St. Croix River, which forms the border with Wisconsin. Like Lake Wobegon, Marine was first explored by New Englanders, who established a large sawmill instead of a college. The town is strikingly New England in character—especially the scant two-block business district on Judd Street.

The easterners who settled Marine first, lived in great homes on the steep bluffs above the river, leaving the flats and bottomland to the Swedish immigrants who would later form the main population base of the town. Marine, as a Swedish community for new arrivals to America, was the setting for numerous exterior shots for the film *The Immigrants*. Swedish architecture dominates the residences in Marine—houses with pointed roofs and bull's-eye windows; lots of gingerbread on porches and stoops of older homes. Some of the residences are referred to as compounds and contain more than one dwelling. Citizens, proud of their heritage and of the antiquity of their homes, will often post the construction date of their houses on fences or gateposts.

Marine's general store was at one time owned by a man named Ralph—the Ralph of the Pretty Good Grocery in Lake Wobegon. And the character Billy the Boy Butcher was a local lad who worked for Ralph.

"Garrison liked Ralph's," Beverly Skoglund said. An English and journalism instructor at Stillwater High School and a resident of Marine, Skoglund knew Keillor during his brief stay there, when he lived in a house on the Wilcox compound. "It was an old-fashioned store; there was sawdust on the floor in the butcher section, and there were old pine floors. The store is the way he describes it. The meat counter was one of those old high ones, and deep. Naturally everything you wanted was down at the bottom of the case, and while Ralph was fetching it, you'd ask about so-and-so, and catch up on all the gossip. And by the way—it's true; if you couldn't find it at Ralph's, you did without," she added, referring to Keillor's slogan about Ralph in his "Prairie Home Companion" "commercials."

There's an outsized gazebo in the small town square on Judd Street. The general store and the Marine Branch Library rise two stories and are identically painted white with green trim. There's a bell tower above the library, indicating probable use as a fire bell or warning for other potential disasters. The Marine Township Hall, where Keillor performed some early programs, is a couple blocks up the hill from Judd Street. Constructed in 1872 for two thousand dollars, it is among the best representations of Swedish stonework crafted by early Minnesota settlers.

Marine, at one time a snug, cozy village, is now giving way to suburban sprawl but has not yet lost its quaint charm. "You're not an independent family when you live in Marine," Skoglund says. "You're part of a bigger family. It's very comfortable, open and friendly."

No Chatterbox Cafe here either, but the Valley Cafe on Judd Street will do as well for coffee and small-town gossip.

There's the Brookside Bar and Grill, but it's a bit too uptown fancy to be Wally and Evelyn's Sidetrack up in Lake Wobegon.

There was no *Herald-Star* newspaper in Marine either, but the weekly news sheet used to be published by Ralph. "It was just one sheet," said Skoglund, "a piece of long yellow paper that Ralph cranked out down in the basement of the store. One side would be grocery specials at the store and the other side homey little personals. But when Ralph sold the store the news sheet was discontinued."

If the Freeport church was Catholic, it's only fitting that the lone church in Marine is Christ Lutheran Church, a handsome white structure up the hill on Oak Street, close to the Oakland Cemetery along County Road 4.

The reason Keillor decided to leave Marine, said Beverly Skoglund, was because of the tiresome drive to the KSJN studios in downtown St. Paul. "It's a long way when you drive from Marine, because you're on back roads, not freeways. I remember once on his show, he talked about how he never thought about the fact he looked funny. But once his car had stalled and nobody picked him up, and it was during the winter and cold, he decided he must have looked funny to all those people who passed him by. When he was creating his personality, he did look sort of funny. Now he looks straight, which is too bad. Then he was bearded with granny glasses, high-water pants and white socks. His shoes were also odd-looking."

If Keillor drew incidents of Scandinavian ambiance and Ralph's Pretty Good Grocery from Marine on St. Croix, it remains clear that geographically he places Lake Wobegon in Freeport. The location of Lake Wobegon is cited in a paper presented at the Dakota History Conference in the summer of 1986 by John E. Miller, professor of history at South Dakota State University, who has never been to Freeport. In "The Distance Between Gopher Prairie and Lake Wobegon: Sinclair Lewis and Garrison Keillor on the Small Town Experience," Miller writes that Keillor provides numerous clues about the town's location, "indicating that it is near St. Cloud, northwest of St. Cloud, and more specifically, thirty-two miles from St. Cloud. That would put it almost exactly at Freeport, the town Keillor lived in when he started inventing stories about Lake Wobegon as a radio announcer for Minnesota Public Radio during the early 1970s. It could hardly be closer to Sauk Centre, which is just ten miles up Highway 52 from Freeport."

Keillor's use of Lake Wobegon predates his acquaintance with Marine. He began referring to it while working at KSJR, the oldest station in the Minnesota Public Radio network. KSJR was started in 1967 by the university with a full-time staff of four. In 1969 a separate corporation was formed to establish a network of stations throughout the state, and this was called Minnesota Educational Radio, later changed to Minnesota Public Radio.

Keillor's job there was to host a three-hour drive-time classical music program each morning. It gradually evolved into a mix of bluegrass and other nonclassical music, and was sponsored by Jack's Auto Repair. When station management complained about the new direction his program was taking, Keillor quit in March, 1971, and tried to live off his writing income.

"Local Family Keeps Son Happy," was his first published *New Yorker* piece. It was a parody of small-town newspaper stories, a sketch that *New Yorker* founder Harold Ross might have called a "casual," and told of a family that hired a prostitute to keep their seventeen-year-old son company so he would stay home. The piece totaled a mere 334 words and appeared in 1970, earning Keillor slightly more than five hundred dollars.

By now he and Mary had a son, Jason, and full-time writing wasn't the answer to financial stability and ease of mind. "He had a hard time with his first wife, living in Freeport," Hochstetter said. "I think one of the problems might have been that Mary was after him to write a book. But you see, he wasn't ready then." The couple was divorced in 1974.

In a lengthy Minneapolis *Tribune* profile, Irv Letofsky quoted Keillor: "I would sell a story and then wait two weeks and call and ask for the money. It bothered me that I was spending so much time doing what seemed like humiliating, adolescent things . . . to look through *The New Yorker* to get ideas on how to write another story they would want. It did me no good and I knew that, but just to be busy and neurotic and try to have a plan about it and go at things straight."

After a six-month hiatus from broadcasting, Keillor returned to KSJN, the MPR flagship station in St. Paul, the next October. He says he got the job because he wrote for *The New Yorker*, a tony magazine that made it all right. He told Letofsky, "I would never have been able to get away with playing the music I did unless I happened to be associated with a magazine which, although it has changed, still in the Midwest stands for being Uptown."

He said he didn't like the educational radio formats at KSJR, and KUOM before that, where an announcer merely said, "We now turn to the music of Schubert."

His six to nine A.M. program on KSJN was broadcast four mornings a week until November, 1973, when he left again to write full time. He returned as morning show host in July of 1974 and continued that assignment until April, 1982.

The daily show was originally called "A Prairie Home Companion," its title taken from the name of a cemetery Keillor saw near Fargo, North Dakota. This show carried with it the foundation upon which the Saturday evening program would be constructed. One of his trademarks is that he has seldom if ever mentioned his own name on the air. Listeners would learn his identity only if a guest or another announcer mentioned it. He never did state his name on his broadcasts.

He "discovered" Lake Wobegon while at KSJR, telling the September 13, 1985 issue of *Publishers Weekly* that it sounded vague and had an "Indian sound to it, as so many towns in Minnesota do. And so it sat around for a time simply as that, a fictitious name, before I even started putting people in it. Lake Wobegon was a location for some 'sponsors.'"

He has, in the main, he recalled, found satisfaction in his radio work. "You sit at a microphone with your favorite music, talk to people and wish them a happy birthday and try to create something pleasant and happy for them. Seemed to me to be a simple, decent service to mankind."

Marvin Granger, who had departed KUOM in the late sixties, became program director at KSJN during Keillor's early years at that station. "Bill Kling [founder and president of MPR] had taken a year's leave of absence to work for the Corporation for Public Broadcasting, and Garrison was doing an early morning program of classical music. But he started to work in a little bluegrass, a little Grateful Dead and the Beach Boys, and his program became an eclectic mix. It made me very nervous because I knew where the money came from—people who wanted classical music. A man who individually sent ten to fifteen thousand dollars to our network stations wrote a letter to Mike Obler, the interim station manager, in February or March, 1970, saying that he couldn't see fit to contribute any more money if Keillor continued playing that music. Obler sent a copy to Garrison with a note that said, 'I will not take responsibility for the loss of this man's support.' Garrison resigned within the week and stayed at the farm in Freeport.

"Obler and Kling pleaded with me to get Garrison back, and I made a number of trips begging him to come back and asking him under what conditions he'd return. Kling recognized way back then, his [Keillor's] genius and must have known that here was a singular talent he could build around. It was vital to Kling that Garrison return."

It didn't happen immediately, however. And Keillor initially seemed relieved he didn't have responsibilities to the station or his program. But Granger persisted, and in October, Keillor came back. "That episode told me more about him than any other single experience," Granger said. "He was a person of uncompromising integrity, and his estimation of public radio as groveling before the upper class was something he certainly wouldn't tolerate. He clearly didn't intend to make a career in broadcasting, at least under those circumstances. It was characteristic of his values back then."

Those values included segues from the Beach Boys' "Help Me Rhonda" to Vivaldi's *Concerto in D Minor* and tossing in, of all things, "commercials." Some of those first commercials were about Jack's Auto Repair, and Powdermilk Biscuits. There was also one about an alarm clock—a life-size brass figure of a matron, everyperson's mother, who, when the hour of rising struck, would smack her hands together. The wakened sleeper would dutifully step to the foot of the bed, tilt his head forward, and the big mama would insert her fingers into his ears and clean them.

On his early morning program, Keillor had been developing a following among the hip intelligentsia, but was simultaneously alienating the downtown dollars. The station had received complaints long before the incident that hastened Keillor's resignation. He told Letofsky he understood the station needing money, and that his programming tastes had soured some longtime supporters. But he didn't like being notified in a memo, and that act caused his resignation.

Dave Matheny, a Minneapolis *Star Tribune* reporter, formerly worked as a cartoonist and caricaturist with the paper. He was an illustrator for the *Daily* and *The Ivory Tower* during Keillor's editorship, though they never actually worked together. Matheny recalls that Keillor has always seemed to be very guarded, and of course, shy. "I went to see him in the studio one morning because I was supposed to draw this caricature of him to accompany a story. He had long, center-parted hair and a beard and mustache. I didn't remember working for him in college, since I worked mainly for the *Daily*. I must have done a couple assignments for the magazine, because he remembered me.

"That morning he was replaying a Rolling Stones track, trying to hear a different phrase, what they were really saying. He played it six or seven times, picking up the needle and putting it down again. His was a quirky show, but apparently management complained, because after he'd answered the phone, he put on another record and left. I assumed he went to the john, but the needle stuck on the record. I'm sitting there wondering whether you do what you'd do at home—pick up the needle and move it—or on the other hand, here's all this expensive equipment around and maybe a microphone is live, and I don't know what to do. I'm waiting for him to come back while this phrase is repeating over and over and over and over. He came quickly to the door and picked up the needle. He never said a thing about it. After the show we went for breakfast at the St. Paul Hilton. What we mostly talked about was the difficulty in quitting smoking. He was struggling and so was I. He smoked a cigarillo at breakfast, and said he allowed himself four a day. His conversation was real quiet. He didn't laugh. I got the impression he wasn't a humorous person off mike."

His absence of personal humor also struck Bill Gilchrist, a local musician, who had appeared on Keillor's program with a bagpipe band. A big fan, Gilchrist visited Keillor on the morning program when two of Gilchrist's friends, Judy Larson and Bill Hinckley, were guests. Larson and Hinckley later became semiregulars on "A Prairie Home Companion," and they, along with many local traditional and folk musicians, frequently stopped by in the early A.M. to perform live on Keillor's program. Gilchrist invited Keillor to breakfast after the program and the host accepted.

"Previously I'd only known him through his voice," Gilchrist said. "I was sort of taken aback by his appearance. He had very long hair and a full beard. He looked even taller than he was because he was thin then. He didn't smile much or laugh at all. He was somber. I remember thinking that somehow I would get a laugh out of him. After quite a while I did tell him a story which made him laugh. But it didn't come easy."

Hochstetter, too, remembers that morning program and its attendant problems. "When he started putting on rock songs, country western tunes, people wrote in and complained. In fact some of the people I taught with in Anoka said, 'I don't like this guy. When I get up in the morning I want to listen to classical music.' But he won people over because he was funny in a wry sort of way. Sometimes I remember, there'd be dead air, silence, as if something had gone wrong, until he'd say something strange. For a while there, when he was starting out, he probably had things written down, and maybe he misplaced his script."

Whatever scripting was done in the early days was dismissed, and there was no manuscript present for his later monologues, the centerpieces on all broadcasts of "A Prairie Home Companion."

But the environs of Lake Wobegon and "A Prairie Home Companion" were gestating during his daily morning shows. The "sponsors'" products were emerging, as was Lake Wobegon, making its appearances on that program in occasional letters from the town written by Barbara Ann Bunsen. The A.M. program featured a sort of laid-back repartee between Keillor and his sports reporter, Jim Ed Poole, played by Tom Keith, sound effects man on "A Prairie Home Companion." Poole, whose delivery is similar to Keillor's and who also leans toward understatement, possesses a voice that is pitched slightly higher than Garrison's. Sketches between the two often centered on the exploits of Poole's pet chicken, Curtis. Keillor also once did a piece on the first-ever softball movie, which premiered in Lake Wobegon.

Keillor was once asked by a radio host about his sponsors—if they were based upon real people or real operations. There was and is a Jack's Auto Repair, formerly located between Anoka and Elk River on U.S. Highway 10. It occupied a renovated church sanctuary that owner Jack Kirchner had gutted and turned into a garage. During his commutes between Freeport and the Twin Cities, Keillor passed the garage many times and admitted to getting the idea of Jack's Auto from the establishment on Highway 10. Kirchner, however, is not a listener, and is blissfully unaware of his notoriety. Like Wobegonians, he regards the native son as small potatoes, pleased that someone has made a mark in the big city but finding no cause to be impressed. Jack's attitude, like that of most Wobegonians, is that Keillor puts his pants on one leg at a time, the same as everyone else.

The old morning program had an impact, and listeners who appreciated the Keillor style were extremely loyal, setting clock radios to 91.1 even earlier than necessary so as not to miss anything, and sometimes fans sneaked into work a tad late because they waited in the parking lot to finish hearing a sketch with Keillor and Jim Ed Poole.

"I found the program by accident in the winter of 1972," said John Moore, a corporate claims specialist from Stevens Point, Wisconsin, who formerly lived in the Twin Cities. Fiddling with his radio dial, Moore happened on to "A Prairie Home Companion" and was drawn to the unusual mix of music. "I sometimes made requests for cuts from albums by Bo Conrad's Spit Band, which he honored, and when I used to drive my wife to work in downtown St. Paul in the early morning, we used to be able to see him do the broadcast through the window in the Park Square Court building. I've been a big fan ever since."

The ex-*Daily* sports editor, Dave Mona, remembers serving on a contributions committee for a local foundation. "We were discussing making a contribution to public radio, and one top officer, who shall remain nameless, said, 'Anybody ever listen to that nut they have on in the morning? It's the worst thing I've ever heard. Boring, terrible music.' We had to argue with him a little before he agreed to maintain the contribution level we'd gone with in the past."

Charles W. Bailey, author and former editor of the Minneapolis *Tribune*, became an early fan of the morning show too. "I moved to Minneapolis from Washington in 1972 and lived alone for a while in one room of my house, which was being remodeled before my family arrived. I used to wake up in the morning to the public radio station and listen to 'Prairie Home Companion,' as it was called then before it became 'The Prairie Home Morning Show.' This was the first I'd heard of him and I liked the way he sounded. I thought this fellow might be able to write good little pieces for the op-ed pages on Sunday. I called him and we had lunch in Minneapolis. He lived in St. Paul, and I offered to meet him there, but he said he rarely got to Minneapolis anymore, and wanted to look around.

"I told him I'd like to try him out as an op-ed contributor. He agreed and we settled on a ridiculously small fee. He wrote these wonderful pieces and I would have liked to have kept him on, but he signed a retainer with *The New Yorker* and couldn't afford to work for us any longer. He was witty, a funny, literate man who livened up our pages for a while."

In the course of the year Keillor contributed fourteen pieces to the *Tribune*, which were later collected in his first book, entitled *GK the DJ*. The book was not distributed nationally but was used as a fund-raising gift to new members of MPR during a pledge-week campaign.

"I got a kick out of the picture on that book of him in that beard," Deloyd Hochstetter said. "You know, he actually turned down a journalism job in North Dakota because they wouldn't let him keep the beard. He needed work, but he told me, 'This is a good beard.'"

Even as Keillor was gaining acceptance and local fame both as writer and broadcast personality, a steady self-confidence was still absent. "He continued to send me everything," Hochstetter said. "Because he knew I was going to put it up on my bulletin board. When he began publishing I mentioned it to other faculty out at school, who were impressed, but not overly. Some of the stories they thought were weird."

They certainly might have seemed so to straitlaced midwestern sensibilities. Some of his stories seemed "pointless," a word often heard around Anoka when his work is discussed. *Lake Wobegon Days* received greater acceptance around the old stomping grounds, some of it being regarded as "pretty darn good" by senior citizens who read it—though one, Bernard Crandall, the garden columnist for the *Anoka County Union*, pointed out a minor error in the text of that book. In one of the early chapters, Crandall noted, "he describes an alfalfa field near the unused depot of the Great Northern Railroad. At that time it would have likely been crimson red clover or alsike clover. Alfalfa was quite new to most planters in the 1800s."

Keillor is not, by and large, considered a native son, and there's little expression of pride of the local-boy-makes-good type. The idea that he would host a live radio broadcast was not part of anyone's assumption, because Keillor was so shy he would not be at ease in front of an audience seated in a theater. However, he did accustom himself to live performances by participating in several readings staged at the Walker Art Center in Minneapolis during the early seventies.

Suzanne Weil, now vice president of programming at PBS, worked at the Walker then and convinced Keillor to do some performance poetry, even though he'd never performed before. "It was one of those crazy shows that people liked to do back then where you didn't really do what you were supposed to do," he said in a St. Paul *Pioneer Press* and *Dispatch* interview in April, 1986. "I did a number of pieces, including a slide show on the penis, which was funny."

Robin Raygor is a psychology professor who used to give poetry performances around the state. He was with Keillor during Keillor's first public performances. "Suzanne Weil had heard Keillor on the radio and talked him into performing, but he wasn't comfortable working alone and attached himself to Gregory Bitz and me, who were used to performance poetry readings," Raygor said. "The first year there were four readings by four different groups. Robert Bly and Michael Kincaid were headlining a couple of those readings, which were done at the Guild for the Performing Arts, and Gregory and I and Garrison did another of them. Garrison didn't think people would want to hear serious poems, so he wrote a couple humorous prose pieces. The first was about walking through the woods and encountering a squirrel that complained about being harassed by nature poets, and the second was an autobiography of Richard Nixon. Both those pieces were pretty funny.

"Later we were asked to do a show at the Walker Art Center.

Because Garrison wouldn't sing or participate in sketches, he became the emcee for the performances. We didn't expect many people at the Walker for our first show because it was Thanksgiving and there was a snowstorm. But our second show was sold out even before we went on with the first one." That performance was called *The Walker Art Center Presents a Poetry Show: Handmade Poems and Prose Pieces.*

"The demand for this show was largely due to the talents of Gregory Bitz," Raygor said. "He had a great comic sense, was a fine writer, songwriter and all-around performer."

Keillor read a couple pieces, Raygor said, but most of the excitement was generated by Gregory Bitz and Tom Arndt, who did songs, poems and sketches and a magic show.

The following year the ensemble was again asked to perform at the Walker, and this time the show was called *A Prairie Home Entertainment: Poems, Songs, Small Prose and Items D'Art.* In previous performances, Raygor and Bitz had received top billing. For this performance, the contributors were listed alphabetically.

"By now, Keillor's show on radio was established, and he used to call himself 'the old scout bringing you "A Prairie Home Companion",'" said Raygor. "Our show was called 'A Prairie Home Entertainment.' Garrison said he didn't want to call it that, because it was too closely connected with his radio show. He really wanted to call it that, but wanted to insist on not calling it that. We met for more than three hours to decide on a name, but he turned down other suggestions. 'No, I don't think that would be good,' he'd say. He said he didn't want 'Prairie Home Entertainment,' but wanted it to be our idea, which it was, finally, of course. He didn't accept any alternatives to it."

Will Jones, a Minneapolis *Tribune* columnist, reviewed the show and described it as "Garrison Keillor and Friends." "Garrison apologized for that, saying that Jones was a friend of his and that was why it came out like that in the paper. Later we took the show up to St. Cloud and there on the marquee was

'Garrison Keillor and Friends.' I don't know if he planned it like that or not.

"Later he talked about taking the show on the road, doing a sort of Chatauqua performance, but none of us wanted to do that," Raygor said. "The next year I read about the show in the paper and discovered that I wasn't in it. Bitz also disappeared the following year.

"Garrison was very ambitious, a career-minded guy, but he didn't seem overt or ruthless about it," Raygor said. "The point is that Gregory had a major role in launching Garrison's career in performance. If Garrison had appeared by himself, he would have read a couple things and would have been mildly entertaining. Of those groups participating in the poetry readings, the only one asked to appear at the Walker was ours. And Keillor wouldn't have gotten there on his own. That's not to say he didn't contribute. He certainly did, and his career might have happened anyway, but back then, Gregory and I were veterans at that sort of thing, and he was a novice."

Raygor remembers, too, that Keillor was quite bored with the bucolic life on the farm in Freeport. "It was supposed to be the great romantic thing to get away from the city, to live in the country and just write. But he was bored, and he used to invite some friends to visit him, but these weren't very successful occasions. Garrison didn't seem to know how to entertain. We went up once and he showed us bound volumes of *The Ivory Tower*, and seemed to act as though we might want to spend a couple hours just reading through them. Then he showed us a galley copy of a story he'd written for *The New Yorker*. Part of it, maybe, was the fact that he speaks so slowly, like he's turning through a thesaurus in his mind as he speaks. He was also a very slow writer.

"At one time back then, we were involved in a poetry collective that wrote poems for occasions. Gregory and I could just churn them out, and it frustrated Garrison that he couldn't do that. We'd have meetings and there'd be a batch of requests on the table. I'd take twenty and Gregory would grab a batch, and

Garrison might take one. The next week he still might not have finished the one, while we had no trouble handling ours."

In November, 1973, Keillor again departed KSJN to devote time to his writing, and his program was replaced with one called "Morning Pro Musica." At this time he became a contributing sports writer for a local weekly alternative paper, *The TC Express.* Its editor and publisher, Tom Berthiaume, had known Garrison casually from overlapping years at the university. Berthiaume was coming on board *The Ivory Tower* at about the same time Keillor was leaving, and Tom eventually became an arts editor at the Minnesota *Daily.*

The *Express* always struggled to find its place in the Twin Cities market, and Berthiaume, hoping to salvage his paper and make it thrive, asked Keillor to contribute gratis. "I never paid him," Berthiaume said. "He wrote for us as a tremendous favor. He was already being published in *The New Yorker* and elsewhere. He was really very gracious."

Keillor wrote a biweekly sports column—"a thinking man's column," Berthiaume said, "that concentrated on local sports, and was often funny." The paper lasted only a year, and Keillor's association less than six months. "He resigned after it was apparent we weren't going to make it," Berthiaume said.

This act of aiding a struggling enterprise was typical of a man Marvin Granger said had deep humanitarian sensitivities. "He somewhat surprises me today," Granger said. "Because back at the university he never would have made business dealings and business kinds of decisions. Promotions, hucksterism just went against his grain. He was a thoroughly decent person. His apparently being involved in that kind of activity today surprises me."

It didn't start out that way. What Garrison wanted was for his radio, the radio programming he had grown to love, to remain viable forever. The type of shows he heard on that old Zenith would be ever fresh, vibrant, and comfortable. And decent folks would gather in a living room around that old set and listen to friendly people—neighbors, really—talk to them and entertain them with songs and stories. It was the way radio used to be, the way radio could be and the way radio ought to be.

"In the old days, radio stations built their audiences by doing remote broadcasts," Bob DeHaven said. In his own long career, DeHaven did many for "Our Own Hardware," broadcasting regularly from stores within the listening range of the WCCO signal for nearly two decades. "There'd be more people in the stores on Saturday mornings than the total population of the town. Farmers would come in to be a part of those broadcasts, which were a lot of fun. Cedric [Adams] did a lot of those too, and audiences would get a kick out of seeing what the announcers and entertainers looked like."

DeHaven's reminiscing smile dissolves as he talks of the cessation of remotes and personal appearances—factors that strongly influenced Keillor's programming sensibilities. "Stations probably weren't making money, and nowadays there is no longer any saleable talent," he said. "You have disc jockeys and newscasters. Stations years ago had orchestras, bands, singers, and actors, but this is no longer the case. So even if stations wanted to start doing them again, they have nothing to send out anymore. Old radio stations had versatility. Now all people do is read copy. Stations made a mistake by stopping the road promotions."

DeHaven talks of emceeing plowing contests and meeting thousands of his fans at the Minnesota State Fair. "I covered state fairs beginning in 1934 until I left WCCO. And here's one thing I think Garrison's picked up on. Everybody loves the state fair because he's from a small town, or he'd like to be from a small town. What makes Garrison successful is he puts it on the air—revives and plays on the yearning that I think is in almost everybody for something small, something different from the big town, different from the jet set.

"Even though people may not have had the experience of the small town, they long for it. They long for peace and quiet, for something that's more their size, something they can handle. And then Garrison adds something we didn't have in the old days—the storytelling. We were selling flour and feed and equipment, so there was no time for stories."

But neither were there stories or monologues for Keillor either, at least not in the beginning. There were bits and pieces, commercials, sketches, reminiscences, comments on the human condition, the relevance of an old essay test from a college literature course. Ken Newhams, a computer systems analyst and fervent fan of the old morning program, said he liked that show more than the Saturday program. "It was really off-beat, a nice way to get going in the mornings, and Garrison matched my own perceptions of the world."

Those perceptions tended toward a liberal social and political posture. "He made people laugh," said Newhams, "and that brought us together. He was a very unique personality in a very bland medium."

Though Keillor's 1974 journey to Nashville to cover the Grand Ole Opry for *The New Yorker* is credited with giving him the impetus to try "A Prairie Home Companion" in its present format, the idea had gathered momentum in the summer of 1973, when he listened to old radio program tapes provided by Twin Cities radio archivist Bill Lund, a former WCCO engineer and former head of KBEM, another Minneapolis public station, which was operated by the local public school system. "He listened to my old tapes of programs done by Bob DeHaven and Cedric Adams," Lund said. "We played them in studio three at MPR's old facilities at the Park Square Court. I also played him old Gene Autry tapes, programs from the Melody Ranch [studio]. That program used to break for a story in the middle of the program, much like he does on his own show today. We also played the old kids' show, Smilin' Ed McConnell, which had a story in the middle, and some of the stuff Tom Keith does with sound effects is reminiscent of the old Smilin' Ed program."

"This isn't meant as a negative," continued Lund, "but what he does dates back thirty or forty years. He took an existing art form and enlarged on it, reworked it and made it better."

"A PRAIRIE Home Companion is like nothing else in this world, and nothing so intimate, charming and evocative is available elsewhere on radio or on television," observed James Taub in the May 1982 issue of *Esquire* magazine, in an article titled, "The Short and Tall Tales of Garrison Keillor." "Garrison Keillor's use of radio is inspired, rarely done," said Chicago Pulitzer-Prize–winning author and radio personality, Studs Terkel, whose own use of the medium might well be considered inspired, or at least perspicacious. Terkel, a decades-long veteran of radio as actor, announcer, and now host of his own daily program on WMFT-FM—a catchall of interviews, music and stories—says that Keillor "brings a basis of life that is noncheap, nonshoddy, nonlying. In a society that is surfeited with ersatz violence—Rambo, for instance—this guy's an out."

Keillor's success with "A Prairie Home Companion" seemed hugely out of synch with the high-tech contemporary American society, and seemed to represent a throwback to a simpler, gentler era, when folks gathered in front parlors on a summer's eve and someone played tunes on an upright piano. Everybody sang and laughed, and then as the evening quieted someone would produce lemonade, squeezed fresh from lemons stored in the icebox, or home-churned ice cream. There would be the stories, reminiscences usually, but memorable, a part of an oral tradition that connected us with our roots, an oral tradition that is vanishing. Terkel laments storytelling as a rapidly disappearing art form. "It's just lost," he growls. "Garrison revives it."

Keillor's old boss at KUOM, Burton Paulu, says he thinks Keillor created a microcosm of small towns and that Americans are ripe for small towns. "They're nostalgic for living out a dream, reaching back for the past when they perceived things as decent and respectful."

What Keillor reached back for are perceptions of how life might be lived as an ideal; like photos from the old *Life* magazines during the postwar forties and early fifties. Think of the old Coca-Cola Santa Claus in ads on the back covers of *Life* and *The Saturday Evening Post*—perhaps the most perfect representation of what Santa Claus would look like if he were real (with no apologies to Virginia)—and a vague image of what Keillor attempted emerges. His monologues took him to the times he nestled in Uncle Lew's lap and listened to stories, and there, surrounded by adults who loved him, he felt secure— nothing could go wrong, all was right with the world.

But grown to adulthood, we remain frightened, unsure, certain only that nearly everything can go wrong and few things will be all right. Still, we hold out hope. And what we hope for is a future that might somehow be like the past we think we remember. And if we remember well enough, our hoped for past becomes real to us, and lives on in stories. Only we have gotten away from our capacity to convey security and magic through stories, and must rely on someone with extraordinary skills; we need then, a Studs Terkel, a Garrison Keillor to tell us how we were, and how we might yet be, and that although our lives may not always be joyful at least we might be loved.

All of this works best on radio, especially for those of us reared in the forties and fifties. Radio was our constant, our comfort.

"The radio Garrison grew up with is the radio he now does," said Keillor's old hero, Bob DeHaven, before Keillor's resignation. "Of course, his literary contribution is what makes him special and unique. Fred Allen once said, 'In radio we can do anything the audience can imagine. In television we can do anything the carpenter can build.' You see, he's able to create that magic for us." Everyone, DeHaven thinks, knows what Lake Wobegon looks like; they know the smell inside the Sidetrack Tap and have fished for sunnies in the lake.

The audience for "A Prairie Home Companion" reached nearly four million listeners each week, over the more than three-hundred-station American Public Radio network. APR, a subsidiary of MPR, was formed in April 1982 by public stations KQED in San Francisco, KUSC in Los Angeles, WGUC in Cincinnati, KSJN in St. Paul, and WNYC in New York. Boston's WGBH came on later. APR is headquartered in St. Paul. While many NPR stations are also APR members, National Public Radio never distributed the program.

But Bill Kling was at that time chairman of the technology committee with National Public Radio and was intimately involved with the planning for the satellite system which came to life on May 1, 1980. Nick Nash, former MPR vice president for programming, and later program director at APR, remembers Kling being instrumental in insuring there would be multiple satellite uplink sites around the country, one of which was in St. Paul. "Kling probably realized before anyone else did that when you have multiple uplink sites and multiple satellite channels, you have at least the potential to create networks of interest. He knew there was enough increasing interest in Keillor to attempt a national thrust. He felt there was a national audience for Keillor. It's a good example of Kling's prescience in things like that."

Kling offered it to NPR, but then president Frank Manckiewicz thought Keillor was nothing more than a regional phenomenon and refused the offer. So MPR bypassed NPR and offered "A Prairie Home Companion" free for a year. Nash said that contracts were carefully written so that either signatory had thirty days to change the relationship. "When the relationship was changed, stations yelped and pleaded and money was charged, but it was in the contract.

"The program just exploded, and was on more than three hundred stations, plus it was offered to commercial stations in markets where there were no competing public radio affiliates. Some programs were sold to Swedish radio also."

And the Australian Broadcasting Corporation carried the programs on a tape delay. Roger Grant, general manager of the North American division of Australian Broadcasting, says the program was popular down under. "It's the old-fashioned radio that people grew up with," he said, "and that's appealing. Midwest America is very much like middle Australia: small town—though his humor escapes people sometimes. It's drawn mixed reactions. Some like it a lot, and some hate it. Some don't understand it. It's very different from what we ordinarily broadcast, but his book has sold quite well, so he must have quite a following."

Keillor's American audience was drawn to Lake Wobegon because it is "real." A writer from *Metropolitan Home* asked in 1985 if Lake Wobegon really existed. "It's still there," Keillor said. "It really is. If you wanted to go back to Minnesota, I'd drive you around and you could see the people—to me they're the people I talk about on the show. And 'Prairie Home' isn't something that I've invented as some sort of fairy-tale populated by warm fuzzy animals who grant our wishes. There are people who are still living in essentially the same way my parents lived when they were young."

Keillor believes that people inherently react against trends and ideas they regard as reckless and foolish, but they do so quietly, maintaining a personal dignity and integrity, not suckered by media hucksters, politicians or trendsetters from either coast. Or as former Tennessee governor Lamar Alexander said, "Our lives are not defined by the network news on television."

Studs Terkel found Keillor's presence on a national medium

vital and necessary. "More and more we listen to 'experts,'" Terkel says. "They know more than we do, those folks up there. So there's less and less connection, and that means less and less participation—debating, arguing, and telling stories. What drew people to Garrison was the sense that 'there's somebody who's talking to me, talking to us.'

"You see, we hunger for stories, and Garrison is telling a story to millions, using an intimate medium. In a way, we can compare FDR and Keillor. Roosevelt's voice was orotund and sonorous, but he and Garrison were messengers of the medium. FDR had the voice of a patrician; he spoke to the farmer and his wife, a young couple in a tiny apartment who worried about jobs. But what all these people had in common was the feeling that the president was 'talking to me, personally.' And that's the feeling that Garrison gave us too. Just look at his audience sometime. Who are they? They were the gentle people, the teachers, librarians, students. Keillor intuitively knows radio well, and he captured our devotion."

That devotion may sometimes be carried almost to extremes. There are those devotees who used to schedule nothing during his two-hour broadcasts and would not take phone calls or engage in conversation. Others were almost willing to steal a radio to try to catch a program, such as the two wilderness trekkers emerging from a month in the bush along the Yukon River.

On a summer Saturday afternoon in 1985, the two pulled their canoe ashore in Ruby, Alaska, population 232, a not-quite-ghost town on the banks of the Yukon River. They were 350 miles west of Fairbanks, where a pilot was to ferry them back to civilization. It had been a quiet week in Ruby, as are all weeks. It's been quiet in Ruby for decades, in fact, and residents—trappers, fishermen and vestigial prospectors—like it that way. There is no saloon there, but there is a small grocery and launderette; until recently, even radio was nearly inaccessible because of the surrounding hills which blocked signals from distant towns.

The trekkers, however, managed to cadge a radio from a wary resident by offering him a bottle of his favorite whiskey, purchased for twenty dollars at the grocery store, which doubles as a liquor outlet for locals. They set up the battery-powered boom box inside the lauderette, where they turned dials until squawking and scratching over the airwaves, a familiar voice crooned,

> "Look who's coming through that door
> I think we've met somewhere before
> Hello, Love."

And after three weeks in the bush, their first link with home was via radio, via their favorite program. And it almost felt like home as the two forsook accumulated tattered coverless magazines in the lauderette and listened to "A Prairie Home Companion," while dirty jeans and socks and underwear were soaped, rinsed and spun dry.

That people would go to such lengths to hear a broadcast does not strike avid fans as unusual. Many have their own stories of trying to find stations to hear the program in unfamiliar parts of the country while traveling. Such people talked owners of motels into affixing radio antennas to television satellite dishes to facilitate reception from a station more than a hundred miles away.

The praise of critics and the adoration of fans for a program so simple in concept and execution began quite modestly in the summer of 1974. However, "A Prairie Home Companion" was undoubtedly what Keillor had in mind all along—what a radio program ought to be like. It took a spring visit to the Grand Ole Opry in Nashville to finally bring the notion to fruition.

The New Yorker sent him to Nashville to cover the last Opry broadcast from the old Ryman Auditorium. While researching the piece, he sat in his room at the Sam Davis Hotel on Saturday night, listening to the Opry on a transistor radio, and got the concept for his program, which he outlined in a memo to Bill Kling.

The New Yorker paid Keillor six thousand dollars for the article, and the chronology of what happened after he received the check comprises the preface to *Lake Wobegon Days*. It's a story of his train trip west, and how he lost the briefcase containing the manuscripts of his two finest stories in the men's room of the Portland, Oregon, train station.

The Opry, he told Michael Schumacher of *Writer's Digest*, "gave us the impetus to think that you could go and do this kind of show, that it was not a museum piece, that this type of show is still valid today. We've taken the format of the variety show and we've done a lot with it. I think we've changed the idea quite a bit from what I saw at the Opry."

What he saw was much of what he'd seen and heard on the "Red River Valley Gang" programs on WCCO and what had been done for many years with programs such as the "WLS Barn Dance," the "Midwestern Jamboree," and the "Louisiana Hayride"—programs that had regional and national impacts during the heyday of radio from the thirties and forties through the early fifties. Such programs were homey, offering hayseed humor and live music and commercials, which were often woven into the fabric of the programs.

The Opry sustained this format and continues to thrive, featuring name performers as well as those who are relatively unknown.

Keillor's program resembled the Opry inasmuch as many performers throughout the years were traditionalists—"the personhood of music," as Keillor called them—fiddlers and flatpickers. Jazz, blues, classics and chorales were booked, and like those old-time programs, there was repartee between performers and the host announcer. "Commercials" too were interwoven throughout the program and done live, with no switching back to the main studio for those announcements. In short, the effect was not of polish and production but of immediacy and intimacy.

At first, though, the show was not live. On May 19, 1974, the Walker Art Center auditorium was home for the first three programs, taped to be broadcast on Minnesota Educational Radio the last three Saturdays in June. The first of these taped programs was broadcast on June 15, and appearing were Judy Larson and Bill Hinckley, who sang blues and work songs; Vern Sutton; and a women's quartet called the West Bank Trackers. The second tape featured a group from the Plymouth Church called the Herrick Family Quartet, Sutton, and Philip Brunelle. On the third show, regulars again performed, and added was Bridget Hardesty, who danced Irish reels, jigs and hornpipes. She danced in stocking feet, and the Minneapolis *Tribune* quoted Keillor as saying she was "one of the finest dancers ever to appear on radio." During the final taping, the audience was invited to come down to the stage and dance, and about forty did.

That taping was particularly memorable to Paul Burpee, who was twelve years old at the time and was taken to it by his mother, a fan of Keillor's morning program. Burpee, now an art student at the Minneapolis College of Art and Design, said his mother told him it was a first show and that the boy might enjoy it. "I didn't have anything to do, and I didn't know anything about him or what the program might involve," Burpee recalled. "But as the taping got underway, Keillor asked if any young people were interested in trying announcing. I was halfway up the rows in the auditorium, and he picked me."

Burpee was given cue cards with which to open and close the program segments, and Keillor said, "I always maintained that radio announcing is an amateur profession."

What Burpee remembers most is the lights in his eyes. "Keillor gave me a few lines and I introduced the commercials and breaks, and made a few mistakes along the way. He said not to worry about it and just read what was on the cards and take my time. I really enjoyed it. It seemed like a folk meeting. It was hip—old, new—a little bit of everything."

The first live broadcast occurred on July 6, 1974, when only eight adults and four children filed into the four-hundred-seat Janet Wallace Fine Arts Center at Macalester College in St. Paul. Eight dollars were taken at the box office. Admission had not been charged for the earlier programs and fans apparently did not want to pay for what previously had been free.

At five P.M. the show started, with Garrison Keillor seeming ill at ease. He was not what one might have come to expect as a broadcast emcee. With long hair and beard he might have been a counterculture remnant from the sixties. He looked at his shoes while speaking into the microphone, perhaps more out of shyness than as a result of the stage lights. The patented shyness would never be overcome, and early in his broadcast career, he told reporter Judith Yates Borger that he was so shy, "I could hardly bear to be looked at even when I was on the air."

He has, of course, overcome it, though he insists it remains at the core of his character. "It stays with a person," he said on the "Fresh Air" broadcast. "I think you can put it aside to do a particular thing. If you are committed to a piece of work to an end, then you can do all sorts of things—amazing things sometimes, that you would not do if you had your choice on them individually. But when you're done with them, then you go back to being shy in your real life."

Motivational seminars inevitably feature speakers who tell us that we can do the impossible if only we overcome the seemingly insurmountable roadblocks, if we can turn our liabilities into assets. And a shy Keillor is infinitely preferrable to a bold, aggressive one. The aggressive, the arrogant who clutter the media are apt to be shills for used car dealers or products ordered through the mail. For Keillor, to be shy has meant success, and the liability is among his greatest assets.

Guests on the first live broadcast included some of the future semiregulars: Vern Sutton, Phillip Brunelle, Bill Hinckley and Judy Larson, along with Bob DeHaven, Ernie Garven (an old WCCO studio musician), and the Briescian String Quartet. Only DeHaven was not a musician, but he represented a link with Keillor's past, a monument to radio nostalgia, and a bridge into the future of a program that would be broadcast nationally within four years and make Garrison Keillor a household name.

DeHaven remembers little of that first program, not anticipating any historical significance to his appearance. "It was fun, I recall," he said. "Garrison and I got along fine on the mike. He was easy and soft-spoken, as was his nature. Easy to work with. We reminisced about early radio, and there was some music, and I think he told a story. No one thought, I'm sure, that it was part of a phenomenon in progress."

Bernard "Buzz" Kemper was technical director for the original "Prairie Home Companion," serving four and a half years, until he resigned in 1979 to return to college, after the initial national broadcast. At nineteen, he was the youngest of the crew members when he assumed the role of tech director. "I had been with MPR just a short time, beginning when I was eighteen," Kemper said. "I started with the show just moving mikes around. Then one day Garrison asked if I wanted to be technical director. It never occurred to me to refuse the offer, because I figured he knew more than I did and had reason to trust me. I'll be forever grateful to Garrison for that chance."

Kemper saw the show develop from a concept into a program with steadily growing audiences. "We used to play small rooms that would hold maybe two hundred people, and more and more people kept coming." The show moved from its first home at Macalester College to the Park Square Theater, which seated fewer than a hundred, to the three-hundred-seat Arts and Sciences Center auditorium, to the College of Saint Thomas, and finally to the World Theater during Kemper's tenure.

"We did outdoor shows then too," Kemper said. "The audience was definitely counterculture—quintessential folkies and hippies who were throwbacks to the sixties. The old show was certainly not a yuppie program."

Kemper, now a technical producer at WHA, a public radio station in Madison, Wisconsin, said the final shows weren't much different in concept from the early ones, except that the latter crop of musicians were better. "In the old days we would get people who didn't sound too good sometimes. I used to listen to tapes after the broadcasts, and people who were sort of amateur might be good on stage; their live presence gave them standing. But listening to the tapes, their sound was terrible. And naturally if you had to see a performer to appreciate him, it wasn't going to work for radio. As the program got bigger, it assumed bigger responsibility, and it took fewer risks."

That old program also never had a tech rehearsal, and only a brief run-through for its first national broadcast. Kemper used to get a list of who was on the show and the order of appearance from then producer Margaret Moos. The program was so loose that sometimes a scheduled performer wouldn't even arrive at the auditorium until a few minutes before he was supposed to go on. Since there were no rehearsals, Kemper would design a miking scheme in his head, not knowing if it would work until the program was live and on the air. "Things going wrong is the magic of live radio," he said. "We did one show where a piano was about to be used, and Butch [Thompson, Keillor's longtime pianist], I think, was supposed to play. But no one had removed a padlock, so the lip couldn't be raised. Ray Markland [a stagehand] came out on stage with the largest screwdriver I'd ever seen, much to the delight of the audience, and tried to pry it off.

"Another time, just before we were to go on, Garrision said there were some tap dancers scheduled and could I mike their feet. Once I had to mike a chicken, and also a duet between players of eight-foot alpenhorns.

"We did a show on Nicollet Island following a folk festival, and Garrison told me there would be only forty minutes to set up following the last act of the festival and the time we had to get on the air. It usually took between two and a half and three hours to set up. But we made it, and I was plugging in the last cord as we went on the air."

Kemper chuckled, recalling one show that emanated from the roof of the Walker Art Center in Minneapolis, when the program was ninety minutes long and broadcast from five thirty to seven P.M. The Walker museum closed at six o'clock on Saturdays, and promptly at six the show was off the air. "My assistant and I thought we had kicked a plug. The audience and Garrison glared at me as though I'd done something wrong. One of the museum guards had forgotten about us and turned the power off. We had dead air for about five minutes before we got back on."

The reason the show was so loose and took no rehearsal time, says Kemper, was to keep costs down. "Everything was working, but it was like walking a tightrope with no net down below. We were all aware even then that we were doing the most popular show MPR was broadcasting. As the show's popularity increased, and as it became in demand nationally, the pressures began increasing."

Kemper left the program before it received national acclaim. But his memories of his association with "A Prairie Home Companion" are fond ones. He enjoyed the tours—the two- to three-week forays into the upper midwestern hinterlands, which promoted the program and built the loyal audience that clung to the show throughout its tenure. For in its first five years, Keillor's show was broadcast only on the Minnesota network, and he hearkened back to the stock in trade of those old programs hosted by Cedric Adams and Bob DeHaven. Keillor took his troupe on the road, touring outstate Minnesota, performing in Waseca; Worthington; Sanborn; Olivia; Brainerd; Hibbing; La Crosse, Wisconsin; and making several stops in Iowa. The program was staged in civic and school auditoriums, and the company toured in buses and small vans.

"The tours were technically difficult," Kemper said. "The hall was never a constant; it changed every night. It was difficult for me personally, because I'm not that fond of bluegrass music, and the musicians always wanted to jam. You couldn't get away from it. Six nights a week for two or three weeks was as much as I could handle.

"Tom Keith and I ran around one night like kids at camp,

and we short-sheeted the musicians. Adam Granger, the guitar player for the Powdermilk Biscuit Band, had never been short-sheeted before, and he thought the maid had screwed up his bed. Through the wall we could hear someone laughing and saying, 'Man, you've been short-sheeted and you don't even know it.'"

"A Prairie Home Companion" didn't find its World Theater home until 1978. The theater, located at Wabasha and Exchange in downtown St. Paul, was originally a Shubert Theater, opened by Sam Shubert on August 28, 1910 to a play entitled *The Fourth Estate*. The great John Barrymore and a host of near-greats trod her boards during the next twenty-three years, until it was converted into a movie house. From 1933 until it closed in November, 1977, it ran mostly second-rate films and occasional foreign features.

The World was slated for demolition, to make room for a parking lot, before MPR took it over for use by "A Prairie Home Companion." To spruce it up, seventy-five volunteers cleaned the theater, scraping gum off seats and layers of soda pop off floors. The World reopened on March 4, 1978 for "A Prairie Home Companion." It would close again several years later when parts of the ceiling began to rain plaster, posing potential hazards to both performers and audience. After a Save the World campaign, renovation restored the relic, and the World remained the program's permanent home. It is ideally suited for the show, or perhaps any theatrical event, as only eighty-five feet separate the stage from the farthest seat in the second balcony, enabling the entire audience to experience an intimacy with performers.

While Keillor was developing an admiring and intensely loyal audience, there was no inkling of national stardom in sight. He was then considered a part of the team, integral and vital, but a team player nonetheless.

He was a man ill at ease in casual conversation. He was

remembered by a music ethnologist who prefers anonymity as one who did not fill conversational gaps just to keep a discussion going. "The obvious niceties to break the ice were not necessary to him," she said. "He didn't fence or take time to build rapport."

The ethnologist recalls the early programs of the mid seventies as loosely structured, informal gatherings. "It was almost like a family," she said. "The performers and the audiences had this great rapport. You'd see the same people week after week. Everyone sort of got to know each other. It was something special."

An indication of that informality was evidenced when some Scandinavian musicians arrived in town for a concert date. A friend phoned Margaret Moos and asked if she wanted to use them on the program that afternoon. Two hours before broadcast, Moos phoned back and said to bring the group on down, they'd been scheduled to perform. In later years performers were booked months in advance, though Nick Nash's view is that Keillor preferred the old, freewheeling style. "He wanted the show put together while they're doing it," Nash said.

Lloyd Hackl, an English teacher at Lakewood Community College in White Bear Lake, Minnesota, was also a fan of the early broadcasts. "Keillor has always seemed reserved, but what I mostly remember is his live audience. People would sit on chairs on the stage at the Arts and Sciences building theater, and everyone would be smiling. It was almost magical. Keillor assumed a persona on stage, and yet he could be perplexing."

Hackl cites a reading Keillor gave at Lakewood as an example. "Coming from a man who was supposedly a humorist, there was a real darkness in his reading of 'Drowning 1954.' His attitude about the swimming instructor who bullied the kids seemed venomous."

That story involves a young man who is forced to take swimming lessons at the downtown Minneapolis YMCA after a cousin drowned in Lake Independence. However, the instructor embarrassed the boys and the protagonist—Keillor—skipped the lessons and instead visited WCCO, where he would catch glimpses of its stars and told of riding the elevator with Cedric Adams.

The early years of the broadcast relied on local folk artists almost exclusively, people such as Claudia Schmidt, Pop Wagner, the Powdermilk Biscuit Band—which originally included Rudy Darling, Sean Blackburn and Dakota Dave Hull, Hinckley and Larson, and "queen of the Autoharp" Stevie Beck, among others. Tenor Vern Sutton and Phillip Brunelle and the Dale Warland Singers also appeared somewhat regularly.

All the while Keillor continued with the morning program, which he didn't abandon until 1982.

In those early days, when he was developing a tone and format for the program, there was no pretense, and no one anticipated the upscale audience that would latch on to Keillor and turn him into a cult figure, though that had already begun to take hold locally.

Once when Keillor went on a brief vacation, he asked Bob DeHaven to fill in as host. He presented DeHaven with a budget for the program, which totaled $325, and was to be distributed among the guests. He also told DeHaven to be sure to allot a portion for his own fee. "He told me he got fifty bucks for the program," DeHaven recalled, chuckling. "So that's what I took."

During one of the mid-seventies road shows, Keillor opened the historic old opera house in Mantorville, Minnesota, a rural community outside Rochester. The audience of farmers and other rural dwellers packed the place, not so much because of Keillor but because they took civic pride in the restoration of the old landmark and wanted to be part of the opening celebration. According to one witness, most of the audience had not heard of Keillor.

Phil DeWolfe, a community college English instructor and antique dealer, happened to be in the area on a buying trip and managed to find a seat in the auditorium. "The place was packed, but some of the mechanical things weren't working, and Garrison made himself obnoxious," DeWolfe said. "He was no doubt frustrated because of the problems, and this audience was extremely cool toward him. He played off that. They weren't responding and he made some sarcastic remarks that made the audience leaden. But when the music started, it lightened the mood, and when he got into the monologue he had absolutely transfixed that rural audience, and we had completely forgotten how he had alienated us. He held us in the palm of his hand. Until then, he hadn't tried to establish contact with the audience and seemed to be addressing the wall on the left side of the balcony and seemed angry at us. He didn't include us until the monologue."

The first national broadcast of the program occurred on February 17, 1979 as a part of National Public Radio's Folk Festival USA. The program aired at eight P.M. from the cavernous Northrup Auditorium on the University of Minnesota campus. Admission was four dollars and five dollars, for a program that had been free for some time, its expenses underwritten then by Cargill Inc. Featured artists included: Pop Wagner, the Powdermilk Biscuit Band, Thelma Buckner and the Minnesota Gospel Twins, Sean Blackburn, Dakota Dave Hull, Claudia Schmidt, The American Swedish Spelmans trio and the Plymouth Church Festival Choir, which sang a choral version of the Powdermilk Biscuit song. Vern Sutton appeared, singing a duet with himself, alternating tenor and falsetto lines. Also appearing were the St. Paul Chamber Orchestra, the Wolverine Classic Jazz Orchestra, and Rio Nido, a jazz vocal trio, whose lead singer, Prudence Johnson, would become a regular guest.

Nick Nash said that particular show was very exaggerated, "almost a circus version of 'A Prairie Home Companion.' A local critic absolutely blistered it and basically said that this wasn't the show that Keillor had been doing, this was some other kind of show, and that if Keillor was going to do this kind of show nationally, he'd better get back to basics. My impression was that Keillor took that to heart. That was a show that opened with Dan Olson as the emcee, welcoming everyone in his deep, old-time radio voice. But there was some positive reaction to that broadcast too."

Ken Newhams remembers it as a special treat for the live audience. "The Powdermilk Biscuit Band and the St. Paul Chamber Orchestra performed an original composition by Libby Larson. The Powdermilks appeared in tuxes and tails, and after the curtain opened, there were people from the chamber orchestra in jeans."

The second national broadcast of "A Prairie Home Companion" was in early 1980, from Kansas City, during the annual NPR convention.

After that initial national broadcast, however, Minneapolis *Star* writer Karl Vick wondered if the national beaming was a good idea. "Would Keillor's wit have a coast-to-coast appeal?" he asked. "Would the rest of America sit still for a deejay who doesn't ignore commas?" And finally, "If we shared the Old Scout, would we lose him?"

To his local audience that aspect was horrible to contemplate. Twin Cities' residents had grown staunchly chauvinistic about Keillor and had in some instances worked to protect his persona and his reputation. Former Minneapolis *Star Tribune* media critic Nick Coleman, who wrote several mildly critical pieces about Keillor and MPR, received dozens of critical letters and calls each time he commented on the sacrosanct. Finally, he says, pressure from MPR officials got to his editors, who insisted he be more positive when writing about Keillor or MPR. "At that point my role there became untenable," Coleman said, and he resigned in 1985 to write a metro column for the St. Paul *Pioneer Press* and *Dispatch*.

ON any Wednesday or Thursday, Garrison Keillor would put aside the potential *New Yorker* or *Atlantic* stories or sketches he'd worked on since Monday and start to think about the monologue for "A Prairie Home Companion." On Friday afternoon he'd rehearse a bit with regulars and guests, and by Saturday he would have completed the monologue. He did not carry any notes on stage with him. The *Time* cover story quoted him as saying that the process involved, "learning to talk until you think of something to say."

The Mother Earth News has published question-answer interviews for years, using a format popularized by *Playboy* magazine. *Mother Earth* called its interviews "The Plowboy Interview," and in its May-June, 1985 issue published one with Keillor in which he said he never used a script for his monologue because it distracted:

> If you make a mistake when you're reading a script . . . then you notice it because you've got the words right there in front of you and panic a little bit. Whereas if you make a mistake when you're standing up there without a script, you don't notice it as much, and neither does anybody else. . . .
>
> Besides that, I don't write very well for the voice, my own or anybody else's. If I were to read off a script, I think it would sound very stilted and literary. However, if I leave the script

behind and just tell a story as best I can remember it, I can sometimes accomplish a kind of natural process of editing whereby most of the literariness is dropped out and just the story remains.

He did, however, compose about four to five single-spaced pages, sometimes using legal-size paper, which detailed the monologues. Though he brought those to the theater, he'd put them away before he started talking.

"The most disastrous thing that a performer could do in telling a story for radio would be to be literary, to do flourishes and put in strange symbolic touches of the sort that people get master's degrees in fine arts for," he told another interviewer. "That would be just awful."

Keillor added that his purpose isn't to manipulate his audience into laughing but rather to lead them along a certain path. His listeners, he said, supply everything that is worthwhile: the details, the sensual surface. The monologues are only a vehicle: "They are just little trucks they are taking for a ride. The point is what you see outside. And that's all supplied by the listener."

The patented Keillor monologues didn't start out to become the tales from Lake Wobegon beloved by millions, and Keillor can't remember specifically when they began to take hold. He told Rick Shefchik in the Pioneer Press and Dispatch that the development had been gradual. "I can remember the Arts and Sciences Center auditorium, standing there and talking under the guise of introducing a song. But as long as the audience seemed to like it I kept on talking and what surprised me was how free I felt, and how they weren't in any hurry for me to sing the song."

The monologue always began with the reference to the quiet week in Lake Wobegon, and if he didn't get immediately into the flow, he'd say that Lake Wobegon is his hometown. After a pause he might have added the phrase "here in Minnesota," and carry on a bit more about weather or other topics until a story took hold. He said the characters in Lake Wobegon are people he's known all his life, and some of them are even named after folks he knew and liked. Deloyd Hochstetter's name was frequently used in various throwaway lines. The name for Skoglund's Five and Dime may well have come from the family Keillor knew in Marine on St. Croix. Other names are familiar to people around Anoka, though none are central characters in Lake Wobegon. Keillor is quoted in *Esquire* as saying the fictional town also includes "most of what has ever happened to me. My childhood, my education, my belief, my disbelief, all go back to that place, and from Lake Wobegon I get my voice."

In a September, 1986 profile in *The Saturday Evening Post*, Keillor said, "Lake Wobegon is as real as my hands on this typewriter, and sometimes more real than that. I once dreamed that I drove over a hill in Central Minnesota and found it. In the dream they weren't particularly happy to see me, but they managed to be fairly polite. I was invited to someone's house for supper, and then I woke up."

Often characters in his sketches were based on his mother and father. But as he told Beverly Beyette, a Los Angeles *Times* writer, "When they [his parents] are in St. Paul, they come to the show and I think they're pleased it has gone well, but they don't tell me how they feel." John and Grace Keillor have lived in Florida since retirement some years ago.

Keillor didn't rehearse his monologues and never composed them as scripts, but he said that in the process of writing, the material goes into what ends up in the monologue. And it works. Alan Bunce, in the *Christian Science Monitor*, observed that Keillor's monologue sounded "as natural and unpackaged as a daydream."

In one of Shefchik's *Pioneer Press* and *Dispatch* articles, Keillor said he was always prepared to deliver the monologue. "I'm not a fool. Sometimes you really change your mind—something that looked awfully good on paper starts to seem hopeless as you come closer to the way you're supposed to do it." In these circumstances, the natural storyteller, the writer-actor took over, and the story may have shifted on its axis, but the listener was not aware of drift or floundering.

Keillor's stories, noted *Mother Earth*'s Peter Hemingson, were "often hilarious, but they're never only funny. Rather, the same story that starts out with laughs, can move to a sad, even tragic note . . . to something disarmingly human and touching . . . then warm and reminiscent . . . then still and quiet . . . and back, closing a loop you probably hadn't even noticed being formed, to a humorous tie-in with its beginning."

Keillor, who tended to be very careful about what he disclosed of his real feelings in public, came close to it in Dan Cryer's *Newsday Magazine* profile, when he talked about the heady sensation he received while delivering his monologue to a live audience:

> For someone as taciturn as myself, and coming from people who tend to keep things in (especially men) it's good to put yourself out on stage, where you're in trouble. Sometimes you almost break into tears on the stage. But sometimes you are talking this story into the dark and you hear sniffling. You start to feel this heat in your eyeballs, and you start to feel this twitchiness in your face. God, it's exciting.

It is that which impels entertainers to seek adoration, universal love from audiences. There is nothing on this earth to compare with that feeling of wave after wave of that love and rolling toward the performer in the form of laughter and applause. It is the absence of that love, and of acceptance, that makes it difficult for performers to simply retire and walk away. It is the moments, moments rare in the course of a lifetime, that are so incredibly exhilarating they cannot possibly be sustained for long, and because they cannot, and because a performer reaching a high for a moment or an hour often cannot bear to lose it, cannot bear to crash, he or she leans on mind-altering drugs.

The lure of succeeding grandly before an audience is what

keeps the performer alive. It was once aptly described by the late high-wire artist, Karl Wallenda, who said for him, "life is on the wire. All the rest is waiting around."

For the performer, life is the performance; time away from the audience is waiting around. What was unique about Keillor was that he may have been the first performer to succeed on so large a scale on the basis of telling stories.

"He captured the essence of drama, of literature, by telling a story," said Studs Terkel.

It was Keillor's manner of storytelling that first drew Jon Fagerson to listen regularly to "A Prairie Home Companion." Later he taught what was probably the only Keillor course for college credit in the country. Garrison Keillor: Our Prairie Home Companion was offered at Inver Hills Community College in suburban St. Paul. Fagerson, an amiable, graying, bearded man, said the course evolved out of a short-story class he'd taught for many years. "Somewhere it hit me that news from Lake Wobegon were short stories with their own coherence and unity and focus and theme and craftsmanship. After listening for years and laughing and being amused, I started assigning the monologues to my short-story class along with their regular readings. The class enjoyed them so much that many who'd never heard of Keillor got excited about it and became fans. I guess I decided there was enough interest among students, and they appreciated it enough, that it would be worthwhile to do a whole course on him."

Fagerson assigned students as texts both of Keillor's books, Lake Wobegon Days and Happy to Be Here. The weekly radio program was part of the assignment too, and the class attended one of the programs at the World Theater.

"It was fun to teach," says Fagerson. "It was new and fresh, and the subject hadn't been done to death by the academics. It wasn't intimidating to students. A kid reads Shakespeare and wonders, Who am I to question the instructor, a guy who's had five classes in Shakespeare? Sometimes under those circumstances students become passive and intimidated. But there we were on Monday morning, discussing a story that was just recited on Saturday. There were no articles or books on it. It was the basis for a healthy student-teacher relationship." Fagerson insists that Keillor is not a regionalist but an outstanding creator of literature who needs not apologize for a regional setting any more than did Southern writers such as Faulkner or Flannery O'Connor.

The popularity of "A Prairie Home Companion" cut across age and sex barriers, with an audience that ranged in age from twenty-five to eighty and divided about equally between men and women. The program's major market stayed at home in Minnesota, where it all began, but it drew significantly in New York, Los Angeles, Chicago, Boston, and other major cities. It also played well in Dallas, according to Michael Mitka, program director at KERA-FM, the public station carrying the program there. "We repeated the broadcast on Sunday afternoons too. It's been very successful. We have a listening audience of about a hundred fifty thousand per week, and thirty thousand or so listened to Keillor. So he was about a fifth of our total audience." Mitka said he was skeptical about the program's ability to attract an audience away from Minnesota or the Midwest, but quickly changed his mind. "It's the humanity Keillor breathed into the program, the way he perceived and said things about behavior and relationships that touched people. Being Scandinavian or Lutheran had very little to do with appreciating what he does."

Bruce Mims, program director at WTSU in Montgomery, Alabama, said that while Keillor's popularity there was limited, it was intensely loyal. "Maybe it was because of the preponderance of country and bluegrass music around here that kept it ["A Prairie Home Companion"] from generating the kind of interest I thought it would. I always thought it ought to play well in any market, thought it ought to have attracted more attention, and it just didn't create the frenzy I thought it would here."

About one-third of the subscribing stations were in the South, and a spokesperson for a station in Murfreesboro, Tennessee, told the Minneapolis *Star*'s Karl Vick that he thought the type of music Keillor featured was a contributing factor. He said he thought the sort of Grand Ole Opry format had a nostalgic appeal, an old-time radio quality that went along with the traditional music.

During the program's early days, Keillor's original producer, Margaret Moos, would arrive at the World Theater about four hours prior to the Saturday afternoon broadcasts. She would supervise the preperformance crew of about twelve as they arranged mikes and speakers on stage. During the early afternoon hours of setup, sound and lighting equipment would be situated in the balcony and tested. About an hour before airtime, musicians and guests arrived and unloaded their equipment. Then they might try to relax backstage, in those days on garage sale furniture—an old green couch, a couple armchairs, and assorted straight-backed chairs.

Stage props have never varied, consisting of a pair of sailcloth drops. The one for Powdermilk Biscuits was huge, of red, yellow, and blue, while the other simply stated "A Prairie Home Companion."

Though the program seemed loose and laid-back, there could be a certain tenseness surrounding the production. Skits were rehearsed sometimes right up to broadcast time, some rewriting and rearranging feverishly taking place. Even then, some skits weren't broadcast because of time limitations.

Meanwhile, staff members may have been chasing about downtown St. Paul during the afternoon, scrounging for sound effects gadgets or obscure sheet music for old songs that the company needed to sing.

The Old Scout would make an appearance on stage about four P.M., and perhaps conduct a brief warmup, introducing musicians who began playing as stragglers filed into the theater, which is now owned by MPR. He returned to the stage fifteen minutes before airtime, as the preshow music wound down and the audience eagerly awaited the instrumental lead-in to Hank Snow's "Hello, Love."

The program's routine would then feature guest artists—most usually musicians—who performed their material and were also sometimes involved with Keillor in commercials for Minnesota Language Systems, Bertha's Kitty Boutique, Raw Bits, or other of the program's "sponsors." Music and commercials comprised the first hour of the program and most of the next twenty or so minutes as well, before Keillor stepped to the podium and announced "It had been a quiet week in Lake Wobegon"—the introduction to his monologue, which would run twenty to thirty minutes. And it was the monologue the audience had come to hear and see. Though the monologue was not visual, as he delivered it Keillor was very much a performer, using his voice with preciseness in the manner of one who owns and plays a priceless Stradivarius. But his body too became involved, mostly through facial expressions: glasses bobbing up and down, the slightest hint of a smile. James Taub in *Esquire* described Keillor's speech as sometimes reflecting "an almost agonizing reluctance to commit the act of assertion, to spill the inner thought. Each word is a sentence with its own echoes, and even words give way to one of the facial expressions habitual with him; a squint in one eye to mark perplexity, an odd thrust of the jaw and widening of the eyes when amused."

Yet what was distinctive, and on the face of it, remarkable, about the monologues, aside from their delivery, was their existence at all. When held up to scrutiny as works of literature, they run between two and three thousand words each—standard-length short stories. Few authors, with the possible exception of the prolific Joyce Carol Oates, would be up to creating a publishable piece of short fiction each week. Yet Keillor did it as a matter of course.

Though the program's audience grew steadily, some longtime fans were less than enthusiastic about it as a weekly as opposed to a daily venture. Keillor admitted this to Letofsky in the Minneapolis *Tribune* article.

> Some people whose opinions I really trust told me that they found it difficult to listen to the Saturday show—that it was too much a piece of nostalgia, even though they knew I wasn't doing it for that reason . . . and the morning show was more where my talents lay. . . . I have a feeling that in doing the stage business, I'm trying to do something that goes against my nature. I'm doing it because I can't do it . . . having been so awkward and retiring and just . . . a person who was afraid to stand up on a stage and try to do humor and sing. I sit back in amazement as I watch myself doing it.

Margaret Moos, the guiding force behind the program's rapid rise to prominence, departed in the summer of 1985 concomitant with Keillor's well-publicized love-at-second-sight encounter with Ulla Skaerved, the former Ulla Strange, at the twenty-fifth reunion of Anoka High School's class of 1960. She consistently refused all requests for interviews.

But as the program was gaining a foothold and drawing national attention, she told Karl Vick of the Minneapolis *Star* that the program's tone and format would remain unchanged. "We intend to keep booking Minnesota musicians," she said, and during her affiliation with "A Prairie Home Companion" musicians hired for the show were largely from the Twin Cities area.

Moos, whose official leave of absence from the program began in October, 1985, had for several years prior shared a large Victorian home with Keillor on Goodrich Avenue in St. Paul. She is a large-boned woman with thick reddish-brown hair and is remembered by former MPR employees as a woman who seldom wore makeup. "She was not a power dresser," said Nick Nash, "but she certainly got your attention." Her wardrobe often tended toward corduroy slacks and sweatshirts, but she worked tirelessly for Keillor and the program. She mailed out scores of news releases to the local and national press, attempting to influence the placement of articles touting the show. Bob Protzman of the *Pioneer Press* and *Dispatch* recalled her persuading him to write a story about one of Keillor's mouth music contests. "I'm not usually talked into writing about something that doesn't interest me," he said.

Moos was, like her soul mate, soft-spoken, but Nash remembers her as being, "always unpleasant to deal with. She was boss cat on the show and by her very nature and very size—and relation with Keillor—had all kinds of room to maneuver that other people wouldn't have had. And when Margaret spoke, everyone assumed it was Garrison who was speaking as well. She was a kind of messenger from the Delphic Oracle. The Oracle would speak, and Margaret would carry the word forth to whichever place it had to go. She, I think, was the one who did a lot of the unpleasant kinds of things, but she turned herself into a very first-rate producer of a very complicated program."

Part of her role was to act as a buffer between journalistic-societal slings and arrows and Keillor, whom she protected, in the words of one ex–MPR employee, "as a mother lion protects her pride."

"Garrison was virtually invisible," said Nash. "He would move through the halls like a wraith, never saying hello to anybody unless addressed specifically, and he never looked at you.

"I didn't like dealing with Margaret Moos—she fought tooth and nail for the program she produced. But when she left under the most difficult circumstances imaginable, I wrote her a note saying that I was thinking about her and wished her well. To go through what she did—and publicly—must have been hell."

Margaret and her sister, Kate, an MPR news reporter, were raised in St. Cloud, in Stearns County, so it seems possible that Margaret may have also contributed notions or concepts concerning Lake Wobegon or Wobegonians. In any case, her contributions toward the success of the program were enormous.

Nash said that Keillor wanted a show put together while it was being performed, and when Margaret was involved, that approach seemed to work.

A group of folk and bluegrass performers were found playing at local counterculture coffee houses, such as the Coffee House Extempore or the Whole Coffee House in Minneapolis. Such performers were more than glad to work for a minimal fee to earn statewide and, eventually, national exposure, which may not have substantially raised their wages but assured them more regular club gigs between the radio work.

Peter Ostroushko and Butch Thompson's trio joined the program early on, becoming mainstays until mid 1986. As the program's success was assured and the budget increased to more than a million dollars annually, Keillor began booking nationally renowned talent such as Chet Atkins, John Hartford, Taj Mahal, Emmylou Harris, Doc Watson, Jean Redpath and Johnny Gimble. The national thrust of the program apparently mandated name talent, but fees remained relatively small. About three hundred dollars—small potatoes, no doubt—is standard, but as show biz celebrities will appear on the late night TV talk shows for minimal fees because of excellent exposure, so were musicians drawn to "A Prairie Home Companion."

Keillor once told Rick Shefchik, entertainment writer for the St. Paul *Pioneer Press* and *Dispatch* that he liked to have people on his show with whom he enjoyed working. "I don't like to have somebody else book them on some theoretical basis. There's nothing theoretical about being out on stage with other people. Either you are comfortable and you like them or it's a slow death. And I believe in avoiding death as much as possible."

Yet he added that most of the people he would have liked to feature on his program are dead. He mentioned Baby Dodds,

King Oliver, Jack Teagarden, and Mississippi John Hurt—old-time blues and jazz artists.

Keillor is not a solo-quality singer but is able to lend a decent bass to a vocal ensemble. But his singing—as was Arthur Godfrey's—is routine, accepted, expected, and appreciated by his audiences. He told Shefchik that "singing is not a technical skill, it's an emotional act, and I always had a lot of things I wanted to sing about that if you were to try to put them in writing, it wouldn't have enough feeling. It would be too smart. I've always had reasons to sing." One of his reasons for singing the opening theme song was that after doing it on his first show, he realized he was going to be the only one present every week who knew the words.

On May 3, 1980, "A Prairie Home Companion" became the first series program to originate from a member station of National Public Radio. One of the program's memorable moments occurred when Keillor read a letter from Jack, of Jack's Auto Repair, announcing he was not pleased that he was paying for a program to beam across country because nobody was going to drive a thousand miles to Lake Wobegon for a thousand-mile checkup.

Over the years, Keillor developed a more polished rapport with his live audience. In the early days the audience was drawn to him because it recognized his creative genius, and in a medium not noted for originality and wit, that was enough. But he shared little of himself then and hid behind a full beard, with a large white hat pulled down over his eyes. What audiences knew of Keillor they knew only from his remarkable voice and storytelling gift. He was later able to look at his audience; he stopped wearing the hat, and the beard too was removed. And he revealed much of himself in his monologues. His friend Russell Ringsack told *People* magazine in the February 6, 1984 issue, "When he gets up in front of a microphone, he really bares himself. He'd never be able to talk so openly in person."

"I think Garrison Keillor has been very truthful about himself in his monologues, his stories and everything else," said Nick Coleman. "I think by studying these you could draw yourself a pretty decent portrait of the man. On the other hand, he is a person who takes things in life that most people take casually very seriously and very intensely."

If Keillor had changed over the run of "A Prairie Home Companion," so had his audience. It used to be comprised of ardent fans of traditional music; folks in bib overalls who belonged to food co-ops and rode bicycles, wore their hair in ponytails, sipped herbal teas, and were into macrobiotic diets. It was a younger crowd; vestigial hippies. And Keillor had said he missed them. In an interview with the St. Paul *Pioneer Press* he added he liked that old audience because they were regulars, and "it seems to me you can have more fun with them. They're a lot more open with you. But this [current] audience is fine. Sometimes for no reason I can think of—not even because the material is weak—the audience seems very studious and very quiet." As the show's tenure was ending he observed his audience as older, with many more people from out of town who wrote for tickets months in advance. In fact, there was often a three-month lead required to purchase tickets for the program.

The World Theater became something of a tourist mecca in downtown St. Paul, and cabdrivers were known to point it out to customers as they drove by, as the place where "A Prairie Home Companion" originated. And for more than five years the Minnesota Department of Transportation included Lake Wobegon on official state road maps, with an asterisk, stating the town is fictional.

Writing in the July 21, 1982 issue of *Christian Century*, Doug Thorpe reported that someone told him he looked up Lake Wobegon in the Rand McNally atlas and expected to find it and drive to it. David Black, in the July 3, 1981 issue of *Rolling Stone*, wrote an article, "Live From Lake Wobegon," and called the program a blend of Sherwood Anderson, Spike Jones and Thomas Pynchon. But Lake Wobegon as a place was universal.

"In some hidden chamber of our hearts, most of us, no matter where we live, are citizens of Lake Wobegon."

When Garrison Keillor broadcasted live each week from the World Theater, he envisioned a family, perhaps a family not dissimilar from the one in which he grew up. And that family was in the living room, where a radio, not a television set, was the focus of attention. Several years ago, *Life* magazine quoted Keillor's references to that hypothetical family. "The children flop down on the floor, the dad reads the paper, the mom does needlepoint, and they all listen to the show. 'When we watch television together, I feel alone,' the mother wrote to me. 'Radio makes us feel close and tight.'"

He wanted all his audience to be that family. Said Nash, "His closing line, 'Thanks for allowing us to come into your living room,' hearkened back to radio in the thirties and forties—that assumption of that's where people were listening, when they were probably in their cars or in kitchens or basements."

In April of 1981 the program the St. Paul papers called "down-home music and uptown wit," was awarded the George Foster Peabody Award—the broadcasting equivalent of an Academy Award. Keillor's response was typical. He told the *Pioneer Press*, "I simply don't understand why it's so important. It's an impossible field to give awards in because the most important things in radio are done every day. . . . [This] is sort of like giving out the Mother of the Year award. Day to day how do you say one mom is better than the next?"

He added that he appreciated the compliment, however. "But there's not one person whose opinion in this world is more important than anyone else's."

Though many fans of Lake Wobegon from the book and the monologues might argue that they find comfort in the town's nostalgic appeal, Rick Shefchik reported that Keillor rejects the notion of the program being based on traditional music and nostalgia. "I'm not a nostalgic person," he said. Nor, apparently, is he a particular fancier of traditional music. Shefchik asked Keillor not long ago if Keillor had always enjoyed folk and traditional music. "He said it wasn't a particular favorite of his and he wouldn't listen to it at home. It's just something he felt worked for the show."

The central element that Keillor insisted on for his show, and to which he attributed a great deal of the program's success, was that it would be delivered live. "The appeal I think is the live radio from a stage with an audience from a particular place," he said in David Black's *Rolling Stone* story. "It's magical, that when you play on our radio show—and I tell this to the musicians over the years—you are not in competition with recordings. . . . You have the benefit of the fact that you are doing it at the same time your audience is listening. So they are with you in a way that cannot be true for other shows." Keillor thought the live aspect created the sense of community and was the basis for the program's appeal. Flubs and snafus, he told reporters, were signs of the program's honesty and integrity, and his reading of greetings from listeners to family and friends perpetuated the magic of radio at its best. "It makes it seem as if they're all somehow back together in the same room," he said in the Plowboy interview.

However, the firm conviction that the program must be carried live softened somewhat. "Keillor and Margaret were very resistant to nonlive use of the program," said Nash. "But that was a totally unproductive perspective. Because you're looking at the time differences and satellite costs. The Swedes and Australians were very interested, but Keillor said no, it had to be live. Well, there's a seventeen-hour time change between here and Australia, and satellite problems across the Pacific are formidable. But then Keillor and Margaret went to Australia for a vacation and had a very good time, and decided that somehow they could see their way clear to take the show there. "It was recorded in Hawaii and heard in Australia on a week's delay."

The original program was ninety minutes long, and Nash thinks it should have remained so. "Two hours was a long time for people. It made the assumption that people had hand grips on their radios. But if you looked at his audience data, people *did* have hand grips on their radios. Normally you would assume people wouldn't sit still for two hours on a Saturday afternoon or early Saturday evening. The last time I looked at the audience research on time spent listening to the show for the Twin Cities, the audience tuned in for virtually the whole first hour. There was a little weakening during the second hour, and I've always thought that when the monologue is over, there was some tune-out. The last fifteen minutes of the program always seemed somewhat loose, and I'm sure that the radio audience departed in significant numbers. It wasn't that well organized.

"The other conceit that Keillor got away with was the business about having an intermission for the people in the theater. The millions in the radio audience deferred to the nine hundred sixty who attend the performance, so they could go to the bathroom and buy popcorn. I thought that was excessively generous to the people in the theater."

Since it's inception in 1974, there were changes in nearly every aspect of "A Prairie Home Companion," except two. The one constant besides Keillor himself was the support for the program by Cargill, Incorporated. Cargill, a large privately held company, deals in bulk commodities, feed grain and bulk foods. The corporation, according to Bill Pearce, senior vice president, routinely awards philanthropic gifts and grants, and MPR has been a recipient. "When the program started on the state network, Cargill gave MPR thirty-five hundred dollars for the first year of broadcasting," Pearce said. "As the program became more prominent, costs went up—costs more than matched by growing support and the audience." In 1985 Cargill supported the TV broadcast of "A Prairie Home Companion" and also helped fund the restoration of the World Theater. "We normally contribute about three hundred thousand dollars to the program," Pearce said, "which was about one third of the total annual cost of producing it."

The Cargill connection was profitable for MPR, but no less

so for the company, said Pearce. "The nature of our business is such that the Cargill label is rarely seen. The program has been a very useful medium for us. Contacts we have around the country will recognize us because of the program. It's happened to me many times, meeting somebody in the business context, and they'll invariably mention that we sponsored 'A Prairie Home Companion.'"

The program was always a perplexing one to categorize. Letofsky suggested imagining Arthur Godfrey doing James Thurber. Dan Cryer called Keillor an unlikely "blend of Fibber McGee and urbane Jean Shepherd. Fibber McGee because monologues are set in a fictional Midwest town and feature regular characters. Jean Shepherd because Keillor does it all by himself."

Jean Shepherd, the humorist most recently noted for films and public television specials, drew a sort of cult following during the fifties and sixties, when he held forth on New York's radio station WOR each evening from ten to eleven. His programs often turned into forms of outrageous, clever monologues or zany reminiscences of his own boyhood in Indiana, where he was a klutz with girls. Though he contributed a blurb for the dust jacket of *Happy to Be Here*, Shepherd is apparently no longer pleased to welcome Keillor to the dwindling species of humorists. When phoned for an interview, a woman testily refused to forward the call and hotly snapped, "He doesn't want to say anything about Garrison Keillor."

Shepherd once suggested his listeners go out in the streets and mill about, and thousands of them did. Keillor loyalists probably wouldn't mill about in the streets, because that's pretentiously quirky, and Keillor would never suggest something that Wobegonians would consider just plain dumb. But they have shown up by the hundreds to have him autograph copies of his books, standing in long queues winding through several sections of department stores, sometimes still standing there after closing hours, for the brief moment of contact with one whom they've come to regard as their hero.

Though these fans tended to be cerebral rather than visceral, they reminded Studs Terkel of the reaction rock stars generate among young groupies. Among those attracted by his humor, gentle satire, and appeals for kindness and understanding, "He matches the rock heroes," said Terkel. "He can do no wrong."

"What he does," affirmed Hochstetter, "he does better than just about anybody. And he says he does it because he can't do it. He really struggled up there in front of an audience."

But that doesn't matter; we live in a new age where men are supposed to share their feelings, to cry, to eat quiche, to admit they're head over heels in love, that they've been failures, that they're shy. Because he could say these things publicly he's a role model for the eighties, for the self-enlightened.

AMERICAN culture grows increasingly diverse, and to many citizens that diversity is fraught with discomfort, uneasiness. We tend not to trust that which we little understand. Ours is a society embracing few absolutes; situational ethics, ironically, being one of them. Apathy and negativism are de rigueur. Many of us even worship at the shrines of antiheroes, but without the sense of security, definition and location that real heroes of the past provided. In the epilogue from the book, *Heroes of Popular Culture* (Bowling Green University Press, 1973) Ray B. Browne writes, "It's basically fear that makes men and women create heroes and heroines."

Thus as the world began to come apart in the war year of 1941, Joe DiMaggio, hitting in fifty-six consecutive games, became a constant, a dependable, a certainty. Paul Simon lamented in 1969, "Where have you gone, Joe DiMaggio? A nation turns it's lonely eyes to you." In an age without demigods, those lines are more than mere song lyrics.

We who grew up in the fifties were used to having heroes. We listened to "The Lone Ranger," "Jack Armstrong," and "Sky King." We watched Roy Rogers in the movies. Wrong was wrong and right was right. Heroes used to be the good guys, the decent. They were manly gentlemen who inspired us. From the post–Korean War era on we have been disillusioned by ersatz heroes—lying, deceitful politicians and corporate officers—by overpaid athletes and actors who consume illicit drugs. And then, through a medium which first presented us with childhood heroes, emerges another; one who makes no claims to lead us from the wilderness but who appears to stand for the old virtues of decency, charity, and honesty. But with a difference. Instead of macho tough, he's gentle without being maudlin or wimpish. In short, Garrison Keillor is a hero for our times.

Throughout history, heroes have been created to meet the emotional needs of their times, observes Browne in his essay. Media hucksters have long realized this, according to Mark Gerzon, author of *A Choice of Heroes* (Houghton Mifflin, 1982). Gerzon says that heroes today aren't born, "they are packaged. They are thrust upon us by marketing strategies. In place of legends, we create personalities. Instead of gods, we manufacture superstars. Instead of admiring greatness, we worship celebrity."

Perhaps this is true, even as the legend grows around Garrison Keillor and the characters he's created, characters of spirit, of quality, of humanness—these are affirming, striving, hopeful. They convey to us that it's okay to be Lutheran, or Catholic, or Norwegian, to live in small villages or neighborhoods, far from the madding crowds of the cities' tumult and shouting; to have glaring character flaws, because God loves and forgives his children. Keillor gives us an affirmation of ourselves, the hope we need to strive toward self-acceptance in its most positive sense.

"Some so-called sophisticates, in a patronizing manner, might say that rubes go for him," said Terkel. "But they recognize there's something there. To recognize the desire for heroes isn't hip. But who decides what is intellectually right? The hip fear something—the simple gifts. Keillor is gifted with simplicity, yet he's a very sophisticated guy. . . . He doesn't oversimplify, and he doesn't make hip comments." In short, he's made it okay for people with masters' degrees to have a hero.

The comprehension of place, of belonging, of security, that FDR, Dwight Eisenhower and John F. Kennedy generated among citizens made us proud to be Americans, and we felt safe with such men at our helm and were willing to make sacrifices for the greater good. As we search among us for heroes, we seek those who encourage and inspire us, who uplift and sustain us, and who, though they come from us, are greater than we are. They are therefore fit to be our heroes, our contact with what is great within the human spirit.

Our grandparents looked to Hobey Baker, the real-life Frank Merriwell, who was a star football and hockey player at Princeton from 1910 to 1914. Heightening his heroic stature on the American scene, Baker was killed in a plane crash during World War I, five years after graduation. He was the prototypical American hero: strong, handsome, athletic, kind to children, courteous to the elderly. He was admired by another Minnesota writer, F. Scott Fitzgerald, who depicted him in *This Side of Paradise*. Baker's name lives on in the trophy that is annually awarded to college hockey's top player.

Baker and those heroes who followed fit Browne's definition, that heroes serve as "a bar on which men and women chin their aspirations and dreams, can stretch and try to become less human and more godlike." Yet, observes Browne, "we want to experience life as bigger than actuality, realizing simultaneously that perhaps it is, in fact, just as small."

Postwar years in America seemed to produce more antiheroes than heroes. We had the beats and Jack Kerouac, Norman Mailer, Bob Dylan, John Cage, and sundry androgynous rock stars.

But antiheroes may espouse the doing of one's own thing, which doesn't work for most of us. We lack the courage and initiative to make that move. Instead, we want to trust leaders who are nobler than ourselves, as D. H. Lawrence wrote in his epilogue to *Movements in European History*:

Now we begin to understand the old motto Noblesse Oblige. Noblesse means having the gift of power, the natural or sacred power. And having such power obliges a man to act with fearlessness and generosity, responsible for his acts to God. A noble is one who may be known before all men.

Some men must be noble or life is an ash-heap. There is natural nobility, given by God or the Unknown, and far beyond common sense. And towards this natural nobility we must live. The simple man, whose best self, his noble self, is nearly all the time puzzled, dumb, and helpless, has still the power to recognize the man in whom the noble self is powerful and articulate. To this man he must pledge himself.

Thousands of us pledged ourselves to Garrison Keillor, though Keillor would have likely rejected this notion and would have been extremely uncomfortable with it. Several years ago, he told a reporter from a small-town Wisconsin newspaper that he considered himself no different from anyone else and certainly didn't encourage the cultlike following that was emerging around him.

Earlier still, he wrote to Hochstetter that whatever success he enjoyed was because God allowed him to succeed, and that God had been good to him.

But as Keillor's fame widened, and pressures on him to sustain his success increased Hochstetter fretted about the health of his former pupil's psyche, his concern stemming from the almost worshipful regard some fans accorded Keillor. Hochstetter is a longtime volunteer at the Minneapolis Institute of Art, manning the gift counter. He said that as magazines and newspaper profiles on Keillor began appearing nationally in the early eighties, some of them mentioned Hochstetter, and a few ran his photo. "People at the institute and people just coming in off the street recognized me from pictures in the paper, and they wanted to see everything I had about Gary. I got letters myself from all over—people wanting to know about him." The former teacher sighs and shrugs. "You know, I brought the wedding invitation he sent me, and folks there grabbed it and mimeographed it to have copies for themselves. I think that's pretty sad. This is a cult and I don't think he likes that.

"He told me once that he liked being famous and successful, but he didn't like being recognized in public. He wants to walk the streets like ordinary people."

He may have preferred to have been considered a first-rate man of letters, with the stature of John Updike or Robert Penn Warren—men who presumably are not instantly recognized in restaurants and hotel lobbies. Instead, Keillor became something of a reluctant hero. According to a former employee, he liked the idea of wealth and fame, but abhorred the price, which is the public's curiosity about this intensely private person. Consequently, he declined to be interviewed for this book, and many reporters who have covered him claim he is difficult to know and that he makes no moves to put a visitor at ease.

Rick Shefchik has covered Keillor since 1980. "I never found him to be the most jovial or cooperative fellow to interview," said Shefchik in August 1986. "But he was never discourteous. One time I was with him about ninety minutes. He pointed out a seat to me in his office, and I turned on my tape recorder, and he turned sideways to me and picked up a box of popcorn and started munching on it, and didn't look at me the entire time I was there.

"He's not particularly interested in talking about himself to reporters. He'd just as soon be left alone if the subject isn't something he wants to talk to you about. He's fairly guarded, fairly closemouthed unless it's something he's anxious to publicize. He's protective. He's a control freak. In the early days, he was as cooperative as he needed to be—never discourteous or harsh—but he didn't enjoy talking to the press. He saw it as a necessary evil, and he did it.

"He's a tough interview. You won't necessarily get what you want out of him, but you will get something readable and quotable, because he does craft words very well. I don't think there's ever a time when Garrison Keillor isn't on. If he's talking to reporters he knows that what he says is going to end up in print. He doesn't want to toss off anything that isn't well crafted. He's slow, he's deliberate, just the way he would be if he were doing the monologue, and you certainly get the feeling he's writing as he speaks. So if you're not exactly getting the information you were looking for, you're certainly getting pretty high-quality conversation. In that regard, he's an excellent interview.

"He's very long-winded. You'll end up with an awful lot of material. He doesn't cut you off. If you ask him a question that strikes his interest, you may sit there for fifteen minutes, twenty minutes before he's through answering your question. It may not have been the question you were hoping to hang your article on, but you wind up using it anyway, because he's found it interesting."

"He's reticent and difficult to talk to," said Irv Letofsky, arts and entertainment editor for the Los Angeles *Times*. Letofsky formerly covered the arts scene for the Minneapolis *Tribune*, and followed Keillor's career almost since its inception on KSJN, making him the journalist most familiar with both the emerging Keillor and the man on whom millions doted. "Keillor never quite responds [to questions] because he's always thinking."

Letofsky, who was also one of the founders of Brave New Workshop, a Minneapolis establishment that features satiric reviews, recalls his first interview with Keillor. "He talked about Brave New Workshop and said, 'The problem is your satire should be more biting and less comical.'" Keillor's friends from the university delighted in Keillor's pungent satirical wit, but the bite of the curmudgeon isn't present in his work, and never was. Keillor no longer thinks of himself as a satirist. "I used to be one," he said in a Los Angeles *Times* interview. "But I've become something else, something odd that I don't understand. It seems to be that on the radio show I took a turn back there somewhere and I got out of the comedy business and veered off away from satire and started being more interested in sentiment and, to some extent, pathos. I became much less a cool performer and more emotional. I'm not sure what to make of it myself, because it's embarrassing in a way."

Kevin Klose, Chicago bureau chief for the *Washington Post*, wrote several pieces on Keillor for his paper. He remembers his initial encounter with Keillor as one in which Keillor didn't seem cooperative. "After a lot of negotiations with APR he finally said he would see me for one hour. My brother Christopher and I were going to meet him in Red Wing, Minnesota, where he was doing a show. When we arrived, he was in the shower in his room and just didn't come out. Finally, about twenty-five minutes into the allotted hour, he had us come up to his room. My brother made a graceful compliment about his work, and that's what got him going. Eventually we had tea on the veranda and walked down to the theater with him.

"The first question I asked him was 'Where is the line between reality and fantasy in Lake Wobegon?' He looked out over the Mississippi River and said, 'Well, you'd have to ask somebody who lives there.' See, what's distinctive about him is that he's created his own world completely, and I had the feeling that it's very hard for him to have people intrude in that world.

"What floors me about him is that he's a one-person literary factory. To function at that level of creativity, doesn't just happen. He knows everything about those people in Lake Wobegon, and his creation has become hilarious. What he's done in this era where nothing lasts very long is to create a durable kind of universe."

His program surprises James Delmont, because the Keillor Delmont knew in college is not the person who presides over "A Prairie Home Companion." "I thought he was a fraud," Delmont said. "The music on the program isn't what he would have been playing back then. I thought that what he was doing was blending some storytelling with elaborate satire, and I still think that at times. I thought he was sincere about the Lake Wobegon stuff but thought the music he played and some of his humor was a put-on. On the other hand, back in college, he was very intellectual, and maybe he went through a stage, which isn't uncommon for a young student, and so perhaps what we see now is what he really is."

In a question and answer interview with Michael Walker in the November, 1985 issue of *Metropolitan Home*, Keillor shared some feelings about the people he writes about and about the place he considers home. Home, he thinks, is a place where one can have clutter without being made to feel it has to be cleaned up. He also said he prefers entertaining in his kitchen rather than in a dining room, which he believes most people can do without.

He's told other reporters that large cities tend to distort the dreams and aspirations of ordinary people and cause them to lose their faith in the decency of humankind.

Keillor amplified his thoughts on small-town life on the radio program, "Fresh Air," telling program host, Terry Gross, "If you live in a small town, you can be an artist, an athlete, a businessperson; you can be a mover and shaker, involved in organizations. You can be all of these things at one time in the same place, and you can have a rounded life that I think would be much harder to have in the city."

Gross asked if he wanted to get out of the small town himself. "I did, because you see I had ambitions along conventional tracks—not conventional for where I lived. I had ambitions to be a writer, which were impossible for me to pursue and stay there. Because I was living among people who didn't value that, who didn't think that that was a good thing for a person to be. But I think often of going back, and I think some day I probably will."

This response was rather curious, because both Brooklyn Park and Anoka are considered parts of the greater Twin Cities metropolitan area, and both towns now serve primarily as bedroom suburbs for Minneapolis. Keillor's reference here must be to his occasional longing to reside in a generic small town, aside from either Anoka or Brooklyn Park. Since the primarily East Coast audience of "Fresh Air" may assume that any area not teeming with overcrowded tenements is a small town, Keillor perhaps felt no obligation to set the record straight: he was not raised in a typical small, midwestern community.

However warm and sincere he feels about living in small towns, and despite the appeal of Lake Wobegon to the small-town citizen in most of us, Nick Nash thinks Keillor's audience is at least eighty percent urban. "I would wager that in some place like Hackensack or LeSeuer there isn't quite the sense of involvement with the program that you'd find in urban areas. Those people, after all, are living the life that he talks about to a great extent, which makes it different for them. I've often thought of the show as an urban fantasy program.

"Yet, I think he represents, in a sense, to our generation what Arthur Godfrey used to in the best days of Arthur Godfrey. He was an interesting person you wanted to spend some time with. With Godfrey it happened to be in the mornings, Monday through Friday. With Keillor it was Saturday night. And Keillor was the most dominant radio personality outside of talk-radio people, and the only one who talked directly to the spirit of people. I always considered Keillor one of the great preachers to the unchurched in the United States. Because he has a moral view, and he communicated that moral view."

"I'm surprised when people use the term *nostalgic* referring to . . . Lake Wobegon and suggest that what I describe is a life that is no longer lived," Keillor told Michael Schumacher.

It simply is not true. People who think that towns such as Lake Wobegon no longer exist lead lives of such isolation that I can only pity them. . . . The life I try to describe is a life that is lived by a great many people—and would be lived by more people if it weren't for the fact that the economy doesn't organize our society that way. The economy wants to organize us into much larger units, into Chicagos and Los Angeleses and New Yorks, rather than into Lake Wobegons. But people are holding out. People are resisting the economy because they want this so badly.

•   •   •

Keillor concluded the thought with perhaps an unconscious paraphrasing of William Faulkner's Nobel Prize acceptance speech, in which Faulkner praised the endurance of the human spirit. Said Keillor, "The people will last . . . long beyond the time when I talked about them. I think they will go on, march on into the twenty-first century."

Keillor, as Hochstetter observed over the years, is at once a man of driving ego and a man who is remote, aloof, cranky and sentimental. Noted his old tenth-grade biology teacher, Lyle Bradley, "I think he looks back in a sentimental manner about his whole life. There are things that not many people know about him. A while back one of his classmates died. She either drowned or died from hypothermia in a canoe accident. He went out to New York, where she taught, for the funeral and even tried to help determine if there'd been foul play.

"Then at my retirement party, some of the folks asked him to come, but he couldn't because he had prior commitments and would be in San Francisco. But he sent me a long telegram, which we read at the party. He's a very sentimental, sensitive, altruistic person. He does not forget his traditions and roots."

"Fresh Air" host Terry Gross probed Keillor's vaunted shyness on her program, asking him which was more difficult, speaking or singing in public. He said he sings on his show because a singer can't be reticent:

"Every singer, I think, has to put their heart out there. I think now that I do that more and more when I tell stories. They are much more an emotional experience than they used to be. I feel good about that. I feel good about leaving craft behind and taking some risks in behalf of sentiment, which when I was a younger writer, we learned to be very careful about sentiment, and about feeling, and to cultivate irony even when there was none. So for me, singing and talking seem to be two poles that come closer together."

•   •   •

Gary Keillor's graduation photo from the Anoka High School yearbook, *The Anokan*.

The Keillor boyhood home in Brooklyn Park, Minnesota, built by John Keillor. *(Courtesy of Judy Fedo)*

From *The Anokan*, Gary Keillor at work on his sports weekly, *Varsity*.

Ulla Strange's graduation photo from *The Anokan*.

Ulla Strange (wearing glasses) was elected to the Homecoming Court in 1960 at Anoka Senior High School.

Garrison Keillor's major broadcasting influence, the late Cedric Adams (second from right), in a personal appearance broadcast during the 1940s.

One of Keillor's idols, WCCO's Bob DeHaven (middle, front row), during a 1940s broadcast. *(Courtesy of WCCO)*

In 1974, Keillor at the mike with a youngster during taping of the first "A Prairie Home Companion." *(Courtesy of the* Minneapolis Star and Tribune*)*

An early 1970s poster advertising one of Garrison Keillor's first performance appearances. *(Poster courtesy of Robin Raygor; photo courtesy of Judy Fedo)*

Walker Art Center presents

TOM ARNDT
GREGORY BITZ
GARRISON KEILLOR
ROBIN RAYGOR

in

A
PRAIRIE HOME
ENTERTAINMENT

Poems, Songs, small prose & items d'art

Saturday, 30 September

2 SHOWS: 8 PM and 10 PM

Walker Art Center Auditorium

Admission $1.50. Students and Members $1 at the door.
Call 377-7500 for reservations.

The "old scout," circa 1978, on stage in rural Wisconsin.

Keillor and friends on stage during a late-1970s tour.

At a rehearsal, Keillor is on stage with musicians. *(Courtesy of the* Minneapolis Star and Tribune*)*

IT'S BEEN A NOT-SO-QUIET WEEK IN LAKE WOBEGON...

The cartoon that appeared in the *Minneapolis Star and Tribune* after *Playgirl* magazine named Keillor one of the ten sexiest men in America. *(Courtesy of the* Minneapolis Star and Tribune*)*

Garrison Keillor and Willie Nelson pose backstage with fans Bruce Lorange and Terry Bratcher (far right) after a performance of "A Prairie Home Companion" at Claremont College in Claremont, California. *(Courtesy of Lorange and Bratcher)*

Keillor poses with a 1940s photo of a Plymouth Brethren church convention. He claims to be related to most of the people in the photo. *(Courtesy of the* Minneapolis Star and Tribune*)*

Keillor and his bride Ulla Skaerved pose with their children after their wedding in Holte near Copenhagen. From left: Morten Skaerved, Malene Skaerved, Garrison Keillor, Ulla Skaerved, Mattias Skaerved, and Jason Keillor. *(Courtesy of AP/Wide World Photos)*

The point being that Keillor does not ridicule sentiment; instead he cultivates it. But he does so without mawkishness, which makes it acceptable to people of education, of culture, who appreciate his approach without a feeling of slumming—such as a professor of philosophy might feel wearing cowboy boots and drinking beer and enjoying himself in a country and western saloon, bothered by the vague feeling that with all his status, education and knowledge, he probably ought to be wearing a dark suit and attending a Beethoven concert. But Keillor, who is clearly intellectual, can speak of sentiment, can draw on the heartstrings, and make us think it's all right to have the feelings we have, and to express them. His emotional gains are never at his audience's expense, and they never come easily or cheaply. Thus, without a traditional military or athletic posture, without strong appeal to children or adolescents, Garrison Keillor has assumed the hero's role for many adults.

8

TO begin to comprehend the complexities as well as the humor of Garrison Keillor, it is imperative to understand the fundamentalist religion of his youth, when he was a member of a Plymouth Brethren assembly. In the *Mother Earth* interview several years ago, Keillor said, "The Brethren were a tiny minority for whom life was strictly an upstream paddle. A great many things that the people of other creeds got to do were forbidden to us. I've felt that restriction as far back as I can remember."

Yet, the restrictions were only part of the impact the Brethren had upon him. On "Fresh Air," he stated:

> People who didn't grow up in a religious background, it's the restrictions that interest them the most. And I can understand that. But that's only part of the story: great love within the group of people who are as closely bound together by faith as the fundamentalists were, and other small religious sects; tremendous affection and a kindness and generosity for other members of the group. We didn't play cards, nobody drank or smoked; dancing was certainly looked down on, movies and television. I guess that was the one that hurt the most. Because every other kid had one, and they'd do bits the next day on the playground. 'How sweet it is,' from Jackie Gleason, other bits from Sid Ceasar or Milton Berle, and I didn't know what they were talking about.

Keillor claims to not have departed from those religious roots, and has said in several interviews that he still believes what he was brought up to believe, though he no longer attends services at a Brethren assembly.

His people were fundamentalists, and often the mention of the word *fundamentalist* is greeted with derision. Keillor objects to this prevalent attitude, telling the Plowboy interviewer that most people think of fundamentalists as narrow-minded, unhappy, sexually frustrated, bitter people who are intolerant and hypocritical, adding, "It's not based on the kind of church I grew up in."

In his church, he says, he felt very secure. "We were so separated from the world with our restrictions and discipline," he said in a 1984 interview with *The Wittenberg Door*, a Lutheran magazine, "it encouraged us to have a greater love for each other—which was more than I have found in any other kind of church."

He spoked about his people in April, 1982, to seminarians at Luther-Northwestern seminary in St. Paul. As recorded by Clark Morphew in the St. Paul *Pioneer Press*, Keillor said:

The people I grew up amongst I always wished would have been more subversive than they were. They were a very devout little bunch and they were sort of subversive in a way. Most of them did not believe in getting on in the world. Most of them were failures out of Christian principle. Most of them felt that this world—the world in which you make it—was not the real world.

On "Fresh Air" he said:

My family, for religious reasons, took and still take a very dim view of success. Fame and fortune never ranked very high in their book, and in fact were considered very dangerous and to be avoided. They take very limited pleasure in what's happening to me right now. And if they'd had their druthers, they'd have rather seen me go into a line of work like teaching, or something a little more modest, something where the sin of pride would not be such a wonderful possibility. Something a little more selfless than being a writer and being a performer. . . . There's a passage in the book [*Lake Wobegon Days*] about how they had modest ambitions for their children, that they could earn an honest living and take pleasure in the Lord, and suffer trouble cheerfully. College and well-paying jobs weren't necessary. Farming is the most godly, and show business the least.

Keillor himself apparently has not been able to completely free himself from this mind-set and has told several publications that his people neither admire nor aspire to secular success, and while he regards himself as a success, his background keeps him from fully enjoying or appreciating his achievements. More recently he seems to have modified that view, for when Gross asked him if he were concerned about the consequences of success, he said he wasn't. "It feels like such a pleasure to me, and most pleasant parts of it have to do with people more than anything else."

Yet he's always aware of the Brethren position on success; they look askance at it. "I'm not the person to say they were wrong. I don't know. I know I'm kind of on an adventure right now, but who knows how it will turn out? It might turn out badly. Maybe they were right."

L. S. Klepp, reviewing *Lake Wobegon Days* in *The Village Voice*, wrote, "As humorist, Keillor owes a great deal to the narrow, repressive religious training that he had to throw off to become a humorist."

But he hasn't thrown it off; indeed, he insists that it remains important to him. In 1985, when the Los Angeles *Times* asked him if he were religious, he replied, "I certainly hope so. I believe the same as when I was young. What's changed is my life, and it's possible, I think, to believe something and not know how to live it. The Christian faith calls us to a standard of which we'll always fall short. The harder we try of course, the farther we do fall short." And when *The Wittenberg Door* asked if he considered himself "born again," he said, "Absolutely."

The fundamentalist hold on Keillor was and is strong, a potent influence in his life. He admits it often embarrassed him, though, as when in *Lake Wobegon Days*, the family leaves a St. Cloud restaurant because liquor had been offered by a waitress. In her *New York Times Book Review* assessment of *Lake Wobegon Days*, Veronica Geng wrote that the Brethren "guard the Wobegonian ideal at its narrowest point, where going east in any way, shape or form means going to hell." For the Brethren were the fundamentalists in Lake Wobegon, stricter than either the Lutherans or the Catholics.

Keillor does not subscribe to all the basic tenets of fundamentalism, however; until recently he chain-smoked Camel cigarettes and is a moderate consumer of spirits. Fundamentalists strongly disapprove of the use of alcohol and tobacco, and this factor has no doubt contributed to a few family problems he's experienced because of his personal habits and chosen career. A while back, after the success of *Lake Wobegon Days* was assured, Keillor reportedly told an uncle he wanted to do something for his parents and sought the older man's advice. He supposedly was told that what would most please his folks would be his engaging in the Lord's work, for some in the Keillor family believe his life, his work, is in rebellion against God.

Jon Fagerson, who was also raised among the Brethren, says, "Any talking about religion that makes anybody laugh is going to make old-time fundamentalists terribly uptight."

While Keillor does not appear to be in rebellion, even by most fundamentalist standards, he may merely be pushing against the strictures of fundamentalism and the Brethren who raised him.

The Plymouth Brethren, called Sanctified Brethren in *Lake Wobegon Days*, is a rather loose affiliation of churches that have early-nineteenth-century roots in Britain. The name is derived from initial meetings in Plymouth, England. The common terminology referring to the group is "Brethren" or "assemblies" or "Brethren assemblies."

There are two main divisions of Brethren: the "closed," or exclusive, and the "open." Keillor speaks of having come from the closed assembly, where only those persons known by members or vouched for by letter from some other assembly could take the Lord's Supper with the Brethren. Visitors to such assemblies usually are seated behind the rest of the congregation. The closed assemblies are known as the Little Flock, which, says Fagerson, "has the concept of being select, a very few. So if Keillor's talking about religious things and so many people approve of it or appreciate it, that may be threatening to the type of person who believes that 'we' are the elect and the rest are excluded."

Though Brethren today are a tiny sect in North America, their beginnings indicated potential for significant growth. With early leadership supplied by the charismatic John Nelson Darby, a minister with the Church of Ireland, who at twenty-eight, in 1828, renounced his ordination to associate with the Brethren. His influence was far-reaching, and his teachings affected the careers of generations of preachers and evangelists, into the twentieth century. Darby, along with most early adherents of the faith, was unhappy about connections between the established church and the British government. The Brethren also found little edification in the dead formalism found in traditional church worship.

Brethren have no generally accepted statement of faith, as they eschew strict creeds, but do uphold the Bible as the inspired, inerrant word of God. Inerrancy, defined by the nineteenth-century Lutheran theologian, Carl F. W. Walther, means that all the declarations of the Bible are literally true, that they correspond to fact. They are true in regard to past events and future happenings. The accepted translations have not diminished in meaning and nothing has been lost from original texts. For the Bible to contain falsehood, wrote Walther, would constrict the truth that God, who has spoken through his holy word, cannot lie or deceive. Therefore God's word, the Bible, cannot contradict itself.

Some mainline denominations make looser interpretations of the scriptures, arguing that perhaps some pronouncements are merely stories used to illustrate important truths. Many such denominations support the theory of evolution rather than the biblical account of a fiat creation in seven days by God. Main-liners may also argue that the account of Jonah and the whale may be apocryphal, and would point to other stories as similarly mythical but effective in imparting truths and principles to a largely illiterate mass during the first centuries of Christianity.

Brethren, as do most fundamentalists, uphold the trinity of God the Father, Son and Holy Spirit, and stress both the deity and complete humanity of Jesus. They hold to the virgin birth of Christ, his physical death, bodily resurrection, ascension to the Father, and intercession in the lives of his followers through prayer. They further believe that man is depraved and is in need of salvation by grace through faith, and that the church is composed of all true believers in Jesus Christ. Brethren practice two ordinances: baptism by immersion, and Holy Communion. They also support a premillenial tribulation, which according to Revelation, chapter 13, will find the earth in torment for three and a half years, ruled by a Satanic minion known as the Beast, or number 666. And before ascendance of all believers to the heavenly realm, fundamentalists believe in the Millenial, or thousand-year reign of Christ on earth.

As Keillor writes in *Lake Wobegon Days* and illustrates in some of his monologues, the Brethren services are unstructured, and all men in the assembly are free to assume oral roles. Brethren refer to this as the priesthood of all believers. There are no ordained clergy, and men of the congregation share the preaching responsibilities. Women may not speak during ser-vices, and all music is sung a cappella.

In its insistence that the scriptures are the inerrant word of God, fundamentalism often stands in radical opposition to Ro-man Catholicism and other church bodies where the historical-critical method of biblical interpretation is employed. Fundamentalists reject this method of historical interpretation because that method understands the scriptures to have human sources and to be products of human literature rather than divine inspiration. But the fundamentalist position sometimes runs deeper than this, moving into the interpretation of prophecy. In Revelation, chapter 17, verse five is a reference to Babylon, the Great Mother of Harlots, which numerous Protestant commentaries believe represents the papacy. This fundamentalist belief is solidified by the caliber of protestants who have held this position since reformation: Luther, Tyndale, Knox, Calvin and many others. Further, some fundamentalists believe Catholics practice idolatry by owning medallions or crucifixes, and by decorating their churches with stained glass. Fagerson recalls his own Brethren assembly as without pictures anywhere, the walls unadorned except with verses from the scriptures.

Coming out of this background, Fagerson believes, Keillor may have been trying to rectify that hostility by depicting Father Emil, pastor of Lake Wobegon's Our Lady of Perpetual Responsibility, as both wise and foolish, but certainly a good man who is concerned about the souls of his parishioners.

While there's something of a mild tension in Lake Wobegon between Catholics and Lutherans, such tension would have been uneasy dating back to Keillor's childhood and might even have been somewhat hostile between fundamentalists and Catholics. There were then and remain today fundamentalist religious tracts instructing the faithful how to witness to Roman Catholics, or even discrediting the infallibility of the Pope. And even in Lake Wobegon, no responsible Lutheran would have casually wandered in, as Clarence did, to see Father Emil for a "second opinion." The uneasy truce between Lutherans and Catholics is still prevalent in small Minnesota towns, where they are the dominant denominations, and there remains family anguish when interfaith marriages occur.

• • •

English Protestantism, from which the Brethren broke away, had an emphasis on negatives—what a Christian ought not do. The concept of the negative plays a role in contemporary fundamentalist faith also. Forbidden by fundamentalists are tobacco, alcohol, social dancing, gambling, motion pictures, card playing, much of what is on television, divorce and more recently, abortion. Positive concepts such as love and forgiveness and concern for the welfare of others sometimes tend to be submerged under the weight of the negative strictures, also called legalisms.

Theologians who reject legalisms say the so-called abstinences stress reliance on one's own performance rather than on God's grace through faith alone. Critics claim legalists pay lip service to grace and convey to peers the impression that if one doesn't perform correctly, one can't be a born-again believer. Thus, during the presidency of Jimmy Carter, a self-proclaimed born-again Christian, when wine was served at White House functions, many fundamentalists questioned the efficacy of the president's faith.

The Wittenburg Door asked Keillor if he'd had trouble with legalisms, and he said occasionally during his teen years, but not when he was younger.

"They'd use real wine during communion, which confused me as far back as I can remember," said a former Brethren "because it was such a terrible thing to have wine in your house to drink socially."

Legalisms have confused many fundamentalists because some traditional taboos are without scriptural foundations, and legalists have been sometimes selective in determining which activities are sinful. The Bible opposes drunkenness but does not teach abstinence. On the other hand, one of fundamentalism's great heroes, the nineteenth-century evangelist Dwight L. Moody, had a prodigious appetite and was overweight, and some Pentecostal fundamentalists jokingly refer to themselves as having a "Pentecostal belly," resulting from heavy indulgence in potluck dinners and picnics.

In the absence of direct spiritual advice concerning alcohol or tobacco, fundamentalists employ the Biblical references to keep the body holy as a temple of the Lord. "Would Jesus smoke a cigarette or drink a glass of beer?" is a frequent rhetorical question posed from fundamentalist pulpits.

The dancing taboo has close ties to smoking and drinking. While the act of the dance does not appear in and of itself to be harmful—witness King David's dance in 2 Samuel, it has evolved into a sinful transgression because it may incite lust, and people who dance may frequent establishments where, presumably, a majority of dancers imbibe. For a Christian to enter such a place invites temptation.

Fundamentalists may strictly interpret the Sabbath as a day of rest. And many former fundamentalists recall childhoods where Sunday afternoons were fraught with tension because they were to "rest," to sit in chairs after the noon meal and contemplate the minister's morning message until it was time to depart for the Sunday evening services.

In politics, fundamentalist activists assume absolutist positions on moral issues such as abortion, pornography, gambling, the teaching of evolution, and prayer in public schools. Though these positions are often ridiculed in the media, some of the antifundamentalist feeling may spring from the resulting unease when the fundamentalist pricks our consciences.

According to Keillor in *The Wittenberg Door*, this is precisely what fundamentalists are supposed to do. He defines their mission as "to bring us back to earth. To bring us back to reality. They are evangelists. They are supposed to shake us up. They are people with a very strong and very clear message. And when they are about the business of delivering it, it's a good message to hear. We need to hear it."

A fundamentalist background such as Keillor's is seldom if ever without major influence on one's life. If one backslides, an omnipresent gnawing of conscience remains. A woman of sixty, who has smoked for forty-five years, said, "I still feel guilty when I light up, and both Mom and Dad are gone. I started smoking just to prove to myself that I could do it, and I wouldn't be struck dead or get the plague or something." She adds that she can relate to what Keillor is saying when he speaks of his background. "You never shed all the guilt." Keillor, by the way, never smoked in his parents' presence.

The conscience of the fundamentalist is always seared, and the residue of guilt for offending the faith, the family, remains for years, and may never dissipate. Fundamentalists assert this is appropriate, that the individual in rebellion against God needs to be convicted of his sins, ask forgiveness and return to the fold.

Because Brethren and other fundamentalists believe that worldly success is not significant in the life of a Christian, Keillor speaks a personal truth when he says he's not entirely comfortable with his achievements. And he continues to regard himself as a failure in formal education.

"You have to consider yourself a failure when you're holding yourself up to a standard that says, 'Therefore, be ye perfect as I am perfect,'" said Fagerson. "Who can be perfect? He probably really did feel he was a failure at that time, in not getting straight A's, in letting his parents down. But I think that gets back to the message I hear from him in everything I read and hear on the radio; that in dragging out these areas where he is not perfect, and in dealing with them and somehow learning to accept them, he's teaching us something about self-acceptance."

In his classic book *The Protestant Ethic and the Spirit of Capitalism*, sociologist Max Weber wrote, "One may attain salvation in any walk of life; on the short pilgrimage of life there is no use in laying weight on the form of occupation. The pursuit of material gain beyond personal needs must appear as a symptom of a lack of grace, and since it can apparently only be attained at the expense of others, directly reprehensible."

This thinking was even earlier expressed by John Wesley, who wrote, "I fear wherever riches have increased, the essence of religion has decreased in the same proportion. . . . As riches increase, so will pride, anger, and love of the world in all its branches."

Brethren take admonitions against pride very seriously. Their attitude may be typified by the example of a nineteenth-century Brethren poet, Joseph Scriven, whose poem, *Take it to the Lord in Prayer*, has become the widely known hymn, "What a Friend We Have in Jesus." After his conversion, Scriven refused even to have his photo taken, because the picture, he believed, would be a concession to vanity.

Keillor, however, remained perplexed by the teaching that calls Christians to be selfless, without pride, admitting in a Los Angeles *Times* interview, "It's not clear to me how a person who's a writer and a performer does that."

Thus, his creative gift must have at times seemed almost a curse to him, as the pressure to conform to established norms within the Brethren assembly would have been enormous. He's regarded himself as a writer since early childhood, but fundamentalists eschew idleness as a ploy for Satan to invade the soul of the unwary. "Waste of time," Weber wrote in his essay, "is the first and in principle the deadliest of sins. . . . Loss of time through sociability, idle talk, luxury, even more sleep than is necessary for health, six to at most eight hours, is worthy of absolute moral condemnation. . . . Thus inactive contemplation is also valueless. . . ."

A writer, however, is almost by definition a dreamer, a seeming waster of time. He may contemplate for hours, days, even weeks without appearing to be performing a job of work. Thus, to be doing nothing, or to be merely writing, would have been viewed by the Brethren as valueless.

As Keillor writes his tales and recited his monologues, the factors of pride and guilt and sin appeared almost omnipresent. But far from making judgments and railing angrily against the restraints of his upbringing, he recognized its force in his life, and treated it with respect, if not reverence. He once told Letofsky, after the journalist moved to the Los Angeles *Times*, that the strength of Lake Wobegon as a place was that its people believed in the existence of sin. "They don't believe that everything that goes wrong is the result of a failure of communications, or a misunderstanding, or a lack of B-1 vitamins. People sometimes spend a great deal of time trying to understand problems—only to come up with a new and different problem . . . whereas in Lake Wobegon, they simply call it sin and forgive it and to hell with it."

Wobegonians take their religion seriously, as does their creator. Persons who have been in his presence and assumed his religious remarks were satire have been caught short by Keillor's insistence that he has not departed his Brethren roots and has no intention of doing so.

The religion he respects is clearly of the old line, traditional Christianity, rather than those denominational bodies that attempt a contemporary, with it approach. Even old Father Emil in Lake Wobegon is vexed that some young priests are cast in this mold, and the good father doesn't want his replacement during a vacation hiatus to be the modernist from St. Cloud who wears a T-shirt with a picture of Jesus waterskiing on it, the inscription reading HE'S UP.

"I'm certainly uncomfortable with churches that I consider a great deal more liberal than the one I was brought up in," he recalled. "I have a very hard time sitting still when a preacher's talking about the value of being a good listener or something like that. When I hear that sort of sermon, I really feel like I ought to get up and walk out."

And in another interview he says:

We don't need the minister unless he has something that the Spirit has put in his heart to say. The important thing is to have something in your heart, look out at the people and try to say what is in your heart right then and there. We don't go to churches to hear lectures on ethical behavior, we go to look at the mysteries, and all the substitutes for communion with God are not worth anyone's time. A minister who stands up and occupies twenty minutes of the worship hour only has to say *one* thing for a sermon to be worthwhile—just one clear image, one proposition that you can take home with you. . . . The gospel message is not easy, and ministers who try to make it more pleasant than it really is are doing a disservice.

It may be attributed to his creative genius that Keillor finds acceptance from conservative Christians as well as from those who perceive his work as lampooning traditional beliefs. In this regard, the monologues with spiritual tenents seem to be open metaphors. "As critics or interpreters we are all saying who we are in the process," says Jon Fagerson. "Whether we see this as humor or profound truth."

Studs Terkel, a Jew, observes of Keillor that "He spans religion, secular humanism; he spans liberal and conservative. Conservatives think he's conservative, and liberals think he's liberal."

In his *Village Voice* review, Klepp writes, "One of the best things in the book is an evocative account of a revival meeting, which demonstrates that guilt is the common denominator of religion and humor."

At the same time, the November 25, 1985 issue of *Christianity Today*, a leading conservative Christian magazine, in its review of *Lake Wobegon Days*, concluded, "Certainly Garrison Keillor is making Judeo-Christian values, a Christian worldview and the pursuit of the spiritual dimension of life more credible and interesting than just about anyone in the public eye today."

Linae Haase, however, said "I'd be embarrassed about how he handles the church if I were his parents. It bothers me a little too, because I don't know how much he is laughing with it or at it."

John Moore, the corporate claims specialist, was also raised a fundamentalist. "He's working through what I did for many years," Moore said. "But I sort of resent him doing this in front of millions. Others might see it as ridicule or sarcasm. His listeners tend to be better educated, more cerebral in their likes and dislikes. And since they aren't fundamentalists, they may be amused at how he presents that style of life."

Keillor seemed curiously cranky in the *Metropolitan Home* interview in October, 1985, and objected to the notion of his program as wholesome, skewing the views that many harbor toward "A Prairie Home Companion" and perhaps corroborating concerns expressed by Haase and Moore. "People who look on the show as a clean, Christian family program write me letters complimenting me on the fact that I don't use bad language. When I get letters like that, I try to find a way to get a word like *bastard* into the show as soon as possible. . . . I'm not in the business of nice."

He recognizes that he has a darker side, and can flirt with the bawdy. Some years ago, about the time President Jimmy Carter was having hemorrhoid problems, Keillor gave a reading at the Coffee House Extempore in Minneapolis, in which his theme was hemorrhoids. According to those in attendance, his descriptions of the affliction were "shockingly graphic," though a woman who was there added, "He was quite funny, though, at the same time."

Early in 1987, he must have received one of the letters referred to in the *Metropolitan Home* interview, because in his monologue he had a minister's wife thinking of calling her husband a bastard.

Keillor does not regularly attend church anymore, stopping because, as he told an interviewer, "I felt like a Pharisee. I felt conspicuous. Most of the people in the congregation knew who I was. They would stare at me and say to themselves, 'Oh, look. It's so wonderful—a semifamous man goes to our church every Sunday. What a wonderful person he must be.' Who wants that? I felt as if I was on display. I felt like people were approving of me for going to church. I don't like to be approved of; that's not why I go."

He also told "Fresh Air" that he won't go to churches where they play guitars and where the sermon deals with being a good listener.

Instead of attending church, he had said he would rather stay home and watch Jimmy Swaggart on TV. "He's a very emotional performer. He knows how to walk right to the edge and put it out there for people. He actually weeps on his show. He weeps for the sins of the world. He's a very passionate preacher. . . . I admire him. He's a rock 'n' roll evangelist from Louisiana. He's an artist."

When Keillor writes of religion—religion aside the Sanctified Brethren—he often takes literary license in his depictions. Bob and Verna, who conduct the evangelistic meetings in Lake Wobegon, are much more apt to come from a fundamentalist perspective than out of Lutheran orthodoxy. Lutherans, by and large, adhere to a formal order of worship, and their services tend to avoid the fervent emotionalism of people like Bob and Verna, who may well be patterned after old line itinerant preachers, or even Jimmy Swaggart or Jerry Falwell. Lutherans, being mostly Scandinavian and German, lean toward stoic unemotional expression in their worship and faith.

And when Keillor tells of Wobegonians ditching their drinks behind the sofa when Pastor Inqvist comes unannounced to the front door, he's not describing Lutherans, who place no restrictions on the moderate use of alcohol.

Despite the popular conception of fundamentalists as humorless and frowning, Keillor has said he often found humor among the Brethren. "The kids I was brought up with at the meetings had a sense of humor about a lot of things," he said in a Minneapolis *Tribune* profile. "Certain members would always preface any remark about the future with the phrase, 'Lord willing,' and in writing, say if one kid wrote a letter saying they planned to be in Willmar on Tuesday, they'd write D.V. after it—Deus volenti—because He could come back at any time and there might not be a Tuesday as we knew it."

Aleksandr Solzhenitsyn has written that "life consists not in the pursuit of material success but in the quest for worthy spiritual growth." This tenent may be broadly applied to many of the Keillor monologues, which have replaced the role of sermons in the lives of some listeners and fans.

Notes historian John E. Miller, "One of the many appeals of

the tales of Lake Wobegon is the way in which it grapples with fundamental moral and religious problems. Beneath the humor lies a serious effort to confront the ambiguities and dilemmas that face us every day. Garrison Keillor's parables contain truths that can instruct us all."

In a monologue from a few years ago, Keillor took up one of his perennial themes: being embarrassed about coming from a small village and being a member of a tiny, unknown religious sect. He meets some upper-middle-class Catholics at the university and is invited to their home. The man is apparently a cultural anthropologist, who is amazed and delighted to discover that his guest is a member of a Brethren assembly. For a long time he's wanted to talk to someone familiar with this minuscule band that sings a cappella in their services.

"That was one monologue where I recognized my Brethren experience," said Fagerson. "I remember being embarrassed by it, and I think Keillor was too, until this experience. I think it is symbolic of what one of Keillor's main appeals to people is— that everybody feels they're not okay, or has some secret they can't share, or they're the only ones who have parents like this. Everybody feels that there's something that makes them different from other people, and then you have Keillor coming on these programs and having his audience vicariously experience this sense of secrecy, shame or embarrassment. I'm sure the audience all plugs in their fears and embarrassments, and what happens in the monologue is that the person makes some insights and accepts them. There's some sense of acceptance of the person in that story, and it makes me as a listener a whole person, in the sense that I can see myself for what I am and not be ashamed. That is a catharsis of which the Greeks would be proud."

Miller notes that Keillor's special status as a close observer but nonparticipant "provides him with a unique vantage point for perceiving and elucidating certain truths about churches and their members."

In Keillor's monologues, however, there was a certain ambivalence about where he might stand on pertinent moral issues of the day. This limited him and rendered him unable to discuss sensitive topics such as abortion, because, he said, there was no way to treat them humorously.

He continued, though, to find religion and Christianity a rich mine from which to cull his unique and gentle humor. In a speech delivered at Goshen College in Indiana he said, "People think it's difficult to be a Christian and to laugh, but I think it's the other way around. God writes a lot of comedy. It's just that he has so many bad actors."

Among the old college crowd, James Delmont for one appreciated how Keillor's monologues and stories had turned. "Garrison acquired a gentle air he didn't have before. A reluctance to hurt anybody. I liked his charity toward his subjects, that is maybe Christianlike. He defended the simple Christian ethics with a New Testament approach and life-style."

Also, Keillor may have seen in himself something of the evangelist, one who was constrained to preach the truth to a mass audience. He strongly hinted at this in his story "Friendly Neighbor." Dad Benson, the main character, was the star of a network radio program called "Friendly Neighbor," a daily drama which keynoted simple messages of love and concern. And in the story, Reverend Weiss tells Dad that Dad was perhaps more a minister than he was himself, because his stories preached spiritual truths far better than most sermons.

"That's why Keillor's uncle wanting him to devote himself to the Lord's work is almost strange," said Fagerson. "Because the beautiful irony is that he is doing that."

9

IN 1982 Keillor wrote to Deloyd Hochstetter telling his
former teacher that he still took
great pleasure in writing. He
said that in writing, unlike
teaching, one may destroy his
failures. He believes that writing is fun, and he writes post-
cards during his travels, sending them to friends around the
country. He told the Los Angeles *Times*, "The postcard is a
great neglected literary form about fifty words in length. Yet
there is something you can do in fifty words you might not be
able to do if you had to use five hundred."

During his college years, Keillor tried writing essays in the
manner of E. B. White and other *New Yorker* stylists. He has
mentioned reading some of White's pieces and counting the
number of words in the first sentence, and then writing an
opening sentence with the same number of words. White, Keillor has stated, was the writer he most admired because the author of *Charlotte's Web* and, with William Strunk, Jr., *The
Elements of Style* was a precise, meticulous wordsmith.

But Garrison Keillor's own work is also wrought with great
care. "His work is absolutely genius," said Hochstetter. "You
could see it already, even way back then at the school. His idea
in writing, and he kept saying it over and over, was how to use
words. He wanted to see it published to show that it was good.
He was very pleased when his early *New Yorker* stuff was never
blue-penciled."

Keillor's writing process frequently involves finishing a piece and putting it away until he can look at it with less emotional attachment. After weeks, or even a few months have passed, Keillor will take out the sketch or story again and may strip it away almost entirely, only its main idea remaining, and approach the piece from a new direction.

In the Minneapolis *Tribune* interview with Letofsky, Keillor was in the process of selecting pieces for *Happy to Be Here*. He said that writing was one way poor people could make a lot of money, and while he hoped his book would be a marketplace success, he didn't think it would. "It's not that I'm shy about the idea [of making money], it's just that I'm a particular kind of writer. I'm a slow writer. I'm a small writer, and I do the kind of thing that it seems to me to have only one home, and that's *The New Yorker*. He added that earning fifteen to eighteen thousand dollars a year writing his way would be almost as good as earning fifty thousand dollars by doing work that wasn't as satisfying.

In the interview he gave Michael Schumacher of *Writer's Digest*, he said:

> I can't think of stories in formal terms until they're written. Then I can look at a story that I have written or that someone else has written, and I can describe its form, as I did when I was in school and was asked to write term papers. Every story finds its own form. Finding that form is the great struggle of writing, for which there is no prescription. I would say that the essential element in storytelling is the passion of finding out how to tell it. If you don't have that passion to tell a story, you will settle for telling it not very well, which is almost worse than not telling it at all. But if you have the passion to tell a story, it becomes a wonderful problem in your life—a wonderful problem like being in love. It becomes an irritation, a splendid misery, that might get some work out of a person who will do his little part in adding to the world's knowledge, in adding to the life of the world.

• • •

Keillor said that he wanted to be a writer from the time he was nine or ten years old, knowing, he said, that he would write, but not being certain what sort of work he'd do or how he'd go about becoming a writer. "But I knew that writing was what I would do with my life—which is amazing to think of now, the fact that I knew something to be true when I was nine years old that is still true."

Keillor believes he's a writer with a mission. "I think that I was put here on earth to write in extravagant praise of common things."

In the main, he said, his pieces are painstakingly developed and worked over:

> At some point in the writing, I will sit down with a manuscript and go over it, word for word, more than once—sometimes many times. I guess I believe that writing consists of very small parts put together into a whole, and if the parts are defective, the whole won't work. But that's a mechanical view. What really comes first is feeling and passion and curiosity.
>
> If the writer is true to personal experience, the reader is offered something recognizable. It's only as you are faithful to the peculiarities and the exact description of personal experience that you create something that other people will be able to take as their own.

What occurs in the Lake Wobegon experiences are many moments, truths, and observations that we indeed take as our own. The small-town values can be almost universally embraced. Jack Bibee, a communications professor, says that Keillor's monologues and Lake Wobegon stories were urban fantasies. "Even among those of us who were raised in urban environments, we can recall rural roots through perhaps our visits to Grandma's farm in Wisconsin. These fantasies strike a chord with people, even with those who've never been in a truly rural small town. In a way, I'd compare these people with upper-middle-class kids in the sixties who wore blue work shirts and sang work and labor-union songs, but who knew little or nothing of that life-style. The dress and those songs represented a fantasy for them in the same way many of his followers fantasize and romanticize small town life. They really don't know what it's about, but in their minds Keillor made it seem like the life he described in Lake Wobegon."

According to Jesse Bier, professor of American literature at the University of Montana in Missoula and author of *The Rise and Fall of American Humor*, Garrison Keillor is bringing back regionalism, or small-town humor. "During World War I and into the twenties as America was becoming urbanized, small towns were passing and were the object of nostalgic regard. Keillor's gone back to that—not that *we* have—but we want to migrate back. There are demographic figures that show there are people who want to reverse the urbanization of America. They want to go back to something that's more comprehensible, and he appeals to them."

Though Keillor is a meticulous writer, he has nonetheless experienced those rare flashes when the mind and fingers on the keyboard are at one; when a virtually finished draft flows forth in a couple hours; when the writing seems automatic, yet retains the heat of inspiration. Schumacher reported Keillor as having written a few stories like that. "It's like washing very fine china," Keillor said. "You're afraid you're going to break this story as you write it down, but you don't. It goes right down on paper. There are a few stories that I have written that are like that, and I'm grateful for every one."

Commenting on his much praised collection of stories and comic pieces, *Happy to Be Here*, published in 1982 by Atheneum, which sold 210,000 hardcover copies, he said, "Some of those stories were labored at pretty hard. And I hope that they don't show signs of it. Some of them started way off in left field and it was only through quite a long process that they became anything. The writing, I think, always begins with extravagance, and the paring down and close examination and going at the piece with a tweezers comes later.

Writing, he added, isn't always writing what you know. "You write in order to find things out."

Happy to Be Here, stories mainly taken from his material published in *The New Yorker*, enjoyed sales far in excess of what most such collections achieve. Many of those sales were no doubt generated among fans of "A Prairie Home Companion." But since those pieces have little in common with stories about Lake Wobegon, there were many who were disappointed with the book. Keillor admits as much when he says that he received comments from fans of his program who weren't happy with that book. People who liked his *New Yorker* and *Atlantic Monthly* stories have sent letters saying they find little to interest them in his radio program, as well.

The enormous success of *Lake Wobegon Days*, with more than 1,200,000 hardcover copies sold, is a direct result of the popularity of the radio broadcast. The skeptics—and there are many—assert that without "A Prairie Home Companion," the book might not have received a second printing.

The selections in *Happy to Be Here* contain elements of brilliance, if not comic genius. The satire in pieces such as "Don: The True Story of a Young Person" cuts close to the bone. It originally appeared in the May 30, 1977 issue of *The New Yorker*. Don's parents are worried because Don plays punk rock music. His band plays for the 4-H County Poultry Show Dance, and the audience becomes enraged and throws feed pellets at the group. Finally a live chicken is tossed, and a band member gets carried away and bites its neck and kills the chicken, initiating a community scandal. But national rock critics hear of it and say the band are geniuses, inventors of a new fad called "geek rock." The piece directly reflects on the psuedo-intellectual posturing of *Rolling Stone* writers and their imitators—the fatuousness typified by the critic in the late sixties who observed that when the rock group the Yardbirds trashed a stage and their equipment the audience witnessed an extension of the group's artistic integrity, but when other groups behaved similarly, they were merely pandering to popular taste.

Keillor's "Shy Rights: Why Not Pretty Soon?" lampoons liberation-rights rhetoric. In "Attitude," he reflects on personal feelings he holds toward slow-pitch softball, a sport he takes seriously. He rails against the absence of seriousness on the part of teammates. He chafes under their attitude that winning isn't important because, after all, it's only a game. Players forgive themselves for making errors, which he finds unforgivable.

This particular piece may have come out of his experience as manager of a team from Minnesota Public Radio that played against other local media-sponsored teams a decade ago. Nick Coleman, whose columns about Keillor and "A Prairie Home Companion" would earn him the enmity of both Keillor and MPR, said he first met Keillor in 1976 on a softball field, where Keillor's team played a group from the Minneapolis *Tribune*. "Keillor didn't play, he watched, and he kind of supervised," Coleman recalled. "He was so intense it was frightening. This was a fun game, not taken seriously by anyone but Keillor, who would exhibit a violent temper if calls went against his team."

The stories in the collection, observed Doug Thorpe in a perspicacious review that appeared in the July 21–28, 1982 issue of *Christian Century*, suggest a writer-narrator who is vulnerable himself and sees vulnerability everywhere: "in shy people, in all that is passing, growing up and growing older. He sees that we can do little to help each other out—even our own defenseless children. Sometimes the best we can do is send messages over the airwaves. Or tell . . . stories."

Garrison Keillor used to write either at home or in his office at MPR headquarters in downtown St. Paul. Every day found him at his typewriter—or word processor, on which he wrote *Lake Wobegon Days*—by nine A.M. A few years ago, he told the magazine *M P L S, St. Paul* that he puts a piece of paper in the typewriter every day. "I don't always do very much with it," he said. "The pleasure of it is the blank paper, the beginning of something, struggling with it. . . . It's sad when it's finished."

The first draft of *Lake Wobegon Days* ran 230,000 words. After revisions, the final version totaled 150,000 words. In an August 15, 1985 interview with the Minneapolis *Star Tribune* reporter Kim Ode, Keillor hinted at a sequel. "I haven't told the whole story. I was very careful to write an unfinished book. It's sort of rounded off, I think. There's a lot more, a good deal more."

As is apparently true with his monologues, he said that much of *Lake Wobegon Days* is based on people he's known and things that happened or might have happened to them. He said, "I don't believe I invent anything—everything comes from experience. But it all sits around for twenty-five or thirty years and simmers. Marinates in its juices. . . . Some secondary characters were based directly on pals of mine. There are names of people in there who are real people, but I use them as part of a wonderful old literary tradition—to put your pals in your work in an incidental, humorous way."

Yet, as he told *Writer's Digest,* using friends and family in fiction that draws so much on his own life violates a taboo of the family:

> You don't tell these secrets outside the circle. You don't go around the neighborhood talking about this, because you were brought up to keep family secrets. I have kept a great many— I've kept most. There's a great deal I won't talk about or write about that in some way I wish I could. It interests me. But when you break the rule, you pay some price. You expect to. There is a great deal of integrity in privacy.

He has often been asked where his stories and monologues come from. In the *Metropolitan Home* interview, he talked about venturing into small-town cafes and taverns and absorbing stories from other customers:

> I get in my car and drive a little bit west of Minneapolis. You don't have to drive far to be out beyond the life of the arts and,

you know, pasta, to get to where my stuff is set. Hutchinson, Hamel, Rogers, Watertown—they're all within easy driving distance. There are taverns in those towns that are really the social centers, where not everybody is drinking to get drunk. You don't want to dress funny; you don't want to look at anybody. You just want to sit there with your head down holding your beer. And a lot of their material is a heckuva lot funnier than what I do on Saturday night. But they don't operate with the same restrictions of good taste.

As a storyteller, Keillor reminds himself of his father or his uncle, Lew Powell. He told one interviewer that as he gets older he is hearing his father's voice coming out of him, "and I find myself saying things he would have said, or Uncle Lew would have said—sort of an apotheosis of what they would have said if they had been writers. I find the satisfaction in doing that that I don't get from writing funny stories."

In the *Time* magazine cover story of November 4, 1985, Keillor said that Uncle Lew's stories sometimes did not come to a point, but to a point of contemplation. "As I got older, of course, life was becoming strange. I just looked to those stories of his, and to the history of the family, as giving a person a sense of place, that we were not just chips floating on the waves, that in some way we were meant to be here, and had a history. That we had standing."

To recognize his own standing, his own place, is important to him, and he maintains it is also vital to others. But so often powerless people are not accorded standing or place. Jon Fagerson remembers hearing Keillor speak to a group of high school English teachers in the mid seventies at a Minneapolis conference. "He wore his white hat and white suit, and he walked up there, and here's all these education types ready to get their in-service credits for attending the workshop. They're all sitting with their notebooks, waiting for three main points of good writing, and he just takes off telling stories; I was profoundly affected by two stories he told.

"One was when he was working writing obituaries for the St. Paul paper, and a woman asked him to write her obituary. She was a cook at a church and was given the status of a cook. What nobody knew, and what she'd never told anybody, was that she had a Ph.D. in social work and had been head of a women's correctional facility for many years and was a respected figure in her field. She vanished from that professional life and became a servant for a family in Summit Hill [a wealthy St. Paul neighborhood] as a cook.

The only tag Keillor put on that story was, what should you write about? He was saying that there are some things you know you have to write about, and he said, 'I know I have to write this woman's life.' There was something about it. For me, I see that as something that was attractive to Keillor—a woman could disappear and do things of service to help people who would not thank her or give her any credit for intelligence and treat her as a servant, and she would go on serving. Keillor is sort of hiding behind being a celebrity. But what a paradox. It can be a mask for Keillor that some people don't know that he can be a preacher or a helper of people, a good Samaritan. He may prefer not to be known as that, but rather as a media celebrity, to protect that part of him.

"The other story was about his father working in the Post Office mail car on a run between Minneapolis and Jamestown, North Dakota. Being on his feet all day apparently gave him back problems. He wanted a transfer, and asked Garrison, who was editor of *The Ivory Tower* at that time, if Garrison would write a letter requesting the transfer for him. His father had carefully compiled three or four single-spaced pages of information about himself and his back condition, the number of years of service he'd had, and commendations he'd received. He asked Garrison to polish it up.

"Keillor was telling the English teachers about the importance of saying things as briefly and concisely as possible. So he was able to take those three or four pages and condense them into a couple paragraphs on one page. He thought it was pretty effective because no supervisor would read through three or four pages. But his father was crushed, just terribly hurt that his son thought that his life—four pages of material—was worth only two paragraphs.

"Keillor never said why he was telling us that story, but I think it must have had something to do with warning teachers how fragile the identities of their students are, and how carefully they have to treat them. They're exposing themselves in writing. He didn't say, but that is his genius, to be able to say such corny ideas as 'be nice to your students,' to reveal the truth behind the cliché. He was able to tell us in such a way that I've never forgotten to this day."

Another English teacher, Beverly Skoglund, who teaches at Stillwater High School, recalls the time Keillor visited her journalism class in the mid seventies. "I had mentioned to him that I taught journalism, and he said he'd like to see our newspaper. I remember sending him a couple issues, and then another time asking him if he would ever have time to come to see us. I really felt I was imposing upon him, because he had to get up so early and take that long drive to St. Paul for his program, and my class was at two in the afternoon, which meant he wouldn't have much time for an afternoon nap. But he was delighted. What he wanted before he came—which I thought was just wonderful—were all the issues the kids who were going to be there had done. That consisted of a lot of writing. And when he arrived he had read every single thing.

"There was one kid there, who was also a tall drink of water, and in the writing Garrison had picked him out, and in their exchange you could just see they were working on the same wavelength. He had picked out all the weaknesses, and he went through each one of the kids' stuff and said, 'Well now, this is where you need to work just a little bit harder.' It was a wonderful experience for the kids. Other people being invited in might come and do a surface thing, not go in depth like that. The kids loved him."

· · ·

Humor has always been the hallmark of Garrison Keillor's work, dating back to that first essay he submitted in Deloyd Hochstetter's journalism class in 1958. As do most humorists, Keillor takes the genre seriously. He is not jocular, given to witticisms or jests; that is for others for whom mirth comes easily, for whom laughter comes naturally. He does not laugh easily, and in fact, Hochstetter, whose enduring relationship with the man dates to 1958, says he never recalls seeing Keillor enjoy a hearty laugh. "He used to be deadly serious about this," Hochstetter said. "He didn't joke around a lot. Once in a while we'd get sort of a smile between us. And that was the extent of it."

The sober, private, shy, reflective Garrison Keillor nonetheless claims that humor is the saving grace of American writing. "American writing that has no laughter in it for the reader seems false somehow," he said in the *Writer's Digest* interview. "I don't think this is true of European writing, and I think that a great deal of what we call serious American writing has looked too hard to English and European writing."

Hochstetter thinks that Keillor may well be considering writing a "serious" novel himself, and that he thinks of himself not as an entertainer but as a writer, and probably as a writer cast in the John Updike or Saul Bellow mold. "He still wants to write the great American novel," said Hochstetter. Six months prior to Keillor's announced departure from "A Prairie Home Companion," Hochstetter speculated about Keillor's future. "I think in a couple years, he's going to stop [radio work] and go to Europe. I think he could. It all fits in now; he's bought his house near where F. Scott Fitzgerald used to live, and that's all part of his plan for his life."

Keillor's old friend Marvin Granger agreed. "He was always first and foremost a writer. And there's certainly another book in him after *Lake Wobegon Days*. One more serious. He is a serious writer and a very serious poet as well."

Fagerson, though, doesn't think such a venture is necessary for Keillor to secure his place as a great storyteller. "While his hierarchy of significance would no doubt place Updike higher than a media celebrity, I don't think Keillor needs to prove himself as an artist to anyone. I think he's gone beyond that. He wrote some powerful stuff in *The Ivory Tower*. What I think is intriguing is his invention of the genre of the radio monologue; he's made that an art form. The delightful joke about the whole thing is that the literary establishment hasn't recognized that yet. They're still making distinctions and saying that he isn't going to make it because he's dabbling among this sort of lower-class popular culture thing, which isn't true literature. I think it is, and that he's pulling one off on the establishment. The monologues stand up to the same criteria you'd use in evaluating a short story."

Some of the monologues have the quality of *New Yorker* "casuals." The term was coined by the magazine's founding editor, Harold Ross, who thought some of the pieces done by Thurber, Perelman, White, et al, weren't quite short stories but weren't nonfiction either, and he didn't know what to call them, so he called them "casuals." A more accurate description of the so-called casual would be the Italian art term, *sprezzatura*, which means art that conceals art. The casual is deceptive, often seems offhandedly simple, but is in fact demanding.

Thus Keillor's monologues often started out slowly, lulling the listener into the web of the story, which takes twists, turns, moving from the humorous to the morose, embracing a man's brooding about his relationship with God, his family, his inner fears and doubts, seeming to lead the listener into a corner, at which point the story, like Uncle Lew's reminiscences, will merely peter out—except that suddenly we were thrust back to the beginning again and recognized the wholeness of it. Along the way we laughed, surely, and perhaps cried too, and may have been changed by the work. "I'm always curious about Keillor's work because I'm conscious of change in myself from listening to his monologues," Fagerson said. "I think probably many people change feelings and attitudes but I don't know if they're aware of it. For example, I may be busy with a number of small tasks on Saturday that need to get done, and I may be short with the family. I may even have been intense about listening to Garrison because it was something I did, and it was an assignment for my class. So I had to listen. When it was over, I'd suddenly seen the silliness of all my small tasks and the beauty of my family. I'd want to love them. I was once more a whole person. For me the monologues had a liberating effect because of the values they asserted. The realm of the spiritual was at work."

Though Keillor's monologues had the quality of the casual, or *sprezzatura*, which made them seem almost incidental and extemporaneous, they did not come easily, despite his claims that writing for the printed page was a bit more demanding.

In the August 20, 1985 *New York Times*, Keillor said that even when he began publishing in *The New Yorker*, he was still torn between radio, which he called intimate and sentimental, and his other writing, which he characterized as drier, "a piece of craft. And in the conflict between radio and writing . . . I arrived at doing this monologue on Saturday nights. It was based on writing, but in the end it was radio . . . there's the sound of the human voice to sort of carry over the imperfections. But in writing on the page you have to create that voice artificially, and it's a very delicate job."

When Alan Bunce of the *Christian Science Monitor* asked Keillor what makes a good story, he replied, "Mimicry; a good eye and ear for detail."

Amplifying on this, he said in *The Mother Earth News* that the most important element of a good story was something recognizable, something people can identify with. Most important, though, he said:

. . . is the necessity of it—the urgency of it. If it's not necessary, the structure you create won't do a thing. . . . When you come up against the great flood of mass culture on radio and

147

television and in magazines and newspapers and books you have to explain your background to people. You have an urgent need to explain what it is that sets your people apart . . . exactly how they talk and exactly the way things look like and the truth about what happened. *That* is storytelling. It is, in a way, a defense against all the things that would make us too similar.

Studs Terkel thinks Keillor is something of an oral historian. "First of all, storytelling predates Gutenberg. Alex Haley in *Roots* tells of the *griots*—professional storytellers, and he traced his family history partly through the oral history of the *griot*. There were projects in the New Deal days where writers interviewed people, and an oral history emerged. The story about blacks, *Lay My Burden Down*, resulted from that. Henry Mayhew, a Dickens contemporary, recorded people in the most humble conditions and worst of all trades.

"So storytelling, oral history, is a part of continuity. What Garrison Keillor was doing was reviving this. There are storytelling festivals around now, but not in his category. Ironically, the art began to decline when radio came along. Instead of telling stories, people listened. TV made things worse. But our universal hunger for stories cuts through all identities."

"You discover that being a semi-celebrity is not nearly so much fun nor as interesting as writing," Keillor once said. "A great many writers, particularly young ones, think they want to be writers, but what they really want I think is not to write a book but to have written one." He told Schumacher that he regards himself as a writer who is temporarily a performer:

As a writer, I have gotten on to a track of writing material for performance, which I feel only I can perform. But I'll get off that track. A show such as this one has a limited life. Performing is work that you can do only with the permission of other people. You need no permission to write, so I am a writer before I'm a performer. Despite all of the changes and upsets and the general disjointedness of so much of the rest of my life, writing is the one seam that runs straight through—one of the few. That is why I consider myself a writer. It is an act I perform every day. It is an act by which I hope to come to some peace with myself and my past, as every writer does. It's an act of discovery. At the same time, it is work that a person can do to earn a living and get by. It's an amazing stroke of fortune to be able to earn money doing this.

Keillor told another periodical that after his father, Uncle Lew and Aunt Ruth, his favorite humorists were Thurber, Liebling, Perelman and E. B. White. All were, of course, closely affiliated with *The New Yorker*. Though he still loves that magazine and takes great pleasure in writing for it, Keillor told *Publishers Weekly* that he was also interested in a different style of writing, a style less sophisticated, more colloquial. This style was what he had developed in his radio monologues, and while these were humorous, they contained sentiment, which most of his *New Yorker* pieces lacked. He was challenged by the notion to turn the radio pieces into a book.

The humor inherent in his work, however, rarely surfaces in the flesh. It needn't, of course, and in the scores of interviews and profiles published about him, few witticisms are quoted. There is a little sarcasm in later, more recent articles; most interviews have tended to be straightforward and factual. Instead of being funny, Keillor discusses humor and analyzes why it works for him. In one interview, Keillor said that a sense of humor is individual: "The journey of art is to somehow take that private laughter and give it to other people—to give that private vision to other people so they will laugh at it. Jokes can get worn out in becoming public, so humor always has to be refreshed by the strangeness that comes from individuals' senses of humor." In this interview he also said he didn't like the term *humorist* because he doesn't feel obligated to be funny. "I have done very well from time to time telling stories in which there were no jokes."

Keillor's attitudes, shaped by his Brethren upbringing, colored his approach toward writing and may yet haunt him, even as he achieved enormous success. The ethical dimension of wasting time comes home to roost, and as he told the Los Angeles *Times*, "Writing is a wasteful, not an efficient line of work." Which is what his Brethren family and peers maintained all along. The anguish of dreaming, thinking, avoiding other tasks to free the mind for the construction of episodes, incidents, sketches and stories is wasteful from most every perspective but the artist's. At the same time, the so-called whiling away of hours contributes to the artist's sense of being misunderstood, and may have made Keillor—a compulsive writer—feel guilty for such self-indulgence.

Keillor considers himself mainly a writer of short stories, finding them an easier medium because he is not slave to the heft and weight of a book. Thus, while *Lake Wobegon Days* is most assuredly a book, it is not a novel, as David Guy noted in his review for *USA Today*. The book lacked narrative thrust, wrote Guy, adding, "when it came time to write a book, he could find no more to do than throw his sketches together, sometimes with transitions that the reader has trouble following."

By making deliberate and painstaking efforts to insure each word is correctly fixed in place, Keillor is probably much like Thurber, who rewrote endlessly and found it impossible to face the prospect of putting sixty to a hundred thousand words into one sustained project.

Yet the short story is to the novel what the one-act play is to the full-length play—an appetizer. The so-called "real" authors and playwrights cut their teeth on the shorter stuff, but eventually move on to the full-blown works. Consequently, there are few playwrights known principally for one-act creations, and few writers have sustained major literary reputations without turning out a novel. In Keillor's case, though, there may be too much money offered for him not to publish a novel within the next few years. But money may not be the sole motivator; he may also think that his reputation demands that he produce a serious novel.

Fagerson, however, doesn't think Keillor should try a serious book because of those pressures. "His main purpose isn't just to make jokes and entertain," Fagerson said, "He's very serious about what he's doing." Underneath Keillor's humor, says Fagerson, "are profoundly serious issues." Therefore, though the work is often set in humor or satire, the intent is not laughter but rather to attempt to draw the reading and listening audiences into self-examination.

As Lloyd Hackl has observed, a dark side occasionally emerges in Garrison Keillor's work. But darkness and melancholy have been endemic among great American humorists, beginning with Mark Twain. Certainly Thurber and Benchley had bleak visions and used humor as a saving hedge against rage and madness. Perelman too was sullen. And today's most visible humorist, CBS's Andy Rooney, poses dourly each week on "60 Minutes." Former APR Program Director Nick Nash, though, thinks Keillor's darker instincts perpetuated his endearment to his audience. "As his own visions became clearer to himself, I think he was willing to express that. Even though it very rarely reflected on him, the fact that he was willing to talk in that context, I think, helped people understand him."

Humor scholar Jesse Bier thinks that much of Keillor's appeal is nostalgic, but Keillor managed also to inject a dark element. "His revelations about his religious background are not only dark, but sometimes furious," said Bier. None more so than the "Ninety-five Theses" left by a former Wobegonian at the *Herald-Star* offices in 1980 and published in *Lake Wobegon Days* as one of literature's longest footnotes. There can be little doubt that these theses are Keillor's own exorcisms of those aspects of his upbringing which he found repugnant. Though the anger expressed in the theses is often seething, it is sometimes funny nonetheless.

"I sometime heard his audience laughing at somber, even

black humor," said Bier. "They were delighted by his technique, of course, but there was a darkness to the humor, a deep criticism of the religious and family restrictions put on his life and lives like his. He doesn't easily forgive."

Stuart Hyde, professor of communication arts at San Francisco State University and author of a standard broadcasting textbook, *Television and Radio Announcing*, agrees with Bier. "There was a lot of hostility," Hyde said. "Keillor's voice submerged his message. He whispered, and he got away with a hostile and obscene wit because of it. His pitch and articulation were good, his volume quiet and hushed—an intimacy that made you accept gossip. Using that soothing sotto voce, he seduced his audience. He got away with the hostility because he's a down-home boy, and in this country we tend to favor the down-home boy over the city slicker."

Though Keillor has claimed that Wobegon has an Indian sound to it, and it does (there is a Lake Wabegoon in Ontario, Canada), it may also be argued that Wobegon is really "woebegone," which usually means joyless, dismal, bleak, bearing out Bier's and Hyde's perceptions.

Interviewed several weeks before Keillor's announced departure from broadcasting, Bier said, "the audience ignores the gray and dark side of him." If the program had endured another five or six years, though, Bier thought Keillor's audience would have at least subconsciously discovered the underlying bleak qualities and possibly turned away from him. They may not have recognized the blackness, Bier said, but rather considered him repetitive, while suppressing the darkness.

In Day Cryer's *Newsday Magazine* article, Bier said that while Keillor's show represented a "nostalgic throwback to rural American humor," and was "almost a last punctuation of small-town rural American values, there's more regret here than happy possession."

Sometimes the anger is not so thinly veiled, and audiences

are caught short by obvious hostility. On one program, for instance, he castigated "feminists, fundamentalists and fanatics," for the letters they'd sent the program, ending the dissertation with a terse "get off my back." But always his audience forgave, forgot, preferring only to remember the whimsical, the nostalgic pieces from the monologue.

10

THOUGH of Scottish descent on both sides of his family, Garrison Keillor is imbued with Scandinavian-American subculture to the extent that he may have been discussing himself when he spoke about Lake Wobegon's Unknown Norwegian, memorialized by the town's residents by a large statue, whose facial expressions seem to change as the day wears on, as the sun's rays catch it at different angles. Not calling attention to oneself is endemic among the fundamentalist Brethren of Keillor's youth, and is also a distinct characteristic among Scandinavian-Americans, who by and large are taciturn folk, undemonstrative, stoic, and whose oral communications are often oblique. Frequently these folks are given to understatement, or often no statement at all. Many Scandinavians, whose population base in America lies in the Upper Midwest and the Pacific Northwest, have chosen to live their lives as unknowns and as people who respect an individual's space.

"My first acquaintance with Garrison was in the summer of 1973, when my daughter, Polly, was going into the sixth grade," said Beverly Skoglund. "The town's sixth-grade teacher always put on a play—an extravaganza like *Fiddler On The Roof*—and my daughter was going to be in it. Garrison was invited to the sixth-grade play by a friend here. He was also going to be at the cast party, and we went to meet with this 'star' and here was this bearded guy with granny glasses, high-

154

water pants, white socks and funny-looking shoes. After the play, at the party, he mainly stood around and didn't talk much. He didn't interact with the kids.

"Once he moved here [to Marine on St. Croix] I got to know him better. I was excited about something one time, and I went up to him and touched him as I was talking, and he backed away and looked a little shocked. He needed his space. I feel so sorry for him now, because he has no space that he can call his own."

Despite Keillor's disdain for the celebrity-type publicity that surrounds him, a certain amount of notoriety is necessary to a writer. Its absence, noted by rejected manuscripts, may reduce the meaning and value of the writer's existence. In the *Paris Review* series "Writers At Work," William Faulkner said that the writer's only responsibility is to his art, and if the writer is good, he will be completely ruthless. "He has a dream. It anguishes him so much he must get rid of it. He has no peace until then. Everything goes by the board: honor, pride, decency, security, happiness, all, to get the book written. If a writer has to rob his mother, he will not hesitate; the *Ode on a Grecian Urn* is worth any number of old ladies."

This is the struggle—the commitment of the serious literary artist to do whatever is needed to secure his place among the published. But to go beyond publication, to rise to the top of best-seller lists, to earn public and critical acclaim requires even more. And in the end, it is not Mother who pays, but the artist himself.

Nick Nash thinks this happened with Keillor and "A Prairie Home Companion." "That show became a kind of monster. Here is an organization [MPR] which is classical music oriented, with some jazz and a healthy dollop of news. Suddenly the organization has this growth, a carbuncle, that in time seems larger than the organization itself. Everybody is aware of what has happened and tries to keep the organization in balance. Impossible, because the show started to produce too much income, too much notoriety."

That was a problem with "A Prairie Home Companion," which became the raison d'etre for American Public Radio, and no doubt increased the pressure on Keillor to continue to capture his audiences' fancies and imaginations. This was a pressure the Norwegians of Lake Wobegon would not have been concerned with. They could live their lives simply in an insular atmosphere and do what needed to be done because it was their choice. They would not have endured what Keillor did to achieve success.

Their space—the space afforded the anonymous—appealed to Keillor. The anonymity that characterizes the Brethren and many Scandinavian-Americans was not to be found on the path Garrison Keillor selected, but neither did he believe that celebrity might exact a great personal toll, that it required nearly as much energy as creativity. Keillor's ideal, perhaps, would be anonymous celebrity: he'd have instant name recognition yet would have retained the freedom to go unrecognized, unbothered in restaurants and airline terminals.

Esquire magazine reported that Keillor parted with his beard after being spotted on a flight by a passenger who made certain everyone knew a celebrity was on board, and sang songs and alluded to routines that Keillor performed. The next day, he shaved his beard.

While Garrison Keillor couldn't escape his celebrity, the unknown Norwegians have no such problems, and they would never have aspired to the notoriety that persistently dogged this shy man.

Keillor insisted that his monologues were not figments of the imagination; they were honest and real and dealt with life the way it ought to be lived, and often is lived. But it was only small potatoes for those who actually lived like Wobegonians, because the life experience for all of us is not based on the nostalgic but on the everyday, the mundane, that which surrounds us—and going through the life experience, none of us believes the time we're living in will be held in nostalgic regard in the future. We live in the present; Keillor does too, though he seems to wish it weren't so. Observed *Esquire*, "Keillor was perched somewhere between a world that was fading and one that was coming into being. He never spurned either world, or either century, and today carries both of them within him; his irony makes him kin to his cosmopolitan listeners, while his unbending, almost quixotic affection for the old-fashioned gives him access to something uncorrupted."

Maybe so, but Norwegian-Americans, like Brethren, don't place much stock in literature, and only one Norwegian-American novel, Ole Rölvaag's stark *Giants in the Earth*, might be considered a classic. If only Keillor were Norwegian, he might change that. Instead, he can only be Norwegian at heart, and his characterizations of Lake Wobegon's Norwegians were warmly received by Norwegian-Americans. Liv Lyons, Director of Sons of Norway, the fraternal organization that serves as the model for Lake Wobegon's Sons of Knute, says the group is honored by Keillor. "He writes about us with such love," she says. "That certain group of Norwegian immigrants were very honest, down-to-earth people. . . . I think the Norwegian bachelor farmers are cute."

Marion Nelson, director of Vesterheím, the Norwegian-American Museum in Decorah, Iowa, enjoyed the humor and the Norwegian bachelor farmers who grow the wheat for Powdermilk Biscuits, but thinks, "The Norwegians get to be kind of a dressing or facade. Norwegians don't take any offense; this rings true for them and for others. Keillor's approach was not specifically ethnic, and that's his real genius. He's an astute observer. Norwegians have all along liked to make fun of themselves, and there were Norwegian-American comics who did a lot with dialect humor as far back as 1909 and 1910. Later on we had the Scandinavian songs of Yogi Yorgeson.

"Keillor's humor, I think, goes beyond the ethnic. There are people who'll say, 'The Irish or the Germans I knew were like that.' He's cut through to basic human frailties and responses that ring true to anyone who's grown up in an agrarian culture, or where the church dominates a set of beliefs."

Acting as an omniscient observer, Keillor noted the small crotchets of a people, and made them nearly universal in his monologues and *Lake Wobegon Days*. He probably enlarged on the character of a people who first spied and set food on the North American continent several centuries before Columbus. But being Scandinavian, the Viking explorers didn't tell anyone, thus losing the opportunity for a sanctified role in American history, no small sack of potatoes. At the time, however, the new land didn't much impress, and since it couldn't hold a candle to home, why bother?

The first early settlers to the upper Iowa River Valley in and around Decorah were Norwegians. Land in the valley was fertile, rich, excellent for farming, and those first settlers knew it. But because they preferred long days of hard labor—as in Lake Wobegon, where bachelor farmers won't buy larger combines because it would mean finishing a job sooner and having to wait around longer until it was time for bed—these immigrants settled the higher, rocky ground, where they were less likely to have neighbors nearby. It was the second and third waves of immigrants who ended up with the good land.

If Scandinavians are traditionally a distant, taciturn people, they also tend toward the oblique in their conversations. A writer once inquired about an elderly Norwegian woman's family, specifically mentioning a daughter-in-law with whom he had attended school. "We don't hear much from her," the woman said. Later the writer learned that the woman's son and daughter-in-law had been divorced several years earlier.

Keillor's characters are amalgams of the more distinct Scandinavian crotchets he's observed throughout his life. "He got a chance to study a generalized Scandinavian culture and observe it rather close up in Marine," said Beverly Skoglund.

The foibles that Keillor ascribes to the Norwegians, who along with the Germans dominate his fictional town, are, however, pervasive. An East Coast English professor stated, "That character is universal. The Norwegians of Minnesota are the Yankees out here, the Down-Easters from Maine. I suspect we'd find some common identity in the South too. Keillor doesn't judge these people but accepts all, is amused by all, and creates a circle of love. . . . Ask a Down-Easter if he knows how deep a particular lake is and likely as not he'll say 'Yeaup,' and wander away. Which is what one might well expect from a Norwegian bachelor farmer in Lake Wobegon."

Lake Wobegon, and its residents, are a celebration of the average, and average is how Keillor sometimes characterizes himself as well. But he is quite clearly wrong, even as he has protested in the past that he does not wish to be regarded as distinct; that he does not encourage the cultish loyalty that arose over the past decade.

There was a time, however, before the program went national, when Keillor was on the verge of achieving what had eluded him as he was growing up: acceptance among peers. In the early and mid seventies, he was considered a member of the MPR family by those who worked on the program, a team player. One former newspaper reporter recalled a party at singer Adam Granger's house in St. Paul. "A lot of people from the show were there. Garrison and Margaret, too, and nobody made any extra fuss over him. It wouldn't have occurred to anyone that he was any sort of celebrity, even though he was beginning to draw that cult surrounding. He didn't seem to be any different from anyone else and joined in the fun and games."

But Garrison Keillor couldn't be like other people, because he never was like ordinary folk, and can't make pretentions to the contrary. He even drew attention from Eastern bloc countries, most notably, Hungary. In a recent magazine article on American life written by a visiting journalist, Keillor and his program were mentioned and damned with faint praise. The writer, who had attended a performance of "A Prairie Home Companion" at the World Theater, mentioned the program as a representation of phony American wholesomeness, a tool to lull the American people into a stupor. The writer likened the program to a Billy Graham crusade but admitted it was enjoyable because it wasn't militaristic and violent. But, claimed the journalist, the show failed because it drew people's attention from the real world's problems, giving them a false sense of security by dwelling on a nonexistent bucolic life-style.

Glyn Hughes, in the March 7, 1986 *New Statesman,* a British publication, tended to agree in his review: "Lake Wobegon retreats into its satisfactions with small-town values. . . . Moreover [Keillor] too often relies upon a winsome and 'fetching' small boy's view of the world. It is this sort of thing that captures a readership and could even form a cult. . . . It is small-town values that make the U.S. such a menace with the arsenal it has at its command. That's not funny."

Another critic of Lake Wobegon is Don Kauls, who writes a column syndicated nationally by Tribune Media Services. In late 1985, Kauls wrote, "I find . . . Lake Wobegon a boring little burg—duller than Brigadoon, even—and his 'Prairie Home Companion' radio show an exercise in tedium, particularly the music. It's like being trapped on a cross-country bus with a jug band."

Keillor was frequently asked to describe "A Prairie Home Companion" and its appeal, a task he found perplexing. In November, 1981, he was asked by William J. Reynolds, writing in *TWA Ambassador,* an in-flight magazine. Keillor responded:

> I think you have to get the word *live* in there. I think that's real important to what the show is. I think the word *variety* has to go in there, just to suggest the format—you know, that it is not a concert. . . . And it's done from a stage in front of an audience, which is also important.
>
> And if you want to go farther than that, you could get in there the fact that it's a family radio show. I haven't any idea what that means, but the connotation is accurate.

The success of the program, he told Reynolds, was more elusive, adding that he actually knew less about the show than most people because he could never hear its live broadcasts, that being backstage was different than sitting home listening to the program over the radio.

Beverly Skoglund, though, thought the success sprang from his living in places like Marine. "I think since he's left Marine, he's gotten away from a close, little society. Being able to go caroling like we used to do at Christmastime, and come back to someone's house and have hot cider, and have all these diversified people sit around the Christmas tree. I think many of his later monologues were no longer as warm or feeling or in touch with small-town America as they once were."

But he continued to draw on incidents from the hinterlands, fed by friends who still live there. When MPR gave a party for Keillor at the historic James J. Hill House in St. Paul, Skoglund was there and Keillor asked her what was going on at the Wilcox house, the compound where he lived during his Marine on St. Croix residency. "I said 'the boys are building a duck blind down in the basement, and hunting season's about to start, and they can't get it out.' He said, 'Wonderful material. Wonderful material for the monologue.'"

And in *Lake Wobegon Days*, Keillor devotes considerable attention to the duck hunters from the Sons of Knute lodge, duck hunting being an annual rite of autumn in the Upper Midwest, especially among residents of rural towns. Many of them don't particularly enjoy eating wild duck because it has a livery taste, but then neither do many Norwegian-Americans delight in the taste of *lutefisk,* a lye-soaked cod that when boiled becomes a gelatinous, quivering mass on the platter. But for Norwegians it's the ritual of the eating that's important, and for small-town citizens, it's the ritual of the hunt that matters, and Friends of the Animals and Cleveland Amory be damned.

Though many Norwegian-Americans are thought to be cautious, careful in their business dealings, Keillor may have been slow to emulate them in this regard. Half the royalties* from

---

* Estimated by one publishing insider to be "two and a quarter to three million dollars."

Lake Wobegon Days go to Minnesota Public Radio, and this not apparently from Keillor's largess. He may have allowed himself to be saddled with a work-made-for-hire arrangement with Bill Kling's network, and thus the work that Keillor created for his broadcasts was considered the property of MPR rather than Keillor himself.

"That fifty-fifty split goes back very early in the relationship," Nick Coleman said. "Keillor wanted to do that program and Kling wasn't very enthusiastic about it. It was sort of a slap in their faces to make music with bones and saws, and it gave them conniptions because of their classical music emphasis. On the other hand, Kling knows distribution systems, politics and marketing, and Keillor knows nothing of those things. So at the beginning, this was a good arrangement for both of them."

"Back in 1980, I would have thought that Garrison would have incorporated himself and allowed American Public Radio to use his programs," Marvin Granger said. "As his popularity surged, Kling needed him a lot more than he needed Kling. Kling's leverage was much weakened. At first, though, Kling realized Garrison was a potential gold mine and saw that by making the best use of Garrison, he could develop the right market. Garrison should have seen that too."

Partly as a result of this lack of foresight, Granger correctly predicted that the program's days were numbered. Keillor also had told reporters that he didn't envision doing the program forever, and might one day take his family and return to Denmark, his wife's home, and abandon radio altogether.

On the other hand, what's he going to do next? Coleman wondered. "What do you do to top this? He's setting himself up for a fall after he leaves. If he writes a serious novel, there will be critics waiting to savage it. If he doesn't succeed, it will be very painful to watch."

IN 1976, Keillor told Irv Letofsky in a Minneapolis *Tribune* article, "I wanted to go there [New York] and live there and be a writer for *The New Yorker* magazine because I would be free from all those people who had known me and whose knowledge of me was a limitation on me. If I left Minnesota I would cease being the person that I was and I would be a glamorous, witty, sophisticated, well-dressed man living a high old life in New York."

But he never really severed his roots, at least, not by moving elsewhere. There were other aspects, too, of his aspiring to attain the unattainable, and even now, though hugely successful, he has not quite fulfilled those aspirations, because Gary Keillor was not destined to overcome shyness and unease among other people. In Letofsky's article, Keillor discussed a scene from his story, "Drowning 1954," when he had ridden down the WCCO elevator with Cedric Adams. "I followed him down the street, down to the Minneapolis Club, and he turned into the gate and I watched him walk into this great mansion.

"I wanted to be there with him, be one of the guys, you know, like Bob DeHaven, just real comfortable and friendly and jovial and not this screwed-up little kid, scared all the time. Be friendly and easy with people."

Being "friendly and easy with people," never characteristic of Keillor's public or private persona, is occasionally possible, especially when he manages to empathize with a fellow shy person or those who are in awe of his celebrity status. With such persons, he is often courteous, and attempts to put them at ease, though he must understand that he never quite accomplishes this. Michael Schumacher said that when he went to interview Keillor for *Writer's Digest,* he brought along a friend, a longtime Keillor devotee, and promised the man an opportunity to meet his idol. "When we got to Keillor's hotel room, my friend froze when he saw Keillor. He was catatonic. He had never met a celebrity before. He couldn't speak. And Keillor's heart went out to this guy. He asked us if we wanted to sit down, and my friend shook his head. Garrison said he was having room service bring up some breakfast, and asked if we wanted anything. I said I'd take a glass of juice but Jim again just shook his head. Finally, as we were about to start the interview, Keillor picked up a copy of *The New Yorker* and said he had a story in the current issue and asked if Jim would like to read it. Jim took the magazine and just stood there. 'I can't believe you're going to read it standing up,' Keillor said, and he invited Jim to sit on the bed while he read.

"After the interview Keillor asked him how he liked the story, and the guy said, 'It was okay.' As we finished the interview, I asked Keillor to autograph a copy of *Lake Wobegon Days,* and Jim had a copy of *Happy to Be Here* but he didn't say anything. I told Keillor that Jim had a book, and where he simply signed mine, 'Best Wishes, Garrison Keillor,' he took a great deal of time with Jim's. He filled an entire page with an inscription, recounting how Jim had come to his hotel and sat on his bed while reading a story that he thought was okay. He recapped everything that had happened since we entered the room."

That incident provided a lifetime of memory for a man whose copy of *Happy to Be Here* may contain one of literature's most lengthy author inscriptions.

On the other hand, if being friendly and easy with people means disclosing, Keillor withheld—except in his monologues.

"I have a photo of my son sitting on his knee at the last Twins game played at the old Met Stadium," said Nick Coleman. "I was recently looking at that, and it occurred to me that all the times we went to Twins games or talked on the phone or at a bar or backstage, he never shared anything of himself. He's not an open person but is very much like those Norwegians at Lake Wobegon. We'd sit at a game and I'd talk and maybe he'd say a few things, but he let me do most of the talking. He's not a loquacious person, but I don't think he's shy. He'd like to believe that some of his behavior is due to shyness rather than to aloofness. I think he's more aloof.

"He went on the air [for] three million listeners every week, so he's not a shy person. He loved it—he loved the adulation. There's a difference between shy and aloof and shy and private. He's a performer, a person who enjoys success and his appeal to audiences, but in personal matters he can be rude, he can be aloof, and he can be very protective of privacy. Shyness is more a fear of sharing, and a little uncertainty, a lack of social grace. I've seen and heard him be incredibly rude, but not shy."

Rick Shefchik of the St. Paul *Pioneer Press* and *Dispatch* tends to second Coleman. "To do what Keillor's been doing, with this self-examination, in a lot of ways he's been an obsessive sort of person. Relationships with him may be more guarded, more precious and shaped—and, in a way, manipulated—than they would be with a lot of people. In a way he's gotten rich and famous by reinventing himself.

"In terms of friendship, the thing I remember being so surprised about, I couldn't find anybody in town who would admit to being a friend of his after Margaret Moos had left. That's not to say I called the right numbers. One fellow who was very close, lived close to him, said he hadn't talked to Garrison Keillor in a year or two. There was no breakup, but that seems to be the quality of friendship that Garrison Keillor likes to have. It struck me as awfully odd—not having to see or talk to a person for months or years. Although the more I know about the man, the more I realize that his idea of friendship is not the same as yours or mine."

Keillor thinks that finding a friend is a miraculous thing, not casual, not ordinary, and not something he expects in life. He once said that he considered all his friends to be miraculous. "Will Rogers said that he never met a man he didn't like. I don't feel that way. I meet people I don't like all the time. When I meet a person I like, I consider that miraculous."

"Somebody was telling me a few years ago," said Shefchik, "that Keillor would come over to his house and would sit in the living room and just stare at the fire or look out the window for maybe an hour without saying anything. He wouldn't do anything particularly unpleasant, but just inject himself into their home at an inopportune time, and then after about an hour, he'd get up and without saying anything just walk out the door.

"He made such a big deal about wanting to live in St. Paul and wanting to walk down the street and be at ease and comfortable with neighbors. But that's really not the way he lives. It's more like he wants to be invisible."

He apparently doesn't react well to criticism either and is not a person who jests easily. For example, a man who had appeared in concert with Keillor as a member of a pipe band corresponded with him off and on over a period of years, until he happened to make a lighthearted jibe at Keillor's singing. "Garrison had sung Hank William's 'Lovesick Blues' on one program, and it didn't measure up to my expectations of how that song should sound. No big deal, but when I wrote Garrison, I told him in an offhanded manner that he shouldn't sing 'Lovesick Blues' anymore. I haven't heard from him since."

Whether or not Garrison Keillor was doing the Lord's work is not for mortals to judge. What can be ascertained, however, is his impact upon literature and broadcasting (attempts to analyze Keillor himself can lead to perplexing stonewalling by the Old Scout). He regards his privacy as inviolable, and so, apparently do many friends and former business associates. "He wants you to know just what he wants you to know and nothing more," Shefchik said.

Some acquaintances are genuinely protective of the man and his persona, while others have been intimidated by the power Keillor and Minnesota Public Radio have. He is a study in contrasts, making out-of-the-way gestures of kindness and concern and at the same time able to curtly dismiss longtime associates and employees. While most former employees are reluctant to discuss their affiliations with Keillor and "A Prairie Home Companion," some shudder at the recollections of his tantrums, which ex-staffers have called irrational. Several former employees characterized "A Prairie Home Companion" as being run in a dictatorial manner, with the operation of MPR under Bill Kling, the president, and his wife Sally Pope, a vice president, "a sort of fiefdom." Independent-minded employees apparently tend to make the MPR power structure uncomfortable, and often don't last long.

After the year-and-a-half hiatus of Margaret Moos from the program (she returned in March 1987, to produce the program for the Disney Channel), Keillor worked with two other producers, Chris Cardozo and Steve Schlow, neither of whom lasted more than a few weeks.

There was a sense about the program that musicians, particularly those from the traditional-folk genre, who have little impact in the commercial marketplace, were made to feel unworthy in the presence of the Old Scout, who may or may not have deigned to acknowledge their presence. These musicians—throwbacks to the sixties and the back-to-the-land movement—have puny economic resources. Many exist on marginal wages, and in former years occupied old, dilapidated structures on Minneapolis's Nicollet Island, where derelicts lived in caves along the Mississippi River during summer months and musicians and other struggling artists tended vegetable gardens in the small yards of sagging, unpainted houses, scratching the soil for tomatoes and beans. Sometimes well educated, these folks have chosen a way of life that allows them their idiosyncrasies and enables them to pursue their art without having to sell out to the establishment. Unless, of course, Keillor plucked them for appearances on his program. Few could resist the opportunity to perform with a national forum at hand. Suddenly, there might have been a future in producing such music—chances to appear at folk festivals, college concerts, club dates, to say nothing of earning at least union scale of about $117 a performance, which beat passing the hat at West Bank coffee houses and other establishments. The opportunity to perform at least semiregularly on "A Prairie Home Companion" was a lure too powerful for most of these musicians to resist. They became entrapped by what the show might offer, much like the creator of the program himself, and in order to remain in Keillor's good graces must have always been obsequious.

In the late summer of 1986, former *Star Tribune* media critic Nick Coleman said, "there's clearly a time when Keillor thinks you're great, and when he gets tired of your face you're no longer on the show. Peter Ostroushko and Butch Thompson were removed as regulars. What I've heard is that they felt frustrated at not being able to perform musically the things they were interested in doing. That the show had become static, more of a Keillor showcase. And they were locked into smaller, less creative roles, and at the same time a lot of pressure was put on them to come up with things for Keillor to do on the show." He said that after Margaret Moos left the program the burden on musicians increased, because the show was basically operating without a producer. "Keillor had been the producer, but he's too busy to be a producer," Coleman said, prior to Margaret Moos's return to complete the last seventeen broadcasts as well as help make the program viable for television, as those shows were also taped for cable television for the Disney Channel. Coleman believed that when Keillor started exerting more personal control over the programs, they became a little less vivid and a little less entertaining.

Robin Raygor who participated in poetry readings with Keillor years earlier, found nothing unusual about this. "He's a controlling guy," Raygor said. "He's difficult too, because you must meet his ideas, but he can't give you any clues into what he wants. In the process you lose sight of what you wanted, and just try to please him." That approach worked for a time, but most performers with long-term attachments to the program didn't function well under that pressure.

For Coleman, and for a number of local fans who had long followed its development, "A Prairie Home Companion" took fewer risks after it became a national fixture. In a column he wrote for the July 1, 1984 *Star Tribune* entitled "Preaching the Gospel According to Garrison," Coleman pointed out that in the first year of his program, Keillor presented himself as an observer of life in Lake Wobegon, and his own connections with the town were nebulous. That role evolved into his having been raised in Lake Wobegon. Coleman's column concluded:

> Looking back, the show seemed to be at its peak in the late seventies, when it was reaching the height of its local success, and before it went national. Those were the days of constant surprises. There were people who tapped out "The William Tell Overture" on their teeth and played music on saws and nose flutes.
>
> . . . The show doesn't have its 'wing it' quality, and that makes it predictable. The question is whether the show can continue another ten years without becoming a parody of itself.

Bassist, Gordy Abel, who also sang with the Almond Tree Choir on the program several times in the late seventies, said the atmosphere surrounding the program was "loose as a goose. One time the Powdermilks needed a bassist because their bass player at the time was playing lead guitar on a piece. They needed a bass and someone saw me come in and said, 'Ah, here's a bass player. Right on the spot we worked up a few tunes and went with it. It wasn't show-businessy at all."

Yet Abel remembers that even as Keillor exuded a shy, quiet quality, his nervous intensity overwhelmed cast and crew. "He sort of reeked nervousness, and this affected people around him. He used to stay to himself; he didn't kibitz, didn't fraternize at all. He used to be off stage right smoking Camels, and other people were stage left, smoking other things." Abel, who was close to many who regularly appeared on the program, said that many who were dropped from the program's roster were never told why. "You were a regular on the program until it ran out, then you were just off the air. He stopped calling you. It's one thing to ease somebody out, but it can be handled a little more deftly. Everybody I've talked to said it was *chop*—that's it. You were gone."

Nick Nash recalled the demise of the Butch Thompson Trio. "My impression was that Butch was extremely cooperative; he did whatever they asked him to do. He read bits, played piano and clarinet. The Butch Thompson Trio just kind of disappeared, sort of a gradual watching of a curtain fall. In the early days, the drummer, Red Maddock, was a personality, a part of the show. There was a lot of interaction between Keillor and Red. Then Red got sick—had a heart attack—and there were no more conversations between Keillor and Red."

Maddock returned to the drums and remained with the trio until Thompson was let go in May of 1986. The trio became more a backdrop for sketches and incidental bridges than an integral force in the program. Red Maddock overcame his heart problem but died of liver cancer on January 12, 1987.

Thompson and crew were removed as the permanent house band in May of 1986, and Thompson has remained rather closemouthed about his connections with Keillor and "A Prairie Home Companion" since then. However, he did tell Bob Protzman of the *Pioneer Press* and *Dispatch*, "We came to a general agreement that it had been nice but it was time for me to do something else."

Some local musicians and others close to the Twin Cities music scene were more vocal in their displeasure over

Thompson's demise. "The music was much better when he was on and people have told me they miss his whimsical humor," said Leslie Johnson, editor of *The Mississippi Rag*, a jazz and ragtime magazine, in Protzman's story, which appeared several weeks before Keillor announced his resignation. "But they put him [Thompson] on a leash."

Principal music arranger Peter Ostroushko's departure coincided with Thompson's, and Ostroushko told the *Star Tribune* that he left because, "rather than being involved in the creative process I was relegated to being a sideman." He also said that as he neared the end of his tenure with "A Prairie Home Companion," "it was, ask not what 'A Prairie Home Companion' can do for you, but rather what you can do for 'A Prairie Home Companion.'"

Jay Peterson is a musician who is also a graphic designer. He designed the logos for Powdermilk Biscuits and the posters for "A Prairie Home Companion." He claims he was treated shabbily by MPR, which reneged on handshake agreements to pay him royalties and to continue using his designs elsewhere. During the late seventies he also performed on the Saturday program, as well as on Keillor's morning programs. "My relationship with MPR started out good, but ended up bitter," Peterson said.

In the relatively small Minneapolis–St. Paul musical community, local musicians initially appreciated the exposure that came with work on "A Prairie Home Companion." But according to Peterson and others, when the locals were used up, they were dismissed, usually without ever knowing why. In short, their phones stopped ringing; there were no calls from Keillor or his staff. "Garrison found it hard to communicate unless he was behind a microphone," Peterson said. "He'd say one thing, Margaret another, and you never knew where you were with them. They never clarified what they wanted and placed great expectations on the musicians. Garrison wanted an intuitive thing between himself and the regulars as well as the irregulars. When they clicked he'd be overjoyed. When you did something he didn't like he'd never say so—he'd just write you off. He never told you not to do that again, you were just off. Maybe this was a way of keeping his own genius going. He didn't want to get wrapped up with his performers. It was sort of like, 'You figure out what I'm thinking.'

"This might be termed sour grapes by people who are no longer in his good graces, but when people were on that program, they were very eager to please and gave a lot of themselves in the process."

The dismissal of the Powdermilk Biscuit Band came about, Nash said, when Keillor told them, "'You're not giving me what I want.' And Bob Douglas said, 'Well, tell us what you want and we'll give it to you.' Keillor's response was to the effect that if I have to tell you what I want, then you don't understand what I want and then I'm not sure I want you on the show."

Other musicians who formerly appeared on the program don't talk to the press for a variety of reasons, not least among them the fact that their recordings are sold through *The Wireless*, the MPR catalogue, and they fear removal from that catalogue and a significant loss of royalties. In the words of Maury Bernstein, a folk music scholar and performer, whose "Folk Music and Bernstein" at one time played on more than 160 public radio stations, the musicians have been intimidated into silence by Keillor and MPR president Bill Kling. "Intimidation is the name of the game at MPR," Bernstein said.

Bernstein, who formerly taught courses in folk music at the University of Minnesota, also said that Keillor never knew very much about folk music. "One time I did a program with Jean Ritchie on the dulcimer, in which we traced the roots of the instrument. A couple days later, Keillor went on the air and started guessing at where the dulcimer came from. He was silly and self-indulgent, and if he'd cared to, he could have found out about the dulcimer." Bernstein believed Keillor used folk music to further his career and never really respected the art.

Yet a cranky, insecure celebrity performer is routine in show business, because a performer of star quality invariably sets standards for himself that few others can match. Sometimes the commitment of extras and sidemen do not equal that of the star. Also, secondary performers are not always satisfied with second-banana roles. Their egos may be as huge as the main attraction's, though with little or no justification. Friction is thus inevitable, and normally anticipated on Hollywood sets. Minnesota-bred performers may not have anticipated a star complex from Keillor, but it should not have surprised them. Any star who has risen to the top of his profession through his talent and hard work wants very much to remain on top, and in order to solidify his position he must use the talents of those who surround and support him to achieve his goals. Misunderstandings and hurt feelings arise, and there are sidemen and minor actors all over who will attest to the reprehensible, even cruel behavior of dozens of stars who are household names.

But "A Prairie Home Companion" seemed at first to them to be not a vehicle for the star but a laid-back program that offered regular employment, where performers and audience shared a good time. The program's success put an end to that notion, which may never have been Keillor's at all. He may have long projected stardom for himself, and early on he took the trappings of it—aloofness, temperament—to himself.

According to Nash, Keillor's program was always treated as a special commodity by MPR. "When I took the job in August 1978, I was asked how I would manage Keillor, whom I hadn't met at the time. You don't manage someone like Keillor. It was very clear that he was not interested in dealing with anybody on the staff. He wanted to deal directly with Bill Kling. Keillor worked with me only in a very superficial way, and he has, as the British would say, a very large bottom. Most of his negotiations, and Margaret's, were with Kling directly. I was merely an expediter.

"When I came to MPR I'd never been in a studio in my life. Keillor didn't want to waste a lot of time with me. He was never discourteous, but neither was he open, helpful or welcoming.

"During pledge weeks I would be assigned to a studio with Keillor. And I always had to fight for my life in there. Because you walk into his studio and it's all you can do to get one cubic foot. His presence just dominates the entire space. I always felt as if I were in a kind of quiet war when I would go into his studio."

Though most former musicians and other ex-employees declined to discuss their associations with Keillor and "A Prairie Home Companion" and were advised by Keillor's attorneys not to talk about their experiences, some have been reluctant to adhere to the dictum. "Everybody's got stories," one musician said ruefully.

Journalists who covered Keillor, however, have been willing to talk about him. Of them, Nick Coleman has been closest to Keillor, and before becoming the media critic for the Minneapolis *Star Tribune* he counted Keillor among his friends. The two socialized together at ball games and restaurants.

In late August 1986, Coleman talked about his relationship with Keillor in a noisy St. Paul Skyway cafeteria. "I think he's insecure and extremely temperamental," Coleman said. "People who work around him are by and large intimidated and cowed and afraid. There's not much personal loyalty around the staff; it's more a fear factor."

Yet, Coleman said, "I have a tremendous admiration for his talent, and have been a fan of his show from the beginning. Being a media critic got me involved at a much more intense level than I cared to be at.

"He and I used to be pals, and this has nothing to do with personal animosity, but it has to do with what I gathered as a personal friend in those days. He does not like newspapers or the news profession in general. He thinks it's a very tawdry, tacky kind of necessary evil, perhaps. We used to occasionally go to a Twins game or have a beer someplace and get into these long discussions about why a newspaper would do what it does.

I may have written a story about an outstate sensational murder or something like that, and he would take the point of view that it was offensive to report bad things like that.

"He'd ask, 'How could you put that kind of a thing in the newspaper?' I would say, 'What do you mean, how can you? This is what happened. This is important.' We'd have these friendly arguments about whether bad news was newsworthy. I really think that on a fundamental level, Garrison is just a good Scandinavian sort, believing that if you can't say something nice, you don't say anything at all. He doesn't like the fact that newspapers are as interested in negative information as they are in positive.

"He's always kind of acted like journalists were people without moral compasses in the first place. When I took the job as TV critic in 1983, I was on the job about a week and I got this very bizarre note from him telling me he was sorry I had lowered myself into the slime.

"I thought he was joking, just being funny, but later I wasn't so sure. My first week on the job I was at a press conference in Los Angeles, and the public television people were there and told the press conference, which was attended by all the media critics, that they were trying to get Keillor to do a television program. So I called him when I got back and asked if that were true, and he said he wouldn't confirm or deny, and he asked me not to put it in the paper. I tried to explain, I told him, 'Garrison, I have to put it in the paper, it was announced at a national press conference, and I mean everybody in the country could be reporting this, and I just want to know what to do.' He asked me again and said he wished I wouldn't write anything about it. I went ahead and did it, and after that he sent me this note saying something to the effect that I was just another washed-up newspaperman hollering down an empty rain barrel to hear myself make a big noise. Which I thought was really strange, because I was only doing my job and obviously did not realize that doing my job was going to cause a conflict with Garrison.

"At his National Press Club appearance a while back, he said he's uneasy with newspeople because these are people who have a professional interest in his violent demise, or something like that. A funny comment, but at the same time, very revealing. I think this is truly the way he looks at the press. He has a very tainted view of the press as kind of a sleazy, analyst-chasing, celebrity-consuming kind of institution. And it is all of those things, in a sense, but he sees it as personally interested in carving him up. When you decide to become a celebrity, there's a trade-off. The deal you make is to surrender something of your personal life. No one makes you do it. But he does not accept that. He thinks it's tawdry, and it may well be. I think he has an inner conflict about what success and fame and fortune mean and require. Something inside him says, this is distasteful to me and so therefore I won't accept it."

Largely due to the conflict with Keillor, Coleman left his post with the Minneapolis *Star Tribune*, moved across the river to St. Paul and became a metro news columnist with the *Pioneer Press* and *Dispatch*.

The roots of that conflict date to 1983, when Coleman wrote pieces that irked MPR—pieces he considered, by and large, mild. "I was surprised and kind of disappointed with all the things that happened," Coleman said. "The upper level at MPR never has and never will accept criticism gracefully. You're either with them or against them, and they can't accept that you can object to certain things even though you're with them in the main. I've written many times over and over that I like and respect MPR and couldn't live without it, but the few critical comments were what they highlighted."

Other journalists also have been treated to what they considered harassment on the part of MPR's management. Articles deemed unfavorable by Kling have often resulted in letters to the journalists and visits by an MPR delegation to their editors. But while most other reporters may have written one or two stories about the operation, Coleman, as media critic, gored the ox on several occasions.

In May of 1985, MPR's fund-raising effort to refurbish the World Theater was falling short, and the organization approached the Minnesota legislature about appropriating money. Legislators agreed to $200,000 of the $1 million requested. MPR secured a second mortgage on its headquarters at Eighth and Cedar Streets in downtown St. Paul, and Cargill added $300,000 to that fund. Contributions from Keillor's fans totaled less than $100,000, though all told about $2 million was eventually raised.

After talking to some MPR officials, Coleman reported that MPR had sought the funding from the legislature in the eleventh hour of its session, implying that if funding were not forthcoming "A Prairie Home Companion" might have to move elsewhere. Kling and Keillor were angered by the piece, even though Keillor was not quoted in the story, nor did Coleman suggest that Keillor initiated talk of moving.

"I had no objection to their asking for money," Coleman said. "What I objected to was that they threatened the legislature and said, 'If you don't give us this money, we'll have to consider some very attractive offers we've received from other cities to relocate "A Prairie Home Companion" on a permanent basis'—Atlanta, Chicago, or wherever. I objected to the blackmail approach on the legislature. So I wrote a very pointed column which lampooned how ridiculous it would be hearing Garrison Keillor emanating from a place like Atlanta. It's not in keeping with the ambiance of the program. It was a pretty acerbic column but did not say Garrison Keillor is a jerk. It said MPR was heavy-handed, and this action smacks of blackmail. And is ludicrous on the face of it. Keillor took this as a personal attack and went to the legislature and said no one had asked him, and he would never permit it, and that the whole thing had been a gross injustice to MPR.

"After that piece appeared, Sally Pope [an MPR vice president, and Kling's wife] issued an edict that no employee was to talk to me. I was cut off their mailing lists too, even though I'm a contributing member to MPR. I give them a hundred twenty-five dollars a year."

This incident triggered animosity from Keillor toward Coleman, and that animosity actually worked its way into some of the monologues and into *Lake Wobegon Days*. "Garrison went on the air and called me a liar—not by name, but the implication was clear," Coleman said. "He set up a straw man and said that I had lied about his moving the program. I never said that. I said that those superiors alleged that, and he was embarrassed."

On another occasion, Coleman piqued MPR by writing a column with a Lake Wobegon dateline after Keillor had appeared on the cover of *Time* magazine. Coleman called it a good-natured parody of how Lake Wobegonians reacted to Garrison's fame. Coleman had "journeyed" to Lake Wobegon to find the town's response to the local lad's success. The piece was not amusing to MPR, which threatened a lawsuit, claiming fraudulent trade practices: by using Lake Wobegon as a dateline and using the town's characters, Coleman was stealing MPR's property, and in order to sell newspapers, the *Star Tribune* was infringing on MPR's trademarks and copyrights.

"It was absurd," Coleman said. "If anyone else had written it, nothing would have happened. There's no pleasing them. From my point of view, they've had a wealth of good stories around the country and beyond, and they've become spoiled. They think the only publicity is good publicity. It's only local people who are in the position to see the dirty laundry out on the line, and when that's recorded, they get all upset. They wonder, if *The New York Times* writes nice things, why can't the local press?"

But Coleman was continuing to widen the gulf between himself and his former friend. The lead on his Tuesday, November 5, 1985 column read "Lake Wobegon's most eligible bachelor farmer is reportedly planning to get married, but all is not well in Powdermilk Biscuitland." Coleman revealed that Margaret Moos, Keillor's longtime producer and housemate, had left the show, taking a personal leave of absence from her job in October, and that Keillor would be marrying Ulla Skaerved, née Strange, a classmate from his 1960 Anoka High School graduating class. This became a major story, making wire services and appearing all around the country.

"It had been around for two months before I ever knew about it," Coleman said. "The press in this state does not snoop around in people's garbage cans. I thought the story was straight as it could be, not like some of the smart-mouth stuff I've often written. It was a genuine, legitimate news story that deserved to be reported. And I knew I was going to pay a heavy price for reporting it. I did. I think in some ways my job became untenable over a period of time, stemming from the flack over this story.

"Kling came over personally to speak with my editors. My assumption is he asked for my head on a platter. He complained that I had an ax to grind against MPR and was out to make them look bad.

"I had never talked to Margaret Moos, and I never spoke to her since. I didn't want to disgrace her, but things like that happen all the time. I wouldn't have written it if he was just living with a woman, but this woman happened to be the executive producer of the nation's most prominent radio program. I don't know what happened between them, and I don't care. The issue wasn't whether he had a relationship with a woman, but that the woman was the producer and shaper of his program."

Irv Letofsky recalled what happened after the Los Angeles *Times* picked up the news. "I had a reporter check on that piece for our 'Outtake' column. Garrison was upset and called my reporter and said it was one thing for the Minneapolis paper to run that story but was altogether different with a big paper such as the *Times*."

Though Coleman tended to draw support from journalism ombudsmen, who agreed he was right to publish the story, Keillor fans wrote letters supporting their idol to the local papers, and excoriating notes to Coleman himself.

Art Nauman, ombudsman for the Sacramento *Bee*, commented in the reader representative column on the *Star and Tribune* pages compiled by Lou Gelfand. "Keillor's privacy was dramatically invaded by the newspaper, but Keillor is a very public person, and like it or not, the price he pays for this considerable success is the loss of a significant portion of his privacy." Nauman added:

> The revelation of his failed relationship with Moos was relevant because during the last month or so he has capitalized on his new love affair by making repeated, broad and treacly references to it in his monologues, and in song. These references suggest a deviation from his previous well-known depiction of himself as a very shy, private individual who eschews even uttering his own name on the air.

And Donald James, holding a similar post with the Kansas City *Star*, noted, "Keillor can make all sorts of claims about his right to privacy, but he is like any other performer. If they put themselves in the fore of the public, seek public approval and money, they therefore sacrifice a certain amount of privacy if it is pertinent to the story."

"In 1984, for their tenth anniversary, I wrote a big spread that was extremely positive," Coleman said. "Trying to hold on to a critic's credibility, I was critical of certain things, but overall it was a lengthy, positive view of what I think was a great show. But you never heard anything about that, until two months later you criticize them for some decisions they've made, like canceling their morning show, and they just hold a grudge. They take things very personally. They have this ocean of publicity to swim in and ninety-nine percent of it from coast to coast has been purely positive. But it's the critic's role to report events inside all media organizations in the Twin Cities—personnel changes, programming decisions that often reflect failures within the organization. It's the critic's job to report and comment on them. They sent emissaries over to my editors saying there was some kind of hidden grudge or secret grievance I was harboring against them, and that I was out to get them and make them look bad. Kling had come over several times and asked that I not be permitted to cover MPR."

In time, however, Coleman noticed himself appearing in Keillor's monologues and in *Lake Wobegon Days*. "In the book you'll notice the reason Lake Wobegon is left off the map is because the drunken surveyors, the Coleman brothers, messed up. He used to have a different story for that—that in St. Paul surveyors couldn't get the whole map on a sheet of paper, so they scrunched it up and squeezed Lake Wobegon off. That story changed about the time we started having problems, and it became the drunken surveyors named Coleman. Then he's used the Coleman boys who entertained crowds at the Mist County Fair by running across an arena and lowering their heads and smashing head-on as hard as they could until their heads became flat. I've laughed out loud at some of these, but taken together I have lost my sense of humor about them.

"There's Rick the TV dog, which is a mangy Irish setter, who watches TV for hours on end, then digs in people's garbage and crawls in bed with them and stinks up their sheets. He came up with this after the November article which reported his marriage, and he told St. Paul TV critic Rick Shefchik that I was like a mangy dog that had crawled into bed with him after I wrote the story."

In other monologues, Keillor used the name Coleman as a pejorative: people who were "Colemanned" had been subjected to inordinate idiocy.

Keillor's veiled attacks on Coleman were departures from his stated comedic objectives, which, as reported by Kevin Klose in the *Washington Post*, must show compassion and concern for the world. Klose quoted Keillor, "Comedy that doesn't care about the world, doesn't interest me. And there's a whole streak in comedy that is cruel, that picks on weaker people. But it's false comedy."

What Keillor did say in Shefchik's *Pioneer Press* and *Dispatch* column was "This is the sort of thing I expect from newspapers elsewhere, following Elizabeth Taylor. I never made a deal whereby I traded my private life for publicity."

Another St. Paul newspaper columnist, Joe Soucheray, on November 8, 1985 reported Keillor called newspapermen, "bookkeepers, scribblers and old dogs." Keillor hinted that he was so disturbed he might leave St. Paul and that the amount of money invested to refurbish the World Theater would not make the slightest bit of difference. He wondered if he might move to New York or someplace else where he'd be allowed his privacy.

That notion amused Coleman, who affirmed that the local press had always treated Keillor respectfully. "In New York he'd know what it would be like to have thirty flashbulbs in his face when he left a restaurant," Coleman said.

Virtually any journalist would vehemently disagree when Keillor asserted he'd never traded his private life for publicity. The deal one makes when seeking a public audience, when laying claim to a public forum, is that in some ways one's privacy will be infringed. This is true for people in show business, professional athletes and politicians. "But you can't make him see that he's mistaken—that he made that deal," Coleman said. "I really agonized over that Margaret Moos story because I spent the weekend thinking about what I should do. I knew if I ran it I was going to get attacked by a lynch mob. I would have preferred not to have written it, but I think in the end it was the only honest thing I could do journalistically. It was a legitimate news story because by this time, you have a radio show whose star was on the cover of *Time* magazine, who has national and international fame, the most successful radio program in America, and its executive producer—who had been there since the beginning, had really helped shape and develop the show, and was such an intimate partner professionally and personally with the show's star—was out. Not just out of his house, but out of his show. And they would have wanted, apparently, that no one mention this. I didn't seek out this information, sneak around in anybody's yard to get it. Actually, after I'd written the parody, I got calls and people wondered how come nobody wrote about what happened to Margaret Moos. I didn't know; at that time I hadn't heard."

Shefchik reported Keillor was extremely petulant after Coleman's piece appeared. "I called MPR and he said he wouldn't talk to me, but Bill Kling, I think, convinced him to as far as damage control, to go public with it. In that conversation he spent the time saying what a disappointment it was to be covered that way in his own city, to have his personal life splashed all over the papers. He'd never asked for that kind of coverage, and said he never made any sort of deal by which he traded his privacy for fame and fortune, which I found really astonishing coming from a person as intelligent as he is, because that is the deal he made. I agree you don't make any kind of deal that says people can peek into your bedroom, and I don't think that's what was going on here. The story was justified, and he overreacted to the totally harmless coverage he got.

Because of the rush of success MPR, APR and Keillor himself enjoyed, pressure built within the organization, pressure on APR to be something other than a one-program network, albeit they did offer other programs. The sense among member stations, however, is that they were on board solely because of "A Prairie Home Companion." The network will have to scramble to sustain member stations, which grew increasingly unhappy with rate increases assessed for APR membership and "A Prairie Home Companion."

National audiences tuned into Keillor for only six years, and most of his fans were only able to enjoy the program over the last several years, as APR increased its member stations to more than three hundred. Consequently, as the national audience widened, local afficionados seemed to drift away. Gordy Abel remembered a tour with a group of musicians who had made appearances on the program. Their connections with the show figured prominently in advertising. "The further away from the Twin Cities we got, the more excited our audiences were," Abel said. "Keillor's program was more of a big deal to them."

In July 1986, Minneapolis *Star Tribune* writer Dave Matheny measured the mood of the local media concerning Keillor. "It's, let's tear Garrison down in the Twin Cities," Matheny said. "When he was doing the morning show, they couldn't say enough good things about him, but now, when he has his picture on the cover of *Time*, everybody takes a shot at him." Matheny added that he thought Keillor was doing much the same thing then as he was back in 1974.

When in December, 1986, Keillor missed an autograph session at Dayton's department store in downtown Minneapolis, disappointing hundreds of fans whose patient lines snaked through the fifth-floor book section, Keillor apologized, claiming that he was to have had his car parked by store employees at the Dayton's parking ramp. But he didn't see them when he drove up, and the ramp and others nearby were filled. So Keillor found a pay phone outside and called the store, but he said his call was misrouted and never reached the book department. When he returned to his car, he discovered he'd locked his keys inside. He used a coat hanger to break into the car, but by the time he succeeded, it was too late for his appearance. Matheny wrote the story, explaining the snafu in the morning paper. Some of his reporter colleagues snickered and asked Matheny if he believed Keillor's excuse. "They just shook their heads when I told them I guessed I did," Matheny said.

Matheny objected to the scrutiny under which Keillor was placed. "It's an animal-pack mentality. People are asking him how he feels about his Lake Wobegon people. Did anybody ever ask Twain how he felt about his characters? Keillor was always a storyteller, but because he's made the green stuff, that's held against him."

Studs Terkel has long observed the phenomenon of performers with esoteric appeal suddenly finding wide audiences. But critics and early supporters don't rejoice at their achievement.

Instead they offer sarcastic sniping. "With his increased popularity, there will be many who want to take shots at him," Terkel said. "This reminds me of early jazz fans and artists. They loved the work of a guy until he made some commercial success. Then he 'sold out,' he cheapened himself. And this is probably happening to Garrison now too."

What has also happened is that the shy young man who was hardly involved in school activities in Anoka is now the most visible, recognizable figure from his high school graduating class. And the scrawny, awkward kid who idolized Cedric Adams and Bob DeHaven has far surpassed the accomplishments and influence of his own early heroes, appealing to a much wider audience than any of the old WCCO gang could have aspired to or even imagined. And he's done this mainly on his own—through his own creative genius and the courage to be true to his personal vision of what life ought to offer the decent citizens of the world.

Other former co-workers, who declined to be named, have said that Keillor could be very temperamental, intimidating and irrational, and that his blowups kept the staff on pins and needles. Apparently some ex-associates were made to feel extremely unhappy and useless.

Dan Donsker was a twenty-one year-old engineer when he began working for MPR in 1976. He occasionally worked the shift during Keillor's morning program. He recalls the host as a difficult person to work with. "If you'd say good morning he usually wouldn't say anything. He wasn't friendly, but he always got what he wanted. He was assertive, but low key, and projected his presence without saying anything. Is his shyness just a cover for rudeness? I don't know. The end result is that he offended people he worked with.

"He didn't seem to hold others in regard. One of the procedures that had to be followed by all announcers back then was that after their show, they had to refile the records they used. Garrison refused to do it, and every announcer who worked shifts after him would have to do the job."

"People who last the longest in show business," Nash said, "are the people who stay the same in all different forms. So you see Bob Hope on a talk show and it's pretty much the same Bob Hope you see on a Bob Hope show. He's consistent. The Keillor on the David Letterman Show was a different Keillor. Part of that is the medium itself. Television is intense and requires faster responses. It's a much hotter medium, in spite of the fact that ultimately it's the coolest of media. Radio is hotter because it gets into your head faster. TV is cooler because it doesn't require the level of concentration a show like Keillor's did. You really had to listen to his show. Take him out of his own show with his own rhythm and sense of style, put him into a television program, he doesn't come across as well. He comes across as hesitant, rural, or in some cases, he comes across as sarcastic."

It may be that an adoring public feeds upon its heroes in such a way they turn into persons whose craving for adoration cannot be quenched. The person attracted to the public limelight as an entertainer or performer is flawed by a characteristic unique to those professions. He or she needs to be loved, and that love must be expressed by wider public acceptance than is necessary for most of us. At its heart lies a basic insecurity—an insecurity coupled with a driving ego that impels the performer to expose himself or herself to the possibility of public failure, but also to public success. A great many performers may not be well adjusted personalities, as witnessed by the number of their failed interpersonal relationships. And many theatrical producers and directors refer to their actors as their "children." That assessment is not always inaccurate.

Getting to the top in show business is exhilarating, but remaining there, sustaining one's position of preeminence while those about you flounder in mediocrity, creates pressures. How does one deal with a longtime crony-performer whose supporting talents no longer meet the standards established by the superstar? Could Butch Thompson and Peter Ostroushko really no longer deliver the goods? Had Keillor merely tired of and discarded them?

It is a rare performer who hangs on to the old associates and pulls them along with him, demanding nothing more than what they are capable of contributing. One thinks of Jimmy Durante continuing to give a few moments on some of his television shows to his old sidekick, Eddie Jackson—a man of modest talent, but a man who was with Durante at the beginning of the Schnoz's long career, and who was not callously tossed aside like a fountain pen that no longer works.

Garrison Keillor, like many performers who reach the summits of their art, has pulled some folks along, offered them exposure and fostered their careers. But this was sometimes done at a cost to their personal dignities, implying that they existed only professionally speaking, and if they failed to produce an undefined quality known only to him, they were dismissed—sometimes unofficially. They simply wouldn't be called to appear on the program again. One musician, puzzled by his prolonged absence from "A Prairie Home Companion," reportedly wrote Keillor, asking what happened. The reply was a terse "Things change."

On the other hand, many local musicians who appeared on "A Prairie Home Companion" would never have ascended to any national spotlight without Keillor. As one Twin Cities reporter said, "I doubt anyone ever would have heard of these people if it hadn't been for Garrison."

In fairness, there are few persons graced with true noblesse oblige. Few would not falter under the pressures weighing upon one who may have taken on the responsibility for the survival of a national radio network. Executive decisions needed to be made, and after Moos's departure, Keillor had to make those decisions alone.

Coleman, who still claims a fondness for Keillor, says the situation as the program entered its final performances was sad, "like an old show-biz cliché about the star who burns out the people who work for him and ends up trying to do it all himself. . . .

"You can see the price of celebrity in his story. It's a price Garrison may be reluctant to pay. . . . He and Kling have created a monster, and now, I think, that monster is growling." Coleman made that observation six months before Keillor's decision to suspend "A Prairie Home Companion."

Keillor, who revealed much of himself through his monologues, also held back a good deal. The public persona he projected was of his choosing. It suited his program; it satisfied his audience. Yet there may have been a downside characteristic too—one best typified by Lonesome Rhodes, the main character in the Budd Schulberg–Elia Kazan film of 1957, *A Face In The Crowd*. Rhodes, a hobo, ascended to national prominence through radio; a man whose open, friendly nature vaulted him to the top turned cynical, arrogant, and even cruel. Rhodes, like Keillor, satisfied the public need for heroes.

NICK Nash remembers getting off a plane in Lapland on his way to Sweden several years ago, in an attempt to sell some of Garrison's programs to Swedish radio. He was cornered by reporters and photographers who asked, "Is Garrison Keillor really shy?"

The answer to the question is terribly significant, so long as the public persona is that of a shy person. Connie Goldman says, "When you host a show that catches on, you develop the personality that works for you." In Keillor's case, shyness sold. And shyness also served as a protection. Querulousness, irritability, temperament, may all be dismissed as an outgrowth of his shyness, his desire for privacy. Shyness may also provide an excuse for quirkish behavior. Shyness not only sells, it can come in handy; it keeps people at a long arm's length, allowing Garrison to use others to run interference. He did not have to bother himself with trifling minutiae, such as how to get "A Prairie Home Companion" on the air and how to market it and himself. This was a program that commercial radio would not have touched, nor was it one that most public stations would have encouraged. It was in fact, anathema to the current concept of public radio in America, in that it offered companionability, personality. The format for public radio generally eschews personality, relying instead on news and classical music. Public radio's demographics suggest a listenership that is largely white, upper middle class, and well educated—a cultural elite. What Garrison Keillor brought to public radio, someone once suggested, was bumpkin chic—getting the longhairs to listen to simple fiddle tunes and mouth music.

Yet Bill Kling, trusting the creative genius of Garrison Keillor, put "A Prairie Home Companion" on the air and promoted it. "Bill Kling is a very savvy guy," Rick Shefchik said. "I'm sure he feels there would be no 'Prairie Home Companion' without MPR, and as much success as Garrison Keillor may be entitled to, I'm sure Kling feels MPR is also entitled to a piece of that success. I think he sees himself and Keillor as partners in this."

MPR's growth might well have been linked to the program's popularity. What began in 1967 as a shoestring operation at Saint John's University in Collegeville, Minnesota, with one station—KSJR—and five employees, now has twelve stations which broadcast throughout Minnesota and to parts of Iowa, Michigan, North Dakota, South Dakota and Wisconsin. Its budget, a modest fifty thousand dollars in 1967, tops eight million dollars today, and there are nearly two hundred fifty employees on the payroll. With sixty thousand subscriber-members, MPR has the largest membership of any public radio system in the nation.

Thus, the network and its subsidiary, the American Public Radio Network, flourished along with "A Prairie Home Companion." When the gala tenth-anniversary broadcast was promoted, sixteen hundred people filled the Orpheum Theater on July 7, 1984, and another four thousand—persons from nearly every state—gathered on the state capitol lawn to hear the broadcast over loudspeakers and enjoy the postprogram party.

But the success of the program made change inevitable. It booked more national name talent than before. Chet Atkins, Johnny Gimble, John Hartford, Taj Mahal and Emmylou Harris appeared nearly as often as Larson and Hinckley, for example. This evolution came about because network stations demanded more "stars" on the program.

But the change from local, little-known talent to major performers was not necessarily for the better. Some original fans drifted away; the loyalists of several years back became only occasional listeners, or stopped listening altogether. Certainly, the counterculture types who peopled the early performances had long since disappeared, and in its latter days, "A Prairie Home Companion" found itself ensconced in the yuppie establishment.

What also changed about the program was its cost to member stations of APR. When the show was first offered to public stations it was free, supported by foundation grants. But as "A Prairie Home Companion" secured an audience, MPR began charging for membership to APR as well as for Keillor's program and other programs it distributed, such as "St. Paul Sunday Morning."

"We were misled," claimed Bruce Mims, Program Director at WTSU in Montgomery, Alabama. "Certainly we won't pay the same price for the program after Keillor leaves and they decide to rerun old programs."

"APR used it very cleverly as a way of milking us dry," said Marvin Granger, whose Billings, Montana, station's membership fees rose from six hundred dollars in 1985 to five thousand dollars in 1986, while program fees for "A Prairie Home Companion" increased from fifty-three to seventy-one dollars a program. "They originally announced that it would be funded by foundations and corporate grants. Because the program's so popular, they're forcing small stations to pay more, and in the process, I think, they'd like to put NPR out of business. Clearly one-third of the member stations will probably drop out after Keillor leaves. He was APR's main source of income."

After Keillor announced on February 14, 1986, that he would be ending "A Prairie Home Companion" with the June 13 broadcast, there were expressions of disappointment, but also some of unbridled glee, from network affiliates. Stations were informed only fifteen minutes before the February 14 broadcast that Keillor was going to announce his resignation, which caught them by surprise. And while many station managers were dismayed at the loss of public radio's most listened to program, some, according to Bill Humphries, director of development for APR member station WEMU-FM in Ypsilanti, Michigan, were ecstatic. Humphries said "they [the affiliate stations] thought they were being stuck up"—as in at gunpoint. "There are some like us who feel they've got us over a barrel and they're milking us. Well, the barrel's going to be gone soon."

For most of the nation, "A Prairie Home Companion" was enjoyed for only three or four years. MPR member stations had the program for thirteen years, a long run in show business. And that long run served to heighten Keillor's remarkable creative endurance. And it also calls into question why his work has not been subjected to more scrutiny by critics and scholars. True, there are only two published volumes, but if each monologue can be viewed as a short story, as Jon Fagerson asserts, Keillor's production of quality stories has been prodigious indeed. He has written and performed nearly 600 monologues, roughly 1,500,000 *words*, or about the lifetime production of three serious writers, each of whom may be expected to create five novels or short story collections of perhaps 100,000 words. How much can the public fairly expect from a writer over a lifetime—and a relatively young writer at that? Garrison Keillor was only forty-four when his program ended.

Though radio is an ephemeral, transient media most of the time, Keillor's monologues were neither; they are as permanent as print, taped for future sales by MPR and pirated by thousands of listeners at home, thereby denying Keillor the occasional flub or slip of the tongue; everything he said in his monologues would endure, to be enjoyed again by fans and critics. Most other broadcasters' works perished as they were aired.

More than a year prior to his announced resignation, Garrison had implied that he considered leaving the program to reside in Denmark, his wife's home, where he would be free of his celebrity status and would devote himself to writing.

When rumors to that effect surfaced during the winter of 1985–86, APR dispatched hasty messages assuring member stations that the program would remain intact for the foreseeable future, and Keillor told the Los Angeles *Times* that despite his wearying of the show at times, his truest feelings about it were good and hopeful; "If it can survive its promotion, I would think we'd have a good, long life."

But that good, long life has been shortened, though many believe the hiatus will be temporary. "Keillor takes pleasure in his success," said Nick Nash. "He's become the thing he hated while he was growing up. He is well known. He was probably a not very attractive, gangly kid. His family background was so different from everyone else's that just getting into the middle class was probably very important. And now he lives just off Summit Avenue. Like Fitzgerald, he has nearly achieved Summit Avenue." This was a reference to a statement F. Scott Fitzgerald once made about the neighborhood in which he grew up, a neighborhood of grand, stately homes owned by persons of great wealth and status.

And yet, like Minnesota's other chronicler of small-town life, Sinclair Lewis, Gary Keillor may not have found what he was seeking in his life and art.

Keillor's writing has brought about altered perceptions of small towns—a vision that changed after Lewis's scathing indictment, which followed close on the heels of somewhat similar fulminations published by Edgar Lee Masters in *A Spoon River Anthology*, H. L. Mencken's *Prejudices*, and Sherwood Anderson's *Winesburg, Ohio*. Since the publication of *Main Street* in 1920, writes John E. Miller in his comparative paper, "No one . . . has been able to think of the small town without the spirit of Sinclair Lewis brooding somewhere nearby."

Though Keillor loathes the use of *nostalgic* to describe his work, it is nonetheless applicable. He touches a nearly universal response, a longing for a place where our faces and names are known, where we are respected and loved, and most of us, having grown up in urban centers in relative anonymity, doubtless have desired to live in a community where one's word is one's bond, and where people who do indeed watch us and know what we are about also look after our general welfare.

This nostalgic, rural appeal did not seem to include black Americans. Keillor's style was cool, even cold, while many black humorists tend to be hot, almost hyperactive, à la Richard Pryor. There is kinesis in their performances, and Keillor moved only his face and mouth; there was no dance, no poetry of posture, only a man behind a podium telling a story. And the story did not have an obvious cadence or rhythm, such as one might find in a black comic's routine. Keillor's delivery, with deliberate understatement, was what one might expect from a Norwegian bachelor farmer, if that farmer were given to public pronouncement, which of course, he is not.

According to John Wright, professor of Afro studies at the University of Minnesota, black characters and life figure very little in Keillor's work because "there's a strong element of nostalgia, and black audiences are not into nostalgia and often recall small-town rural roots not with warmth, but with some degree of bitterness."

Professor Bier says that Keillor represents regional literature, and can't include everyone. "It would be to his disadvantage to broaden and then falsify. A writer works best in the milieu in which he is knowledgeable." While Southern blacks have rural traditions, Northern blacks do not, and in small-town Minnesota there are very few blacks, thus an attempt to locate them there would ring false. "In a racial or cultural context," Bier said, "Keillor may be more insulated than normal."

Maybe so, but to millions of Americans, cultural diversity may not be an attraction. They'll eat Italian or Chinese cuisine, but much prefer homogeneity in neighborhoods and communities. In Lake Wobegon, practically everyone is of Northern European stock, either German or Norwegian, and practices Catholicism or Lutheranism. The differences are neither deep nor widespread.

Despite his own occasional bleak visions, Keillor differs from

Lewis in his depiction of small-town life: where Lewis's alter ego, Carol Kennicott, the protagonist in *Main Street*, found Gopher Prairie mean, drab, ugly, Lake Wobegon is clearly more human, more revealing of honest characteristics, and it is the honesty of the place that listeners and readers found appealing. Garrison Keillor likes and respects the small-town characters— people whose behavior may be a little off the wall, and who might, if they lived in cities, be suspect. In the *Metropolitan Home* interview, he said:

> I'm sure a lot of people think that if they lived in a small town then they would be what they imagine a small-town person is like. A person whose life is somehow simpler than their own. Of course, it's not really like that in a small town. And without glossing over the meanness or the cruelty of small towns, which is simply human nature, their attraction to me is that in a place where people know you and your business is open, you can live with integrity. It's not a great sin in small towns to be different or eccentric. Even crazy. Just so long as you don't upset anyone.

Lewis would not have looked kindly upon those persons; but the eavesdropper in Lake Wobegon would have raptly listened to their stories, would have appreciated, rather than vilified their crotchets.

On the other hand, when deciphering the small-town experience, Lewis and Keillor are soul-mates at least in part. Keillor's alter ego in Lake Wobegon Days must be Johnny Tollefson, whom he describes as tall, a beanpole—as was the teenage Gary Keillor. Young Johnny also aspires to literary achievement. However, Keillor's exorcism in the form of the "Ninety-five Theses" is "an unrestrained manifesto against the putative parents and neighbors of a former son of Lake Wobegon who still suffers from the results of his overly protective childhood," writes John Miller. "Nothing in Sinclair Lewis's work is more scathing. . . ."

In the theses Keillor rails against bad food, religious strictures, fear of sexuality, fastidiousness, and his own apparent ineptness at sustaining interpersonal relationships. Foremost among the latter is thesis 7, which states: "You have taught me to fear strangers and their illicit designs, robbing me of easy companionship, making me a very suspicious friend. Even among those I know well, I continue to worry; what do they *really* mean by liking me?"

Thesis 79 may also be somewhat telling concerning Keillor's taste in music: ". . . I hate folk music. I don't care for most of the sensitive people I feel obligated to hang out with. Many of them play guitars and write songs about their feelings."

The theses aside, Garrison shares Lewis's contempt for small-mindedness. But where Lewis was unable or perhaps unwilling to look at the overall pictures of the characters who populated Gopher Prairie, Keillor cares about Lake Wobegon's people, and like a loving God, forgives them their transgressions, their foibles, and continues to love them. Writes Miller, "Where Garrison Keillor differs [from Lewis] is that he realizes there is no escape. We all carry the burden of our history, our beliefs, our habits and customs. His stories are parables of patience rewarded, or adversity endured. These are the messages they teach: life is fraught with peril, doing without makes you appreciate things more, life is full of disappointments, it's good to wait, nothing should come easy, you'll appreciate it more if you work for it."

The late Ben Dubois, who was the last survivor in Sauk Centre, born the same year as Lewis in 1885, and a sometime childhood playmate of the author, recalled Lewis as a homely, ornery chap, whom no one in town thought would ever amount to much. Gary Keillor was also an awkward kid, and according to Deloyd Hochstetter, people in Anoka—some teachers and quite a few fellow students—made a similar assessment of him. About Lewis, Dubois said, "He was never at ease. Plainly he was a man looking for something, but if he ever found it, he wouldn't have known what it was."

Keillor too is searching for something. His personal angst

may have arisen from his having found it—fame and good fortune—and having known that he had found it. He has more than become what he most admired and respected as a young student in Anoka—those radio heroes on WCCO. Keillor, unlike Lewis, cared about the area and people he wrote and spoke about. He told the Los Angeles *Times* that he'd gone through many different feelings toward his father's family, from "wanting to get away from them, to satire, to trying to talk about them with admiration and piety, but also some humor. . . .

Lewis's novel *Main Street*, however, had more of an impact upon people who knew the author than do Keillor's stories and monologues. Old acquaintances are pleased to find their names in Keillor's works—quite unlike the situation in Sauk Centre, where townsfolk were angered by what they alleged were depictions of them in *Main Street*. Yet any author who only thinly disguises his settings, his characters, his own upbringing, is bound to step on toes. Keillor said in the *Writer's Digest* article that he was certain there were parts in his book that would cause some pain to his people. "It's tough to tell the truth, especially when, as is so often the case with fiction, we're not absolutely sure of the truth. You're looking for the truth, and you are just putting out some markers. People may be surprised to hear how many writers have been concerned about their families' reaction to their work—even writers who are well grown up."

Keillor, like Lewis before him, has become a public person, recognized in restaurants and hotel lobbies. He is sought out, interviewed, his pronouncements treasured; his photograph graces the covers of important magazines. And he has become wealthy.

Yet he seems vaguely discontent, afraid of being recognized in public, while at the same time fearing that he will be unrecognized. *The Washington Post*'s Kevin Klose once observed Keillor and his family check in to Chicago's Blackstone Hotel. "Keillor looked covert, extremely strained," Klose said. "Yet there he was with six inches of his patented red socks showing between his shoes and cuffs."

There is discontent too because notoriety, success and fortune bring no enduring exhilaration. And perhaps there's been too much prestige. One cannot long endure as an object of idolatry, with thousands worshipping the water one seems to walk upon. So what may be next for Garrison Keillor? What does he do for an encore?

13

FOR most of Garrison Keillor's audience, peaking at nearly four million listeners, it didn't matter where his program originated, for the sound quality remained constant. But after stretches in St. Paul's Orpheum Theater and in Red Wing, Minnesota, the World Theater reopened on January 11, 1986, and "A Prairie Home Companion" welcomed back old standbys Robin and Linda Williams, Vern Sutton, Jean Redpath, and Stevie Beck. The program had been away from its home for about two years.

Though the show was mainly performed at the Orpheum during restoration of the World, problems forced it to do an extended road tour in October, 1985. Beseiged by maddening delays, the staff found it increasingly hectic to locate auditoriums in which to book the program. According to Cathy de Moll, MPR publicity director, the road manager would be on the phone backstage during rehearsals trying to lock in theater and ticket arrangements for the show two weeks in advance.

But in the two-year absence from the World Theater, international fame had come to Keillor, and his program had begun to change. No longer were Butch Thompson's Trio and Peter Ostroushko regular performers, and guiding producer Margaret Moos also departed. During her hiatus, the program floundered, first in search of producers, then in spite of them. A nationwide search for a person with film and television experience turned up Stephen Schlow, who produced only six programs during the fall of 1986 before being dismissed. According to Tom Lieberman, one of the contributing writers on "A Prairie Home Companion," Schlow wanted to bring in more writers, but Keillor, intensely aware of the delicate threads that sustained the magic on the program, was quite hesitant to send out an open call. Though Keillor handled nearly all the writing during the program's early years, as the program's stature grew, it relied more and more on outside writers such as Lieberman and Howard Mohr, creator of the Minnesota Language Systems, another program "sponsor," to write sketches and satirical songs. Keillor always wrote the monologue himself, and it does not seem that he saw the creative well drying up. In fact, in 1986 he told the *Washington Post* that he thought he could continue the broadcast another three or four years, adding, "I'll be curious about the people of Lake Wobegon longer than the radio audience will."

In the two months prior to Garrison's announced resignation, there had been rumors the program would make the foray into television. This occurred when the Disney Channel began taping "A Prairie Home Companion." And the probability of filming *Lake Wobegon Days* also looms imminent. Noted film director Sydney Pollack appeared on the program and had been seen with Keillor scouting the area around Saint John's University for potential shooting sites. A logical step for Keillor would be to provide the narration for a feature film about Lake Wobegon.

Since Keillor has on several occasions eschewed involvement with television and has been a staunch advocate of radio, some of his most loyal fans may have felt betrayed by the move to Disney. But even at the height of his popularity, Keillor was not enormously well paid by contemporary show-business standards. His salary at MPR was about $200,000 annually, which is a fraction of that earned by commercial television stars. It's only reasonable to assume that he'd have to consider any significant financial opportunity, and that would most likely come from television or films.

Jean Shepherd, who apparently regards himself as something of a rival, has enjoyed success in translating his Indiana boyhood chronicles into television specials and films. There's no reason to believe the Keillor sketches also wouldn't work on the screen, unless we're considering a tangible factor that makes the stories work for many of his fans: the presence of Keillor's voice. A Minneapolis psychologist, John Robertson, says he has long been a devoted fan and rarely missed a broadcast. But he said he has not been able to make much headway with *Lake Wobegon Days* because he thinks the stories need to be orally rendered by Keillor. His voice is at least as important as his wit and his pen in creating vivid characters and settings. A Keillor film without the Keillor voice may be just so many small potatoes to his fans.

If, as Marshall McLuhan wrote two decades ago, the medium is the message, then Garrison Keillor's medium is not really radio but rather his voice. The distinctive voice is the instrument he never learned to play as a youngster. He became a virtuoso, however, as a broadcaster, and his voice is as vivid, as memorable as any that has preceded it, including Edward R. Murrow's, or the old commercial pitchman and announcer Frank Gallop's, or even Arthur Godfrey's. The voice of a great broadcaster is his signature, his imprint on the airwaves, a uniquely personal instrument. Murrow and Godfrey used to be done by impressionists, but none so far has attempted Keillor.

While a radio communicator's voice is more important than a television star's, a radio program such as "A Prairie Home Companion" was a great curiosity for television viewers. It looked like the radio shows people over forty-five may remember attending from the thirties through the mid fifties. But people who are younger have never seen live radio and are attracted to the novelty, while older folk are caught in its nostalgia. Which is why the limited run on the Disney Channel was a worthwhile undertaking.

When "A Prairie Home Companion" was televised on April 26, 1986, Nick Coleman wrote in his Minneapolis *Star Tribune* column, "Keillor's radio show never looked . . . well, it never looked at all before except to the people who've seen it in person. But it looked better than Keillor, who used to say it wouldn't translate to TV, was afraid it might. . . . The TV broadcast proved 'Prairie Home' would make it as a regular TV show."

The televised program received the highest rating ever for a local public television station in Minnesota. In the Twin Cities it had a 14 rating and a 27 share for station KTCA. It outrated "Magnum, P.I." and NBC's "Salute to Billy Wilder." Fourteen percent of all TV households in the Twin Cities tuned in. The program earned an eight percent in Chicago, six percent in San Francisco, five percent in Philadelphia and Los Angeles, and only three percent in New York, where it was broadcast on Sunday instead of live.

This apparent audition on public television dismayed staunch fans, including Bruce Mims, program director at WTSU in Montgomery, Alabama, who was saddened that Keillor had ventured into TV. "He's always been a proponent of radio, and his prominence has heightened the national awareness of public radio, which was good for all of public radio. Part of our problem in the South is that public radio is relatively young. We haven't had widespread support. We started in 1976 here, but until 1984 there was no public radio in Mississippi at all, for instance."

During its heyday, the program attracted the attention of musicians and other performers who believed their talents would translate well on "A Prairie Home Companion." While the program did employ many musicians during its tenure, none who performed with Keillor were themselves vaulted to stardom.

As "A Prairie Home Companion" ascended to national prominence, twenty to forty audition tapes were sent each week to MPR from aspiring performers eager to work for the modest wage, plus airfare and accommodations at the St. Paul Hotel.

A consultant, whose name was never revealed by MPR, reviewed each tape and recommended one or two to be added to a list of performers who might work well on the show. Helen Edinger, the program's talent coordinator, would listen to each of the tapes recommended by the consultant, as would Keillor.

While this was the most normal routine for performers to bring their talents to the attention of Keillor, one musician, whose exploits were recounted in a Minneapolis *Star Tribune Sunday Magazine* article by Jan Godown, made the program without auditioning. Velma Lee Frye, a classically trained singer and composer who sings bluesy tunes to her own piano accompaniment, happened to play a benefit for a low-income housing project in Tallahassee, Florida, her home, and Keillor appeared at the same benefit. She sang a duet with him on that show and provided piano backup. Later, at a reception, she handed Keillor her card, and followed up with a letter. Her persistence paid off, and she was booked for September 27, 1986. At the Friday rehearsal she learned she would play background music and play through the fifteen minute intermission in addition to appearing in a skit and a duet.

Keillor never liked a lot of rehearsal, wanting the program to maintain a kind of spontaneity and freshness, which was part of the show's charm but placed a strain on performers, who were sometimes asked to come up with something at the last minute, a *je ne sais quoi*, a vaguely defined quality that Keillor wanted in a certain spot. In Frey's case, she was asked to play some "outdoor" music. She spent Friday night trying to come up with something suitable for the Saturday broadcast, and apparently succeeded, for she was asked to make future appearances on the show.

Richard Allison is an actor who appeared on "A Prairie Home Companion" six times in various skits. "Garrison was talking with Vern Sutton and he said he needed an actor and Vern recommended me. I liked the improvisational quality on the show. One day Garrison came to the green room about an hour and a half before the show and asked if I had any talents he didn't know about. 'I sing,' I said. 'No, that's not what I mean,' he said. 'Anything unusual?' I said I could whistle loudly without putting my fingers in my mouth.

"He said, 'We'll use that. Anything else?' I could make a horse galloping sound by clapping my hands together and on my thighs. 'Oh, that's good. Why don't you do these things?'

"In the skit he was working out I was supposed to be auditioning for the program and was to say, 'I whistle and do horse hands.' I love telling this story, that in the midst of getting everything ready, he kept the pressure to himself. I never saw him upset or losing his cool."

In all the skits that Allison appeared in, he said that Keillor's true person would be present. "One I remember was about the anniversary of the national anthem, a thing on Francis Scott Key. He fantasized about what happened to Key after he wrote the anthem. In the skit, Key had become a celebrity and was everywhere identified as the man who wrote 'The Star Spangled Banner.' He would go to parties and you could just picture Garrison going through this stuff. Key agonized over 'What am I going to write next? I don't want to be known as a one-song composer.' You could just hear Garrison's soul coming through here."

Allison, as a trained actor, occasionally felt a little out of synch with the intent of some of the skits. "I sometimes thought I tended to make the script sound more polished than he wanted it to be."

Allison said that Keillor's work, for him, has an almost immortal quality. "The first time I was on, I was in seventh heaven," he recalls. "I was there listening to his monologue and the thought crossed my mind that forty years from now this will be impressive to my grandchildren, in the way Mark Twain is to me now. I felt very privileged. Mine was a wonderful experience."

Neither Fry nor Allison have approached stardom in their

careers, nor have most other performers who frequently appeared on "A Prairie Home Companion" over the years. But it was never the program's function to develop stars other than the host. Keillor was always the centerpiece, the linchpin. His monologue *was*, for many, the program. They'd tune in about ten minutes into the second hour of the show and listen through the monologue, then eat dinner—supper, in the case of midwesterners.

Dan Cryer in his *Newsday Magazine* story observed that Garrison Keillor wasn't an artist struggling to overcome his roots: rather, he has come to terms with them and made them the source of his art. Sinclair Lewis never really came to terms with his roots, and he lamented to an acquaintance that the only thing he ever wanted in life was to please his father, and that he had failed. Keillor may know that his work cannot be completely pleasing to his father and mother, not because the work per se is evil or sinful but simply because it exists in a totally secular arena and because it brings pleasure to so many. His is a gift not understood by his Brethren peers, and Keillor may have at last been able to accept their not understanding and to continue to treat them with respect and dignity even as his words bring smiles to the faces of his listeners and readers.

Keillor's roots—his semirural rearing, the years of involvement with the Brethren Assembly, on through the young intellectual aesthete at the University of Minnesota—have given his work a remarkable uniqueness—the qualities of the open metaphor. It can and does mean what his audiences choose it to mean. Thus, for the religious, his work carries a strong spiritual dimension, while the agnostic is able to conclude that the thrust of meaning is satirical.

"Satire and seriousness do coexist at the same time," said Fagerson. "But I'm not sure that the satire is one of the things he's serious about. Keillor can satirize Father Emil or Pastor Inqvist. And one of them can say something 'religious' and be very stupid in saying it, but Keillor can still believe that what they're saying may have value. So he may be satirizing what he's doing and he's stumbling—like the monologue where he [the minister] had two note cards, and one said 'conclusion' on it. It was a delightful spoof on some poor preacher winging it from the pulpit. On the other hand, Keillor is very serious about religious values and the importance of ministers and what can happen in a church. He can satirize the flawed, sad instrument of truth, but that person can still be a vehicle for truth."

What Fagerson sees as extremely valuable in Keillor's work is that in dragging out his own roots, he forces us to accept ourselves and our culture. "It's like he's conducting one giant AA session, enabling people to say, 'My name is Tom. I'm a midwesterner,' or 'I thought I was the only one whose parents dressed funny,' or to accept their church as odd, their town as strange, whatever. There's a sense of relief, that 'Ah, I'm not the only one.' I think that's the beauty of what he does. It's also the significance of the motto on the Lake Wobegon crest: *Sumus Quod Sumus:* we are what we are."

There is also beauty in the certainty that Keillor never hit below the belt, with the possible exception of the Nick Coleman incidents, or reached for the cheap laugh, straining for humor like a desperate, overwrought nightclub comic working an apathetic crowd. As he told Michael Schumacher:

There's nothing less funny than someone who is trying too hard to make you laugh. Laughter is always a surprise. It's a spontaneous surprised reaction. I do not promise people to make them laugh; if I could promise people that I could make them laugh, they would not laugh. Maybe that's the difference between comedians and humorists. Comedians have this agreement with an audience—that they will laugh at what they do— so the audience is manipulated according to a formal little dance to which it agrees. When Morey Amsterdam gets up and does jokes, we agree to laugh, and we enjoy laughing even though those jokes predate the pyramids. It's as formal as the tango; we all move in time to the music. I tell stories and I'm not a comedian. I'm a writer, and writers do not accept the same strictures nor lead the audience to the same expectations.

What writers crave, though, is feedback, especially positive feedback. In Keillor's case, that has come in abundance. There's been very little criticism of him or his work in the press, and reviews of his two books have been mostly raves. Kirkus Reviews said of *Happy to Be Here* that it was "mostly minor-league humor . . . but with enough one-of-a-kind touches . . . to rise just a little above the crowd." D. Keith Mano, writing in *National Review*, however, said, "There aren't two weak pieces among the twenty-nine collected here. . . . Garrison Keillor is so derivative that he might well be one of our most original writers." Keillor's friend and sometime guest on "A Prairie Home Companion," Roy Blount, reviewing *Happy to Be Here*, in *The New York Times Book Review*, concluded by stating, "This book will leave you either dumbfounded or happy—almost deservedly happy—to be anywhere."

Of *Lake Wobegon Days* Veronica Geng, in the August 25, 1985 *New York Times Book Review*, wrote that the town "joins Thurber's Columbus as an absurd definition of a very real Midwest," and Sally Vincent in the *Sunday Times* wrote, "The days of the small township of Lake Wobegon unfold, strange and compelling as an exotic blossom, emitting alien odours of pungent, eternal childhood. Keillor knows how to tell a story like nobody's business."

But Keillor fans—the zealots in particular—aren't concerned about reviews, except that they expect them to be positive. Many of his fans are not only loyal, but protective. When Nick Coleman's writings in the Minneapolis *Star Tribune* were known to arouse Keillor's ire, Coleman received a full measure of wrath from outraged loyal listeners—many questioning his intelligence and lineage. One, who would not allow his name to be printed, castigated a writer seeking information about Keillor. "He's a genius," the man stated. "And if you don't want to destroy your geniuses, you've got to make allowances for them. There just aren't that many of them who are doing a lot of good, instead of trying to make bombs and lasers that will hasten the end of life here on earth as we know it. Finally one comes along who's got something worthwhile and hopeful and fun, and you guys want to crucify him. Give the man his space. You'll only be satisfied after you've driven him out of town— maybe even forced him to retire. Then where are we? Then all we got left are the so-called geniuses who make bombs."

While Keillor himself isn't on public record regarding his position on national defense, we can assume he squares with his loyal fan on that issue. Keillor is a liberal who participated in fund-raising for Joan Growe, the Minnesota secretary of state, in her ill-fated 1984 attempt to unseat incumbent Republican senator Rudy Boschwitz. Keillor also remarked on David Brinkley's program that he was ashamed at the plight of America's homeless, whom we remember during the Christmas season but forget the rest of the year.

"It seems like the people I admire who really produce things, like farmers, are not doing all that well," he said in the Los Angeles *Times*. "And people who manipulate, who don't do anything well, are successful."

He voted against Ronald Reagan for president, he said in the *Wittenberg Door* interview, "because he is lazy, inattentive, and cynical. I think he has been very cynical regarding fundamentalists. He has absolutely used them, and he's given them very little in return. Reagan himself is not one of them, and I feel very badly that fundamentalists have been used by him in the way that they have been."

That Keillor may be politically liberal and theologically conservative, may seem contradictory. However, the fundamentalist in him enables him to avoid pat, knee-jerk liberal responses to issues, and thus he would not espouse the slogans so popular among self-styled populists. He discussed this with *Mother Jones*, saying, "A lot of liberals don't see populism as the complicated thing that it really is. There's a certain powerful

strain of anti-intellectualism in populism that has to be overcome if it is ever to take hold. Farmers are basically conservative."

And so are his beloved Wobegonians, who unlike reporters
and reviewers would probably not say anything at all concerning Keillor and his success. Which is the way he wishes it
could be. He told Michael Schumacher, "My people are awfully
polite. Too polite. My people are likely to feel, out of loyalty to
one of their own who did something big, that maybe they
should hold their tongues."

Or in the case of journalists, they should hold their pens. It
must have especially irked him to read Kevin Klose's comment
in the *Washington Post*: "We have a right to know everything
about him—shyness be damned."

Therefore, when Nick Coleman reported in his November 5,
1985 column that Keillor and longtime producer-housemate,
Margaret Moos, had broken off and that Keillor was planning
to marry Ulla Skaerved, Keillor was shaken and disturbed, an-
noyed that Coleman also reported that his salary increased from
$75,000 in fiscal 1983 to $173,186 in fiscal 1984. Not a mon-
strous salary by contemporary entertainers' standards, but a far
cry from the $12,000 Keillor earned from radio and writing
combined ten years earlier.

But it was the impending wedding that was front page news
around the state of Minnesota and was a major story elsewhere
too. Reluctantly, Keillor agreed to talk about the event with
Rick Shefchik for his *Pioneer Press* and *Dispatch* column. He
declined to discuss his relationship with Moos, and made it
clear he thought that press coverage of his personal life was a
violation of his privacy. He was forthcoming, however, concerning his bride-to-be. He said that they had corresponded for
four years until she married in the fall of 1964. "I was married
in 1966," Keillor said, "and we were not in touch with each
other until August of this year." Keillor was divorced in 1976
and Skaerved in 1981. They officially reunited at the twenty-
fifth reunion of the Anoka High School class of 1960.

Keillor said that he'd heard she was coming to the reunion about a week before she arrived, and later in the summer, he flew over to Denmark for a couple weeks and had gone over there since for several days between shows:

> It's a wonderful deal, and good luck; it makes the success seem like very small potatoes to me. That's how I felt all fall—that my book was incidental, a little accompaniment to the main fact of my life, which has been her. . . . I told a few of my friends about the most amazing thing that had ever happened to me in my life, and I had no idea it would happen at forty-three. She's the most amazing woman I've ever met, and I was absolutely dizzy at the idea of meeting her. It changed my whole fall, and then it winds up in the paper as a piece of trash.

Shefchik was not able to reach Moos for comment, nor did she comment since about that sensitive situation.

According to MPR officials, Shefchik reported, the press outside the Twin Cities had been quite respectful. At a Denver press conference, they said, after the questioning ended many reporters sought autographs from Keillor. But as Shefchik noted, in the Twin Cities reporters weren't so much interested in Keillor's autograph as they were in his personal life—a fact he found extremely distasteful. He said it was the sort of thing he expected from newspapers elsewhere, where reporters were celebrity hounds.

Reaction to that story and to Coleman's presentation in the Minneapolis paper was predictable—mostly pro Keillor. His Twin Cities fans rallied to his support, demanding that journalists get off Keillor's back, and charging that if he did decide to leave the area, it would be directly linked to the relentless, bloodsucking reporters who hounded the resident genius.

This, in fact, was the reason Keillor gave to Frank Farrell of "Monitor Radio" in his first interview after announcing the demise of "A Prairie Home Companion." He said that he first considered leaving the show in January, 1986, after returning from Denmark. "I've had a sort of running disagreement with the two papers in town over what constitutes private life, and there really isn't any way to resolve it. . . . But in the end they are right when they say that a person who chooses to be in the public eye really forfeits any legal claim to privacy. When I came home and found a picture of my house in the paper, the address and everything, I thought to myself, I can't really live here."

14

AN institution such as "A Prairie Home Companion," if it were to have survived, would of necessity have endured continual evolution—an evolution so gradual, however, that its constituency would not have been jolted by the changes.

But the program did change, and avid listeners were, in some instances, jolted. Perhaps, as some former MPR staffers and media critics suggested, the program seemed in need of patching after Margaret Moos's departure. She had seen to the details in a way that enabled Keillor to exploit his creativity without being bothered by niggling concerns and doubts about the business of production or program distribution. Neither Chris Cardozo nor Steve Schlow, who successively replaced Moos before her return, were able to meet Keillor's expectations and demands. And the old staff musicians had apparently burned out trying to sustain the magic. But magic of the sort that "A Prairie Home Companion" sustained over time was born of a chemistry that clicked. Such magic rarely can be programmed or planned. It just happens, as it did for years when Peter Ostroushko and Butch Thompson were regulars. Some longtime fans resented the departure of the two, who were considered fixtures on the program. Contributing writer Tom Lieberman, however, remembered that when Thompson joined the show he told Lieberman he considered it to be "just a gig." "He knew that any week could be his last," Lieberman said. "I took my cue from him. As long as I didn't depend on it, it could be fun, but I wouldn't rely on it for a living. I think Butch had that attitude."

Charlie Devore, a musician with the Hall Brothers Jazz Band, a Dixieland group that counts Thompson as a member, said that he was glad to see Butch get national exposure. "Butch is a marvelous musician," said Devore, who also made a number of appearances on the program from the late seventies through 1981. Devore also said that "A Prairie Home Companion" was an indirect benefactor to the band's club, The Jazz Emporium, at a time when the club was struggling financially. "Because the program paid airfare for some outstanding New Orleans musicians, we could book those people at our club," he said.

Even if the Butch Thompson Trio hadn't left the program in 1986 its personality would have been seriously altered, because of Red Maddock's death. Maddock was a great favorite with World Theater audiences; he had a showman's flair and was the only original staff musician on the program who had flirted with national exposure previously. During the 1940s he was with the Al Trace band, and was vocalist on the nonsense megahit "Mairzy Doats." Keillor gave the eulogy at Maddock's funeral, calling him a fantastic drummer and a great artist who brought joy to his audiences.

At least a part of the program's original appeal and sustained success lay in the mutual trust performers had in each other. The ensemble concept worked well, with each performer's best abilities allowed to flourish. However, as the program received increasingly more national and international attention, the tendency seemed to move more responsibility to Keillor, to spotlight him more, and to replace the largely local retinue of performers with people who had national name recognition.

Name attractions for "A Prairie Home Companion" helped APR sell the program to new markets, but some longtime listeners sensed that Keillor may have been losing interest. "He may have felt his contract was too restrictive," said one former

MPR employee, "and that he needed to get out from under Kling's thumb."

If that was the case, few could argue that television and film would be in Keillor's best financial interests. MPR owns the trademarks from Lake Wobegon on T-shirts, mugs, posters, and bumper stickers, and that arrangement has meant many thousands for the organization's coffers, a good share coming from half interest in *Lake Wobegon Days*.

It has caused minor controversy among public radio adherents that Keillor's program has been "commercial." Former public radio personality Maury Bernstein asked, "And what is 'noncommercial' and 'public' about a program like 'Prairie Home Companion,' when every time somebody mentions Lake Wobegon it sells a thousand T-shirts, a million books, all sorts of cassettes? Keillor's 'pseudo-commercials' are nothing of the sort. With all the products to back them up, all of them owned by [MPR], these are *real* commercials for *real* products, and they are on noncommercial radio illegally." Indeed, *The Wireless*, the MPR product catalogue, lists numerous spin-offs from Keillor's program, including Powdermilk Biscuits and Raw Bits, T-shirts and towels from the mythical Hotel Minnesota. These products bring in more than a quarter million dollars a year to MPR.

Despite the loyalty of the "Prairie Home Companion" audience, it was never vast. No national television program would survive with three or four million viewers per program. But the program generated much interest and excitement because it represented more than twenty-five percent of the national public radio audience. According to former APR Program Director Nick Nash, an estimated half of Keillor's audience did not listen to other programs on public radio, and just over five percent of the U.S. population listens to public radio at all.

Since Keillor's program represented a substantial number of public radio's listeners, its departure from the airwaves could prove horrific for the APR network. Marvin Granger looks for nearly half the member stations not to renew their affiliation with APR when current contracts expire. This despite the network's ability to carry on for about six more years with taped programs that have not been aired nationally. The live aspect of "A Prairie Home Companion," Granger thinks, remains a strong attraction, and stations simply won't be willing to pay fees demanded by APR for recorded programs.

Beyond APR's ability to remain viable, however, Keillor's leaving could also cripple public radio in some smaller markets. If twelve to fifteen percent of the total public radio audience listens only to "A Prairie Home Companion," a significant drop in individual membership support could result.

Despite denial by some of its spokespersons, public radio is elitist, catering to the educated, the well-heeled, who support and cherish classical music, news, and jazz programs not normally found on commercial stations. As Maury Bernstein says, "The public feels different about public radio than about commercial radio. Regular commercial advertisers support commercial broadcasting, while all sorts of people with nothing to advertise give money to public radio and television. They get no commercials in return, but always figure they should have some input. They feel as if they own a piece of the action. They are 'members' of a station which is 'public.' That is not the same as listening to a commercial station in which you haven't invested at all."

Bernstein, whose broadcast experience includes both commercial and public radio, thinks that public radio doesn't meet its original intentions—to provide programming that could not be found on commercial bands. He and Nick Coleman maintain that instead public radio belongs to those who pay the bill—those who can afford memberships. However, Keillor's program has altered the conception of mainstream public radio in the U.S. While personality is vital in commercial broadcasting, content carries the day on public radio. "It's been interesting to note," said Nash, "that the program on public radio with by far its largest audience is the one that features a strong, companionable personality." Thus, public radio has lost its leading personality, and in order to hold on to the segment of its audience that remains attracted to a vital broadcast personality, it may find itself forced to develop characteristics that more closely align it with commercial broadcasting, thus blurring the line between public and commercial.

On February 14, 1987, Garrison Keillor stepped to the microphone after singing "Hello, Love," the opening theme, and said he had an announcement to make. He told his audience that the June 13 program would be the last live broadcast of "A Prairie Home Companion." "I want to resume the life of a shy person," he said. "I'm tired." He removed his glasses and cleaned them, while telling his stunned audience, "It's time to go." He indicated he wanted to live for a time in Denmark, his wife's country, and expanded on that two weeks later in an interview on "Monitor Radio": "My plans are to work on a number of things I need to write—a piece for *The New Yorker* about Denmark." It would be an article about walking in Denmark, he said. Interviewer Frank Farrell asked if he thought he'd return to broadcasting. "I think so; I hope so," Keillor said. "But it's time to let go, to take three years off and write, earn an honest living."

Three years absence for a media celebrity, however, is a long time. And Keillor's departure raises the question, how will his subsequent books fare in the marketplace without his public prominence? The sales of both his previous books achieved dazzling totals directly resulting from his presence on "A Prairie Home Companion." *Happy to Be Here*, the collection of short stories and sketches, sold 210,000 copies in hardcover. One New York editor estimated sales for that volume would probably not have reached even 15,000 copies if Keillor had not been a well-known radio monologuist. "And certainly *Lake Wobegon Days* would have been only a modest success at best without his program," the editor said.

Keillor's next book will apparently be another chronicle about Lake Wobegon, titled, according to his "Monitor Radio" interview, *Lake Wobegon Loose*. He called this project "rather an adventurous book for me, and I'm not sure whether to let it go and find its own results or whether I ought to pull it in a little bit. A lot of strange people are coming into this book and I'm not sure whether to let them in or to lock the door."

Certainly his millions of fans would be eager for more news from Lake Wobegon, particularly if *Lake Wobegon Loose* is published within a year or two. But as his radio voice dims, so too may his chances for another mega-best-seller.

Quite aside from his future as a media celebrity, the most significant change for Keillor was not the removal of former regulars from his program, or even his ultimate departure from "A Prairie Home Companion." It was, rather, his marriage to Ulla Skaerved, on December 29, 1985. Except for exchanging letters for several years following their 1960 high school graduation, the two hadn't met until August, 1985, at their class's twenty-fifth reunion. However, other class members said that Keillor and Ulla weren't observed together at the reunion either, though Gary seemed to his former classmates uncharacteristically surly.

David Olsen reported that Keillor had attended several of his class's earlier reunions, but had been barely noticed, chatting only occasionally with others, and because he sustained his shy nature over the years, some classmates wondered why he bothered coming at all, since he kept mostly to himself. Olsen recalls, though, feeling as though he and others were being observed at these occasions, that Keillor was a specter whose presence was somehow felt, and that he was perhaps making mental notes that would one day surface in his stories. Nearly everyone, however, was surprised to learn of the impending marriage between the animated Ulla and the reticent Gary.

"No one outside the show was aware of anything happening in his life," Nash said. "But students of the program say if you go back and listen to the monologues he wrote after his high school reunion, he talks about meeting this foreign student after twenty-five years."

The rapidly burgeoning relationship ended Keillor's association with Margaret Moos and must have been at least mildly embarrassing for him, because it coincided with the publication in hardcover of *Lake Wobegon Days*, which was dedicated, "To Margaret, my love." That inscription was removed from the softcover edition, though Moos retained an acknowledgment in the preface, along with Butch Thompson, Bill Kling, and others.

Numerous monologues, as the wedding day approached, centered on Keillor's discovering true love and bespoke a tenderness that was at once touching and treacly. After the wedding, which took place in a Lutheran church near Copenhagen, Keillor and his bride moved with their children—his son and her three offspring—into a two-and-a-half story ninety-year-old home with four bedrooms and a walled back yard in St. Paul's Crocus Hill neighborhood. This is an area that has been home to the city's established wealth for generations, and the Keillor home is near the boyhood residence of F. Scott Fitzgerald, the house where he lived while writing *This Side of Paradise*. The neighborhood served Fitzgerald as the setting for his Basil Duke Lee stories, which were regular features in the old *Saturday Evening Post*.

Kevin Klose reported in the *Washington Post* on the first broadcast of "A Prairie Home Companion" after the marriage that Keillor's monologue was strikingly different from any that had preceded it, because he used a manuscript and carefully read each line. Said Keillor, "I am too much in love to notice much. I'm aware of nobody and nothing except her, my wife."

Instead of appearing in his usual white suit, which reinforced comparisons with Mark Twain, Keillor wore a black tux with a red rose in his lapel, a red bow tie, red suspenders, red socks and black sneakers—but no cumberbund.

Klose called Keillor's homecoming for the official reopening of the World Theater "bouyant . . . to this northern city where he rose to fame, but which he recently seemed ready to spurn."

In order to hang onto the privacy he craves, however, meant that Keillor had to remove himself from the public spotlight as a performer. The lane in which he'd traveled was not merely fast—at least by standards shy, retiring folk are accustomed to—it was supersonic. Though the ride was no doubt exciting, Keillor felt the need to get off. The presumption is that he had his breathtaking ride, but that he did not relish the freneticism and the demands on his time—encumbrances incumbent upon celebrities in America.

His departure from our airwaves was opportune, appropriate. The program had been losing its freshness. He was able to end his program before his audience considered deserting him. He may not, however, be able to remain out of the public consciousness for long, if his book sales show a dramatic decline.

Still, Garrison Keillor survived fame as well as fortune, and seems not to have been consumed by either. In the process of acquiring both, he has given enormous pleasure to millions of readers and listeners—most of whom didn't latch on to his darker visions, choosing to ignore them or simply forgive them.

Several years ago, *Life* magazine labeled Lake Wobegon as the Camelot of the eighties. It is a valid comparison. In King Arthur's mythical kingdom goodness could not forever endure. Lake Wobegon was never presented as entirely good, but uppermost in the minds of most listeners of its tales was the nostalgic ideal of life in a small midwestern town. And that ideal doesn't survive any more than goodness did in Camelot. But Wobegon and Camelot both call to mind our best potential selves and our less than perfect selves.

Camelot had its one brief shining hour that would not be forgot; Lake Wobegon is seared into our consciousness as "the little town that time forgot and the decades could not improve." But through Keillor's imagination, Lake Wobegon surpasses Camelot, because it is real rather than ephemeral. Lake Wobegon has always held out for Keillor fans a quality of recognition, because we have been there. We have known and loved its characters and establishments. And what is fiction, after all, but the imagination hewn into reality? Thus Garrison Keillor's Lake Wobegon is assuredly real—as real as fiction.

In the "Monitor Radio" profile, Keillor summed up the future of format radio programs such as his own as well as his place as an American humorist. He told interviewer Frank Farrell that radio had not lost any of its romance, power and beauty since its inception, and that he thought his show was very primitive: "Much better things could be done by people who have a natural bent for performance."

When asked to assess his ranking in the tradition of American humorists, Keillor said the tradition was a great colorful parade of characters starting with Mark Twain. "I do believe I'm in the procession," Keillor said. "But I don't imagine I'm riding up front of it, or even sitting in a convertible. I think I'm one of the foot soldiers."

When Garrison Keillor stepped aside as a broadcaster, his fans reacted with regret and sorrow. Keillor had generated enormous goodwill during his tenure, and could have basked in the afterglow of that goodwill for at least the forseeable future. However, he had harbored bitterness toward the press, and its coverage of his activities had rankled him. In March 1987, he granted interviews to several large dailies and during those sessions elected to vent his ill will toward the St. Paul *Pioneer Press* and *Dispatch* in particular. He complained that local newspapers viewed him as a symbol of excess and unearned wealth, and as a distant figure without morals. "It's like you're a display of creamed corn, you know," he said, of his annoyance at continually being recognized in supermarkets. Keillor is a careful wordsmith, and it's not likely his choice of words in the interview was slapdash. Thus the comment may have a figurative connotation. Being creamed means thoroughly pulverized, and he may have felt pulverized by the press, or that the press was trying to demolish him.

If so, his reaction seemed especially graceless. The local press treated him with respect, recognizing him as a cultural icon. There may have been only one time when a paper overstepped its bounds. After his marriage, the St. Paul paper published his home address on the front page. Noticing that, Keillor said he knew he could no longer live in St. Paul. "I live in a town with a lousy newspaper. It's a newspaper which, as far as I'm concerned, is weird." He claimed the local press covered him as if he were a cross between Joan Collins and Watergate.

In departing, Keillor might have simply signed off without commenting about how he was perceived after he became a celebrity. Nick Coleman, in a March 24, 1987 column in the *Pioneer Press* and *Dispatch* said that rubes pointed at him in local grocery stores and make him feel conspicuous. "If that weren't bad enough, a St. Paul celebrity faces daily aggravation from people who purposefully look away from him."

Continued Coleman, "The newspapers here took down his every word and printed his every press release. Although Keillor graciously restrained himself from complaining until now, the papers celebrated his every accomplishment, trumpeted his every success and reveled in his appearance on the cover of *Time* magazine."

Coleman also wrote that Keillor's parting shots seemed less a plea for privacy than "the anguish of someone who isn't happy doing what he is doing, the frustration of a stand-up funnyman who wants to write sit-down novels."

Local fans of Garrison Keillor who had previously defended him against the perceived onslaught of a zealous press, still defended him but with diminished enthusiasm, and some of them agreed that maybe it was the right time for his departure. "If all this attention got to be too much for him," said one fan of more than fifteen years, "then he did the right thing. I mean if he kept on complaining, he'd have turned people off."

Perhaps, and there were signs that his audience was dwindling slightly before he made his decision to leave the broadcast. But he probably could have held his hardcore fans indefinitely, and they will find it difficult to get along without him. The twilight hours on Saturday afternoons will not be the same for them. Observed the Minneapolis *Star Tribune*, "They'll miss that soothing voice, that gentle humor and all those insightful stories about life in small-town Minnesota. Lake Wobegon may be the place that time forgot, but it's one that the legion of loyal listeners to "A Prairie Home Companion will long remember."

POSTSCRIPT

AS I WRITE this postscript, weekly live broadcasts of Garrison Keillor's "A Prairie Home Companion" have been absent from American airwaves for more than a year. Many public radio stations, however, continue featuring the program, rebroadcasting tapes from the PHC's thirteen-year tenure. Some stations continue playing the program in its old familiar Saturday afternoon time slot. Most public stations that carried Keillor's program now schedule its replacement, "Good Evening," during that time.

What remains clear, despite the demise of "A Prairie Home Companion," is that Garrison Keillor continues to arouse considerable attention, to say nothing of curiosity among his fans and the media. Nearly all media profiles and interviews lavishly praise the shy man who forsook the Midwest for anonymity in Manhattan. But adoration has been customary for Keillor, especially during the last several years.

Samuel Johnson once wrote: "Praise, like gold and diamonds, owes its value only to its scarcity." For a long time now, praise has been anything but scarce for Keillor. Yet praise, whether well-meaning and sincere, or from sycophantic hangers-on, finally grows tiresome, and since we intuitively know that laud and honor should be scarce, we begin to doubt the praisers—or, worse, believe them. If we believe them, we may think we can do no wrong, and that the fawning will continue indefinitely.

The highly-touted Second Annual Farewell Broadcast of "A Prairie Home Companion" has come and gone with much hoopla, though that particular program did not rank among the more memorable Keillor shows. Here in Minnesota, it generated little excitement; most reviewers ignored it. But maybe that's because we're still smarting a little over remarks Keillor has continued to express about our state and, specifically, the Minnesota media. In March 1988 he told Paul D. Colford of *Newsday* that he would never live in Minnesota again. It was significant that his site for the second farewell broadcast wasn't the World Theater in downtown St. Paul, but Gotham's Radio City Music Hall.

This is far from the last chapter to be written about the life and work of Garrison Keillor, because of his choosing, Keillor remains a public person. Following his move to New York after a summer's vacation in Copenhagen, he quickly became something of a darling with that city's press, granting interviews, dining out, and making appearances at fund-raisers and guest spots on television. He has seemed a man very much at home with attention.

He may be, in fact, rather uncomfortable without it. Public notoriety is a publisher's delight. The author who knows how to access the media may sell millions of copies of books. And while Garrison Keillor was and remains a major American humorist, he knows that his books were huge bestsellers because millions of his radio listeners were already familiar with his broadcasts.

Doubtless, Keillor will continue to produce first-rate fiction and humor as well as unsigned "Talk of the Town" sketches for the *New Yorker* magazine, and there will be books we can look forward to as well. But without that national radio forum, without his "Prairie Home Companion" persona, it seems unlikely his future books will receive seven-figure printings.

To be sure, sales of his 1987 book, "Leaving Home," are impressive by any standard—one million hardcover copies in print. But in his hometown Twin Cities, bookstores reported less-than-spectacular sales, and the sales total for "Leaving Home" falls well below the more than three million copies of "Lake Wobegon Days" that have been sold. This despite the fact that casual readers find more to like in "Leaving Home"—an edited collection of some of Keillor's best radio monologues—than in "Lake Wobegon Days," which many fans found ponderous.

In order to continue to ring up mega sales for his books, it is imperative that Keillor keep his name and persona before the public. Articles in *The New York Times, People* magazine, *Newsday, Parade*, and elsewhere help, of course, but they hardly qualify as the type of enduring publicity that Keillor enjoyed each week on "A Prairie Home Companion."

It was really no surprise that Keillor's sojourn in Denmark, following his resignation from the popular radio program, was short-lived; there are no American media in Copenhagen. And it would certainly not be surprising were he to look for a re-entry into broadcasting. His numerous benefits, guest appearances, and the second farewell program may be harbingers of a return to regular radio and television.

A performer who has experienced the live audience and an adoring national following, as Keillor has, does not simply abandon them. He can't. He misses contact with audiences the way old-time vaudevillians missed their audiences after the advent of motion pictures. Many of those veteran performers did not withdraw from show business, but scrambled for work where it was available—in burlesque, carnivals, or even donkey baseball—anything, in short, to work an audience. Actors nurtured by live audiences are rarely able to leave them. On the other hand, audiences sometimes forget and abandon performers who formerly pleased them. Certainly Keillor's audience was the elixir that nourished him, and the following which devoured his books. Without that sizeable, worshipful audience, his future books may not be guaranteed bestsellers.

Within weeks after leaving "A Prairie Home Companion," Keillor said he thought he'd miss his audiences more than they would miss him. Perhaps this is now coming to pass.

Noah Adams, late of NPR's "All Things Considered," and host of "Good Evening," has been slowly earning critical and audience acclaim. "Good Evening" is carried by nearly two hundred public radio stations nationwide, down from the three hundred that broadcast "A Prairie Home Companion" during its heyday. But "Good Evening's" figures are respectable, especially when the show naturally invites comparisons to its legendary predecessor.

That "Good Evening" succeeds at all is in part a credit to Keillor, who proved that a quality variety show could sustain a national radio audience. Ironically, Keillor's efforts may mean that a program host need not be a storyteller or star entertainer in order for a variety program to attract and hold that audience.

Should Adams and other producers of variety programs continue to succeed, a Keillor return to radio—even with the old format—may not recapture the magic that delighted millions.

I'm reminded of another *New Yorker* writer of a couple of generations ago, Alexander Woollcott, who was also a broadcast personality. Like Keillor, Woollcott left broadcasting for other ventures, but after a hiatus, returned, saying, "I'm going back to the microphone like a drunkard to his bottle." I think Keillor will too—but the question is, will his audience return to him when he does?

—Michael Fedo

NOTES

Sources and references for each chapter are as follows:

Chapter 1

1. Material on the history of Anoka, Minnesota, was obtained from the Anoka County Historical Society.
2. Quotations by Garrison Keillor regarding his family's radio listening and reading habits were provided by "Fresh Air," produced by WHYY Radio in Philadelphia.
3. Keillor quotations about his old family radio appeared in the magazine, *Metropolitan Home*, "Interview, the Met Grill," November 1985.
4. Keillor quotes reminiscing about early radio came from Dan Cryer's *Newsday Magazine* profile.

Chapter 2

1. Quote by Keillor about why he uses Garrison instead of Gary appeared in an interview by Diane Roback, published in *Publishers Weekly*, September 13, 1985.

Chapter 3

1. Keillor's quotes about his St. Paul *Pioneer Press* experience were printed in *The Los Angeles Times*, September 18, 1985.
2. Quotes about radio work are from the Roback article cited in previous chapter.

Chapter 6

1. The Keillor quote about radio storytelling was published in the *Christian Science Monitor*, September 6, 1985.

Chapter 8

1. Keillor's comments on liberal churches are from *The Mother Earth News*.
2. His quotations about the role of the preacher appeared in *The Wittenberg Door*.
3. Keillor's comments about why he no longer attends church were also published in *The Wittenberg Door*.
4. John Miller's material first appeared in *The Lutheran Journal*.

Chapter 9

1. Quotes about the book *Happy to Be Here* were from the *Writer's Digest* interview.
2. Keillor's quote about his mission as a writer appeared first in the *Minneapolis Star Tribune*.
3. The quote about Keillor's use of personal experiences and basing some characters on friends of his were published in *Publishers Weekly*, as were Keillor's references to Uncle Lew Powell.
4. The references to Keillor's favorite humorists appeared in *Life*, May 1982.
5. Keillor's discussion of the sense of humor is from *Writer's Digest*.

Chapter 10

1. The discussion of friends being miracles came from *The Wittenberg Door*.

Chapter 12

1. Bill Humphries's quote was given to the *Minneapolis Star Tribune*.

Chapter 14

1. Kevin Klose's comments about Keillor's return to the World Theater were syndicated by *The Washington Post* and appeared in the January 18, 1986 edition of *Newsday*.
2. Keillor's "creamed corn" remark was published in the *Minneapolis Star Tribune*.
3. His comments about the St. Paul newspaper were published in the *Detroit Free Press*.

SELECTED BIBLIOGRAPHY

In researching this book, numerous periodicals and newspapers were consulted, as were the articles, books and stories of Garrison Keillor, including *Happy to Be Here* and *Lake Wobegon Days*. What follows is a selected bibliography containing material that was particularly helpful in the preparation of this book.

Anderson, Dave. "Keillor Show Airs Tenth Anniversary Edition," *Minneapolis Star Tribune*, July 9, 1984.

Andrews, Terry. "Five Writers," *Mpls. St. Paul* Magazine, August 1981.

Beyette, Beverly. "Fishing for Meaning in Lake Wobegon Waters," *The Los Angeles Times*, September 18, 1985.

Black, David. "Live From Lake Wobegon," *Rolling Stone*, July 23, 1981.

Bordsen, John. "All the News from Lake Wobegon," *Saturday Review*, May-June 1983.

Borger, Judith Yates. "Your Companion on the Prairie," Lutheran Brotherhood *Bond*, Winter 1985.

Browne, Ray B. *Heroes of Popular Culture* (Bowling Green: Bowling Green University Press, 1972).

Bunce, Alan. "Minnesota Public Radio's 'A Prairie Home Companion' Show Viewed," *Christian Science Monitor*, September 6, 1985.

Coleman, Nick. "Averted Eyes, Stares Too Much for Our Big Frog," St. Paul *Pioneer Press* and *Dispatch*, March 24, 1987.

———. "Preaching the Gospel According to Garrison," *Minneapolis Star Tribune*, July 1, 1984.

———. "Lake Wobegon, Ga?" *Minneapolis Star Tribune*, May 7, 1985.

Covert, Colin. "'A Prairie Home' Exit Draws Mixed Signals," *Minneapolis Star Tribune*, February 21, 1987.

Cryer, Dan. "America's Hottest New Storyteller," *Newsday Magazine*, October 13, 1985.

Dalzel, Tom, and Zoloth, Joan. "Populism on the Air," *Mother Jones,* May 1983.

———. "Favorite Son of the Town Time Forgot," *People Weekly,* February 6, 1984.

Geng, Veronica. "Idylls of Minnesota," *The New York Times Book Review,* August 25, 1985.

Godown, Jan. "Can 'A Prairie Home Companion,' Make a Career?" *Minneapolis Star Tribune Sunday Magazine,* January 4, 1987.

Gross, Terry. Interview with Garrison Keillor, "Fresh Air," produced by WHYY Radio, Philadelphia.

Grossman, Mary Ann. "Keillor Juggles Celebrity, Shyness," St. Paul *Pioneer Press and Dispatch,* August 16, 1985.

Grow, Doug. "Look Who's Walking Out the Door . . . G'bye Love," *Minneapolis Star Tribune,* February 17, 1987.

Gustafson, Paul. "Keillor's Praise Surprises His First Writing Teacher," *Minneapolis Star Tribune,* February 27, 1986.

Guy, David. "Garrison Keillor, A Miniaturist of Small-Town Life," *USA Today,* September 6, 1985.

Hemingson, Peter. "Plowboy Interview," *The Mother Earth News,* May-June 1985.

Hughes, Glyn. "Grace and Fate," *The New Statesman,* March 1986.

Jones, Will. "After Last Night," *Minneapolis Tribune,* May 19, 1974.

Judge, Paul. "Garrison Keillor, Making Waves from the Heartland," *Life,* May 1982.

Kauls, Don. Syndicated column, Tribune Media Services, St. Paul *Pioneer Press and Dispatch,* December 29, 1985.

Keillor, Garrison. "Broadsides," *Ivory Tower,* May 4, 1964 and October 5, 1964.

———.1985 *Current Biography Yearbook,* pp. 219–223.

———. "The Man Who Locked Himself In," (short story), *The Ivory Tower,* October 7, 1963.

———. "Two on Hockey: A Conversation with Minnesota Center, Doug Woog," *The Ivory Tower,* February 1, 1965.

Klepp, L. S. "Garrison Keillor Cooks With Small Potatoes," *The Village Voice,* September 10, 1985.

Klose, Kevin. "A Public Love Notice," *Newsday,* January 18, 1986, distributed by *The Washington Post* Syndicate.

———. "The Keillor Instinct for the Truer than True," *The Washington Post,* September 15, 1985.

Letofsky, Irv. "For Garrison Keillor Fantasy is a Lot More Fun than Reality," *Minneapolis Tribune,* July 29, 1976.

———. "Garrison is Guru of Middle America," *Minneapolis Star Tribune,* July 26, 1981, distributed by *The Los Angeles Times* Syndicate.

———. "Report on the Popularity of Garrison Keillor," *The Los Angeles Times,* July 28, 1985.

———. "Lake Wobegon's Garrison Keillor Finds Love that Time Forgot and the Decades Can't Improve," *People Weekly,* November 25, 1985.

Mano, D. Keith. "Here at the *New Yorker,*" *National Review,* December 11, 1981.

Marshall, Richard. "The World Theater, An Elegant New Prairie Home," St. Paul *Pioneer Press and Dispatch,* April 28, 1986.

Mead, Frank S. *Handbook of Denominations in the United States,* revised by Samuel S. Hill (Nashville: Abingdon Press, 1984).

Meier, Peg. "Keeling Over Keillor," *Mpls. St. Paul* Magazine, December 1981.

———. "Seeking Obscurity Again in Denmark," *Minneapolis Star Tribune,* March 22, 1987.

Miller, John E. "Garrison Keillor's Parables," *Lutheran Journal,* July 1986.

———. "The Distance Between Gopher Prairie and Lake Wobegon: Sinclair Lewis and Garrison Keillor on the Small Town Experience," paper presented at the Dakota History Conference, Spring 1986.

———. "Lake Wobegon, Minnesota, Investing in the Heartland," *Small Town,* May–June, 1986.

Monahan, Terry. "A Musical Borscht," *Mpls. St. Paul Magazine,* January 1987.

Monsour, Theresa. "It Can Be Tense in Lake Wobegon," St. Paul *Pioneer Press and Dispatch,* April 28, 1986.

Ode, Kim. "Novelist Keillor Basks in New Respect," *Minneapolis Star Tribune,* September 6, 1985.

Patterson, Katherine. "Tales From the Town that Time Forgot," *The Washington Post Book World,* September 1, 1985.

Perry, Gale. "A Real Live Radio Show Revisited," Chippewa *Herald-Telegram,* (Chippewa Falls, Wisconsin), November 8, 1978.

Reynolds, William J. "Medium: Hot," *TWA Ambassador,* November 1981.

Roback, Diane. "Interview With Garrison Keillor," *Publishers Weekly*, September 13, 1985.

Roberts, Michael. "Garrison Keillor, Shying Away From Fame," *Detroit Free Press*, March 15, 1987.

Schumacher, Michael. "Sharing the Laughter with Garrison Keillor," *Writer's Digest*, January 1986.

Shefchik, Rick. "Garrison Keillor Ready to Plunge into Deeper Waters," St. Paul *Pioneer Press* and *Dispatch*, April 28, 1986.

———. "Keillor Hit Hard by Love and Publicity," Duluth *News Tribune and Herald*, November 7, 1985, syndicated by St. Paul *Pioneer Press* and *Dispatch*.

Singer, Mark. "Welcome to Lake Wobegon, The Town that Time Forgot," *Blair and Ketchum's Country Journal*, January 1982.

Skow, John. "Let's Hear It for Lake Wobegon," *Time*, November 4, 1985.

Soucheray, Joe. "Celebrity Status Irks Garrison," St. Paul *Pioneer Press* and *Dispatch*, November 8, 1985.

Sutin, Lawrence. "Lake Wobegon: The Little Town that Time Forgot," *Saturday Evening Post*, September 1986.

Taub, James. "The Short and Tall Tales of Garrison Keillor," *Esquire*, May 1982.

Thorpe, Doug. "Garrison Keillor's 'Prairie Home Companion,' Gospel of the Airwaves," *Christian Century*, July 21–28, 1982.

Vick, Karl. "Radio America Hears Our Prairie Home," *Minneapolis Star*, February 20, 1979.

Vincent, Sally. "Desire for Small Potatoes," *Sunday Times*, (London), February 23, 1986.

Walker, Michael. "Interview: The Met Grill," *Metropolitan Home*, November 1985.

Wall, James M. "The Secret Is Out About Lake Wobegon," *Christian Century*, November 13, 1985.

———. "What's Up at Lake Wobegon?" *Time*, November 9, 1981.

———. "Wittenberg Door Interviews Garrison Keillor," *The Wittenberg Door*, December-January, 1985–1986.

Youngren, J. Allen. "The News From Lake Wobegon," *Christianity Today*, November 22, 1985.

INDEX